P9-EGN-010

Janet McCabe is Lecturer in Media and Creative Industries at Birkbeck, University of London. She is the author of *The West Wing* (2012) and *Feminist Film Studies* (2004) and co-editor of several collections on contemporary US television, including *Reading Sex and the City* (2004) and *Quality TV: Contemporary American TV and Beyond* (2007) (all I.B.Tauris). She is a co-founding editor as well as managing editor of *Critical Studies in Television*. Along with Kim Akass, she is series co-editor of the *Reading Contemporary Television* series for I.B.Tauris.

Kim Akass is Senior Research Fellow and Lecturer in Cultural and Contextual Studies (Film and TV) at the University of Hertfordshire. Among the books on television drama she has co-edited are *Reading Six Feet Under: TV To Die For* (2005), *Reading the L Word* (2006), *Reading Desperate Housewives: Beyond the White Picket Fence* (2006), and *Quality TV: Contemporary American TV and Beyond* (2007) (all I.B.Tauris). She is the author of *Telematernity: Watching Mothers on Television* (I.B.Tauris forthcoming). She is a co-founding editor and managing editor of *Critical Studies in Television*, editor of the website *CSTOnline* (www.cstonline.tv) as well as series editor, with Janet McCabe, of the *Reading Contemporary Television* series.

'This terrific and timely collection's distinct focus on the *Yo soy Betty, la fea* phenomenon allows for an impressively expansive inquiry into contemporary television and global popular culture.

The essays herein are strong individually. Cumulatively, they offer unique and important insights into globe-trotting formats and their local adaptation. Spanning the complex interdependencies of industry practices, national politics and audiences' tastes, television aesthetics and representation, evolving genres, enduring stories and more, *TV's Betty Goes Global* is a veritable primer for what global television is now, and why.'

Tasha Oren, Associate Professor of Film and Media Studies
at the University of Wisconsin, Milwaukee

READING CONTEMPORARY TELEVISION
Series Editors: Kim Akass and Janet McCabe
janetandkim@hotmail.com

The *Reading Contemporary Television* series offers a varied, intellectually groundbreaking and often polemical response to what is happening in television today. This series is distinct in that it sets out to immediately comment upon the TV *zeitgeist* while providing an intellectual and creative platform for thinking differently and ingeniously writing about contemporary television culture. The books in the series seek to establish a critical space where new voices are heard and fresh perspectives offered. Innovation is encouraged and intellectual curiosity demanded.

PUBLISHED AND FORTHCOMING

TV'S BETTY
GOES GLOBAL

From *Telenovela* to International Brand

Edited by Janet McCabe and Kim Akass

I.B. TAURIS

LONDON · NEW YORK

Published in 2013 by I.B.Tauris & Co Ltd
6 Salem Road, London W2 4BU
175 Fifth Avenue, New York NY 10010
www.ibtauris.com

Distributed in the United States and Canada Exclusively by Palgrave Macmillan
175 Fifth Avenue, New York NY 10010

ISBN: 978 1 78076 267 8

A full CIP record for this book is available from the British Library
A full CIP record is available from the Library of Congress

Library of Congress Catalog Card Number: available

Printed and bound by CPI Group (UK) Ltd, Croydon, CR0 4YY

FSC
MIX
Paper from
responsible sources
www.fsc.org   FSC® C013604

Contents

Acknowledgements

This book has been a long time in gestation, and our first thanks must go to our fine authors for their outstanding contributions and enduring patience: Michele Hilmes, Yeidy M. Rivero, Jean Chalaby, Andrea Esser, Bianca Lippert, Alexander Dhoest and Manon Mertens, Stefania Carini, Xiaolu Ma and Albert Moran, Divya McMillin, Laurence Raw, Amit Lavie-Dinur and Yuval Karniel, Betty Kaklamanidou, Irena Carpentier Reifová and Zdeněk Sloboda, Elena Prokhorova, Paul Julian Smith and Dana Heller. We would also like to thank those industry insiders who generously made time to speak to authors and gave invaluable insights into the Betty trade as well as the production of local adaptations: Jeff Ford, Alicia Remirez, Dr Michael Esser, Jonas Baur, Vasha Wallace, Jo Frangou, Thanassis Tsaousopoulos, Dieter Debruyn and Reinhilde Dewit, Jan Creuwels and Gitte Nuyens, Hugo Van Laere, Valeria Schulczová, Roberto Sessa – and last but no means least, creator of *Yo soy Betty, la fea* Fernando Gaitán.

What never gets printed, however, are the intellectual conversations that guide and nourish any scholarly enterprise, and this project is no exception. Additional thanks must go to Bianca for her electrifying paper at the Manchester Metropolitan University conference in 2006, which inspired us to take the Betty journey in the first place. Thanks to John Sinclair for helpful advice.

It is impossible to measure the support of the inspirational Philippa Brewster, our editor at I.B.Tauris. She has been stalwart in her encouragement of this project (and the series), and the very definition of patience in believing that this collection would some day, somehow, arrive on her desk. We are also indebted to the production team at I.B.Tauris.

It has been extremely difficult for us to find, in the last few years, time for writing and editing. We have both been fortunate to have supportive families that have given us that time. Janet would like to thank Mike for his endless insights and emotional sustenance, Olivia for believing that I will one day emerge from the study and Chris for taking Olivia to groom a horse deep in rural Somerset. Kim would like to express her thanks to husband Jon for his continual belief not only in this project but also in his often conflicted wife and to Daryl and Caitlin for putting up with only half a mother for much of the time.

Contributors

Kim Akass is Senior Research Fellow and Lecturer in Cultural and Contextual Studies (Film and TV) at the University of Hertfordshire. Among the books on television drama she has co-edited are *Reading Six Feet Under: TV To Die For* (2005), *Reading the L Word* (2006), *Reading Desperate Housewives: Beyond the White Picket Fence* (2006), and *Quality TV: Contemporary American TV and Beyond* (2007) (all I.B.Tauris). She is the author of *Telematernity: Watching Mothers on Television* (I.B.Tauris forthcoming). She is a co-founding editor and managing editor of *Critical Studies in Television*, editor of the website *CSTOnline* (www.cstonline.tv) as well as series editor, with Janet McCabe, of the *Reading Contemporary Television* series.

Stefania Carini is PhD in Communication at the Catholic University of Milano, where she also teaches. She is a TV columnist for *Europa* and collaborates with *Corriere della Sera*, the main Italian newspaper. She is the author of several articles on TV and animation, as well as a book on quality TV (2009).

Irena Carpentier Reifová is Lecturer and researcher at Charles University in Prague. Her research interests include popular television culture, with an emphasis on Czechoslovak and Czech serial television fiction. She was an editor of *Media Studies* and a member of the editorial board of the film studies journal *Iluminace* until 2010.

Jean K. Chalaby is Professor of International Communication at City University London. He has published extensively in leading journals and his most recent book is *Transnational Television in Europe: Reconfiguring Global Communications Networks* (2009).

Alexander Dhoest is Associate Professor at the University of Antwerp. He teaches and researches on television, focusing on representation, reception and social (national, cultural, ethnic and sexual) identity, and has published widely on these issues in edited collections and journals such as *Media, Culture & Society* and the *European Journal of Cultural Studies*. He is currently working on 'quality' in contemporary Flemish TV drama and diversity in audience studies, focusing on queer audiences.

Andrea Esser is Senior Lecturer in Media and Communications at the University of Roehampton. Her current research focuses on the phenomenon of television formats: the growth of the format business, formats' role in production and broadcasting, patterns of flow and the complexities of local adaptations. She is the principle organizer of the 'Media Across Borders' network, dedicated to the localization of audiovisual content (www.mediaacrossborders.com).

Dana Heller is Eminent Scholar and Chair of the English Department at Old Dominion University. She writes about popular culture, television, queer studies and most things considered to be in bad taste. A four-times Senior Fulbright Fellow and recipient of the State Council of Higher Education in Virginia Outstanding Teaching Award, her most recent books are *The Great American Makeover: Television History, Nation* (2006), *Makeover Television: Realities Remodeled* (2007), *Hairspray* (2011) and *Loving the L Word* (forthcoming 2013, I.B.Tauris).

Michele Hilmes is Professor of Media and Cultural Studies and Chair of the Department of Communication Arts at the University of Wisconsin-Madison. Her most recent book is *Network Nations: A Transnational History of British and American Broadcasting* (2011). She and Jason Loviglio are currently editing *Radio's New Wave,* a collection of articles on radio and sound in the digital era.

Betty Kaklamanidou is Lecturer in Film History and Theory at the Aristotle University of Thessaloniki. She is co-editor of *The 21st Century Superhero: Essays on Gender, Genre and Globalization in Film* (2011) and her book on the millennial Hollywood romantic comedy is forthcoming from Routledge. Her fields of study include film and politics, adaptation theory, genre and gender, and contemporary Greek cinema. In 2011 she was awarded a Fulbright scholarship to conduct research in New York.

Yuval Karniel is Senior Lecturer at the Sammy Ofer School of Communications, IDC, Israel. He earned an LL.M. in International Law from the American University in Washington DC and an LL.D. from the Hebrew University of Jerusalem.

Amit Lavie-Dinur is Vice-Dean and the Head of Visual Content studies at the Sammy Ofer School of Communications, IDC, Israel. She earned an MA in Communication from New York University and a PhD from the Hebrew University of Jerusalem.

Bianca Lippert is currently working as a consultant in an agency for corporate communications and develops e-learning formats including different forms of mediatized storytelling. She worked as script consultant for a German TV production that adapted an Argentine *telenovela* for the German market, before completing her doctorate at the University of Siegen. Her thesis is on *telenovelas* and their local and global success, and is published as *Telenovela Formats: Localized Versions of a Universal Love* (2011).

Xiaolu Ma is a PhD candidate in the School of Humanities at Griffith University in Brisbane. For five years, she worked as a journalist for the Beijing Youth Newspaper. She became a scriptwriter for China Central Television (CCTV) and also worked for Sina.com, which is the largest Chinese-language infotainment web portal. She has also worked in the Chinese film industry as a scriptwriter. Research interests include the Hong Kong and Mainland China film industries, Asian cinema, international film co-production and Chinese media.

Janet McCabe is Lecturer in Media and Creative Industries at Birkbeck, University of London. She is the author of *The West Wing* (2012) and *Feminist Film Studies* (2004) and co-editor of several collections on contemporary US television, including *Reading Sex and the City* (2004) and *Quality TV: Contemporary American TV and Beyond* (2007) (all I.B.Tauris). She is a co-founding editor as well as managing editor of *Critical Studies in Television*. Along with Kim Akass, she is series co-editor of the *Reading Contemporary Television* series for I.B.Tauris.

Divya McMillin is Professor of Global Media Studies and Director of the Global Honors Program at the University of Washington Tacoma. She is author of *International Media Studies* (2007) and *Mediated Identities: Youth, Agency, and Globalization* (2009), and has been published in several journals including the *Journal of Communication*, the *International Journal of Cultural Studies*, *Continuum: Journal of Media and Cultural Studies*, the *Indian Journal of Gender Studies* and the *International Communication Bulletin*. She also works collaboratively with the Internationales Zentralinstitut fur das Jugend-und Bildungsfernsehen of the Bavarian Broadcasting Company (Germany) to promote quality programming for youth television worldwide.

Manon Mertens has an MA in Media Culture from the University of Antwerp and an MBA from the Antwerp Management School. She currently works in the private sector.

Albert Moran is a Professor in the School of Humanities at Griffith University, Brisbane. He has edited or authored more than 25 books on film and television and his research interests include Australian media history, global TV formats and geographies of communications. His most recent books are *New Flows in Global TV* (2009), *TV Formats Worldwide: Localizing Global Programs* (2009) and (co-edited with Michael Keane) *Cultural Adaptation* (2009). He is currently writing a business biography of Australia's pioneer TV format importer and exporter, executive producer Reg Grundy.

Elena Prokhorova is Assistant Professor at the College of William and Mary, where she teaches in the Russian and Film Studies Programs. Her research interests include twentieth- and twenty-first-century Russian film and television, cultural theory and media constructions of national identity. Her articles have appeared in *SEEJ*, *Slavic Review* and *The Journal of Russian Communication*, as well as edited volumes. She regularly contributes to the online journal, *Kinokultura*. She is currently working on the book-length monograph *Film and Television Genres of the Late Soviet Era.*

Laurence Raw teaches in the Department of English at Baskent University, Ankara. His recent publications include a book of theatre reviews from the Turkish stage (2009), and most recently *Exploring Turkish Cultures* (2011), an in-depth look at the Republic of Turkey's relationship with Europe and North America, as represented in a variety of contexts including film, television and the theatre.

Yeidy M. Rivero is Associate Professor in the Department of Screen Arts and Culture and the Program in American Culture at the University of Michigan, Ann Arbor. Her areas of interest are television studies, race and ethnic representation in media, and Latin American, Spanish Caribbean, Latino and African diaspora studies. Her work has been published in journals such as *Media, Culture & Society, Feminist Media Studies, Television & New Media, Global Media and Communication, Cinema Journal* and *Critical Studies in Media Communication.* She is the author of *Tuning Out Blackness: Race and Nation in the History of Puerto Rican Television* (2005). Her current book project focuses on Cuban commercial television, 1950–60.

Zdeněk Sloboda graduated in Media Studies at the Faculty of Social Sciences, Charles University in Prague, and is currently studying for a PhD at the Institute of Sociology, Charles University in Prague and Institute of Communication and Media Studies, University of Leipzig. He teaches and publishes on sexualities, gender, media education and qualitative methods. He is a member of the Czech Government Council for Human Rights.

Paul Julian Smith is Distinguished Professor in the Hispanic and Luso-Brazilian Program at the Graduate Center, City University of New York. He is the author of 15 books including: *Desire Unlimited: The Cinema of Pedro Almodóvar* (2001), *Amores Perros* (2003), *Television in Spain* (2006) and *Spanish Screen Fiction: Between Cinema and Television* (2009). He is a regular contributor to *Sight & Sound* and *Film Quarterly.* Follow him on Twitter: @pauljuliansmith.

Introduction:
'Oh Betty, You Really Are Beautiful'

Janet McCabe

The Face that Launched a Modern Global Phenomenon

The first shot of ABC's stylish primetime dramedy *Ugly Betty* (2006–10) opens on its eponymous heroine Betty Suarez (America Ferrera). Filmed in tight mid-shot, slightly from below, her image fills the screen. And what an image it is. A fresh, callow face adorned with little make-up. Dishevelled hair, unruly eyebrows, red-rimmed spectacles framing a wide-eyed look. She appears less than comfortable. As she nervously bites her lip, a flash of metal can be seen inside her mouth. The kitsch title 'Ugly Betty' in bold red and yellow flashes on the screen. Returning to Betty, something has caught her eye. She beams. And we have our first glimpse of her big, metallic smile, heavy, 'train-track' stainless-steel braces on her top and lower teeth. All the while musical motifs (from the theme by Jeff Beal) add texture to the visual. A whimsical, quirky tempo: a lyrical violin evoking a certain old-world charm slightly out of step with the staccato percussion rhythm with its distinctive Latin beat. Immediately, in less than 12 seconds in fact, the US Betty brand is established.

Brands and branding become crucial to the next sequence. There is a cut from Betty to a two shot, as the glamorous Charmaine (Abigail Foreman) joins her on the long bench. The contrast between the two women could not be starker. Everything Charmaine is Betty is not: less is more. Tall and willowy, Charmaine is the definition of contemporary sartorial elegance: black knee-high boots, classic black dress, poncho in subtle shades of oatmeal/biscuit with matching long, thin neck scarf. Her hair is pulled back into a smooth ponytail, her skin is flawless and make-up perfect. Next to her Betty looks gauche in her heavy, plaid, woollen suit and fussy blouse. Bright colours, bold prints and vintage style define Betty's discordant sense of fashion, which in time takes on its own 'geek chic' charm – think Betty skipping through the *Mode* corridors after flirting with Henry Grubstick (Christopher Gorham) in her Marc Jacobs wedges ('Fake Plastic Snow', 1: 7).

Not yet, though.

Betty strikes up a conversation with the haughty Charmaine. 'I like your poncho. My Dad got me one in Guadalajara,' chirps Betty. Charmaine delivers a condescending grimace. 'Milan. Dolce & Gabbana. Fall.' It appears all too obvious who will climb the corporate steps behind them, leading to the offices of Meade Publications, and secure that entry-level position. Charmaine's transnational lifestyle, jetting from one international style capital to another, belonging to the rarefied world of exclusive designer labels and *haute couture*, seemingly has the edge on Betty's border crossings: a child of immigrants who migrated from Central Mexico to America's East Coast, now a commuter from a local, ethnically defined, working-class Queens neighbourhood to the cosmopolitan Manhattan metropolis, claiming that Meade magazines have allowed her to imagine multiple worlds far beyond her own.

Transnational shifts and cross-border exchanges, international trading patterns, global brands and consumer habits, migratory movements and tourism define this ever-so-brief encounter between these two women in motion. Involving image and 'imagined worlds' (2005: 33), media and migration, it recalls Arjun Appadurai and his work on understanding globalization. 'The new global cultural economy has to be seen as a complex, overlapping, disjunctive order that cannot any longer be understood in terms of existing center-periphery models' (32). Image – of lifestyle, culture and politics, self-representation and identities – so finely drawn *in* and *across* these female bodies produces a sense of how the story of Betty has circulated internationally through different *mediascapes* (the production and distribution of images) and *ideoscapes* (political and ideological messages) and often translated in surprising (not wholly anticipated) and inventive ways. Appearances are always deceptive. Nothing is ever quite as it seems in the fabulous and funny world of *Ugly Betty* where those at the margins migrate to the centre and the downtrodden eclipse the social insiders.

Later Betty will wear the 'Guadalajara' poncho on her first day at the office as an assistant to newly appointed editor-in-chief Daniel Meade (Eric Mabius). Of course, this poncho trend will never make the cover of *Mode*, but it brands Betty nonetheless. It was a gift from her beloved father, Ignacio Suarez (Tony Plana), a man identified profoundly with family, strengthening the 'Mexican family' and keeping alive Mexican traditions and identity. Purchased on a trip to Guadalajara, the capital of Mexican culture (home to Mariachi music, as well as host to international film and book festivals), the garment has since crossed national borders as part of migratory movements and diasporic communities journeying (temporarily) back and forth. Before it turns up on Betty at the *Mode* offices as a statement of arrival – of where she has come from and where she aspires to go – similar to Charmaine in her Dolce & Gabbana poncho. As Silvio Horta, creator of the US *Ugly Betty* declares, '[Betty] comes in with a look that is the opposite of what is expected of her, and she triumphs' (Donahue 2008: 28).

That striking visual of Betty in her 'Guadalajara' poncho defined the 'look' of the first series, its sartorial kitschness venturing beyond conventional norms to speak instead of a 'cosmopolitan outlook' (Beck 2007: 72). German sociologist Ulrich Beck describes 'cosmopolitanism' as 'a non-linear, dialectical process in which the universal and the particular, the similar and the dissimilar, the global and the local are to be conceived, not as cultural polarities, but as interconnected and reciprocally interpenetrating principles' (72–3). It is this intermingling of cultures and identities, entangled media networks, global markets, local broadcasting practice and regulation, travelling narratives and trans-media storytelling, reception and preferences of taste, that lie at the core of this anthology, *TV's Betty Goes Global*.

Central to this edited collection is the desire to chart how the tale of the Ugly Duckling growing into a swan migrated from one broadcasting context to another and back again. It is a story of acquisition and movement serving a multi-channel, multi-platform media environment stimulated by 'new distribution technologies ... and new computer software' (Moran with Malbon 2006: 10). One finds that the traffic is no longer a 'one-way flow' (Nordenstreng and Varis 1974), beyond any claims of trade dominated by Western-produced programming (Schiller 1969; 1991; Herman and McChesney 1997). Instead, the story is enmeshed in what John Tomlinson calls a 'complex connectivity' (2004: 26) involving television cultures and industries, as well as multiple discourses of identities – socio-cultural, economic and consumer, ethnic and racial, global and local (even regional), gendered and the feminine. Placing the Betty trade into some kind of historic and institutional context is the aim of the next chapter by Michele Hilmes. Following this, authors adopt a variety of different theoretical and conceptual approaches to understanding the appeal of the original story and why it took off and was adapted in so many different territories – 'broadcast in 13 languages and 74 countries' (Kraul 2006), with 19 official versions, to say nothing of the re-productions and unofficial copycats. In analysing the flow of the tale about an un-comely heroine with glasses, braces and bangs, what emerges in and through its acquisition and movement is a complex, multi-directional, entangled narrative about television industries, cultures, production and storytelling. What gets mapped within the pages that follow is how various media spaces or strata of television production, exchange and reception dialogue continually with multiple cultures and identities, entwine deeply to make the story of Betty a truly modern TV phenomenon.

Exploiting Betty: *Telenovelas*, Geolinguistic Regions and *Yo soy Betty, la fea*

Betty's initial humiliation at Meade, having the door quite literally slammed in her face, cuts to another suffering Latina. The scene is from *Vidas de Fuego* (*Lives of Fire*), a clichéd, Spanish-language *telenovela* that is watched in the Suarez household. Esmeralda, a maid played in the 'Pilot' by an uncredited Salma Hayek, is brandishing a gun. Her hand quivers violently, her countenance is overwrought. The camera pulls back to reveal her pointing the pistol at a dark, handsome Latino, his tie loose and shirt undone. He reaches out and grabs her wrist. Seizing Esmeralda, he crushes her to his body. The camera zooms in on a close-up of her distress. She tries to resist. 'No! No! No!' she sobs. But he gains mastery over her with 'a punishing kiss' (Modleski 1999: 51). The music swells.

Esmeralda drops the gun. As anguish gives way to desire, she wrenches the shirt from his back revealing his muscular physique. 'Eroticized dominance' (56) packaged as romantic fantasy: and it is still only teatime at the Suarez household.

The high drama of uncommonly beautiful people histrionically acting out a familiar tale of passion, corruption and revenge immediately reminds us that *Ugly Betty* has its roots elsewhere. This stylish US primetime hit was in fact the ninth incarnation of a truly global TV phenomenon that began life as a Colombian *telenovela* back in 1999. Produced by Radio Cadena Nacional (RCN), *Yo soy Betty, la fea* (*I Am Betty, the Ugly One*, 1999–2001) was created by Fernando Gaitán. No other *telenovela* had caught on like it, enthralling the Colombian population for almost a year and a half (Hodgson 2000). It gained an average market share of 50 per cent for the private channel ('Betty la nuestra', 2000). At its peak *Yo soy Betty, la fea* attracted 3.3 million viewers, translating into a 72 per cent market share, 230 per cent above RCN's ratings average for the time slot (de la Fuente 2006). Viewers tuned into the five-episodes-a-week *telenovela* to follow the smart but less than attractive Beatriz Aurora 'Betty' Pinzón Solano (Ana María Orozco) climbing the corporate ladder at the fictitious fashion empire, EcoModa, where she finally became an executive, tamed her feckless boss and found love. So popular was it in other Latin American countries that the ratings in March 2001 were higher in Ecuador (58.9 per cent audience share) and Panama (56.5 per cent) than its native Colombia (50.7 per cent) with Venezuela trailing with 'only' a 41.5 per cent share (IBOPE Media Information 2001). When the tale finally ended after 335 episodes in May 2001, more than 80 million people in the region, as well as in the United States, tuned in to watch (Hernandez 2001).

But that was not the end of the story.

Yo soy Betty, la fea in the original (with its source language as well as dubbed or subbed) initially broadcast (almost concurrently) in 22 countries (Morales 2001) as varied as Indonesia, Japan and Malaysia, all over Latin America as well as Spain. It also found success in the US market on Spanish-language channels airing both 'the Colombian version and a Mexican re-production' (Miller 2010: 209). Long before *Ugly Betty* moved the genre centre stage, the first time that 'any *telenovela* format' (ibid.) advanced into primetime on an English-speaking US network, the original had already entered the US media space and found an eager audience of those who had made their home in the United States. *Yo soy Betty, la fea* attracted unprecedented ratings when it broadcast on America's second major Spanish-language network, Telemundo, owned by NBC Universal since late 2001 and aimed at over 35 million Hispanics. Of its 'spectacular run', James McNamara, the then-CEO of Telemundo, said: 'At the time, our network was getting killed every day and Betty helped put us on the map' (Kraul 2006). The original *telenovela* may have first belonged to the US Latino community, but with Spanish-language TV networks firmly affiliated to powerful media conglomerates aimed at the burgeoning (and lucrative) US Hispanic market (Lippert 2011: 139–43), this was no minority TV – and this complex media flow and cultural exchange continues *in* and *through* the US *Ugly Betty*.

As the music swells and passion intensifies in the spoof *Vidas de Fuego* the camera pulls back to reveal the Suarez living room, where 12-year-old Justin (Mark Indelicato) stands, remote in hand, watching. 'I hate *telenovelas*', pouts the third-generation Suarez and only son of Hilda (Ana Ortiz). Justin may speak English and dislike the genre, but watching *telenovelas* in Spanish, without subtitles or dubbing, is as central to the Suarez household as Ignacio's authentic Mexican cooking and the 'Dia de los Muertos' ('Day of the Dead') collectible displayed in the kitchen (see Paxman 2003). The cheesy *telenovela* so popular with Ignacio recalls the work of John Sinclair, Elizabeth Jacka and Stuart Cunningham (1996: 8), who determined language as the principal indicator of 'cultural proximity' (Straubhaar 1991), insisting that canned (unaltered) *telenovelas* tend to flow well within 'geolinguistic regions' (see also Sinclair 1999). As Sinclair later adds, Spanish-language networks in the United States create 'a national market of Latinos', predicated on an appeal 'to Latin-origin people on the basis of a vague pan-Latin identity and their speaking of Spanish' (2009: 35).

The US Latino programming market is controlled largely by the Mexican broadcast behemoth, Televisa – the channel responsible for airing the Mexican *Yo soy Betty, la fea* adaptation, *La fea más bella* (*The Most Beautiful Ugly Girl*, [2006–7]). Headquarters in Mexico City, the multimedia conglomerate, the largest in Latin America and in the Spanish-speaking world, supplies the majority of primetime *telenovelas* to Univision, America's number one Spanish-language network, with which it has an exclusive deal (Kraul 2006). Univision later not only aired *La fea más bella*, but TeleFutura, Univision's second network, re-ran *Yo soy Betty, la fea*, following its airing on Telemundo, and after the ABC primetime series had become a hit and renewed interest in the original. *Yo soy Betty, la fea* in its second run continued to draw strong ratings of nearly a million in its Monday night slot (Ugly Is Beautiful for TeleFutura 2009).

Contained and uncredited in the small-screen, fictional world of *Vidas de Fuego*, avidly consumed by Ignacio, are Mexican television stars, such as Sebastián Rulli (*Mundo de fieras – World of Beasts – 2006-7*) and Eduardo Rodrigues in recurring cameo roles. Their presence calls to mind that Mexican shows still dominate the US Spanish-speaking TV market. But as the spoof Mexican *telenovela* existing only as fragments inside the Colombian-based US adaptation also reminds us, the Colombian television industry is fast gaining on Mexico. It is important to add, however, that the Mexican television companies are prone to strong-arm tactics, for, as Yeidy Rivero demonstrates in her chapter, the industry based in Central America flagrantly flouts piracy laws, 'copying Colombian *telenovela* ideas and scripts without paying royalties', and there is little the South American country can do about it. Still, Colombia remains a major producer of *telenovelas*, second only to Mexico as a supplier of the genre to US networks, in front of Venezuela and Brazil (ibid.) – thanks to the phenomenal global success of *Yo soy Betty, la fea*.

Catapulted by international triumph, Colombian studios are hard at work turning out their particular brand of *telenovela*. Combining humour with quirky stories (different from the Mexican soaps with their social realism and taboo breaking [Paxman 2003]), these *telenovelas* are being sold as far afield as China and the Czech Republic (ibid.). Another reason why Colombia has thrived in recent times is its low production costs, which are often as much as 20 per cent less than Mexico (Kraul 2006), because of its cheap (but highly skilled), non-unionized labour force. Sales of the original and adaptation rights to *Yo soy Betty, la fea* have made RCN a great deal of money, with sources estimating that the company's most profitable *telenovela* ever had earned them at least $50 million by 2006 (de la Fuente 2006). The show has reportedly 'almost single-handedly' rescued the TV network from financial ruin (Martinez 2001). But, as Rivero details, the creative workers have received few (if any) financial benefits. She contends that since the Bogotá television industry for so long remained a local enterprise and non-unionized, when Colombian scriptwriters sell a script to a television company they also waive author's rights. Labour and copyright laws also proved powerless in helping the creative talent once *Yo soy Betty, la fea* propelled Colombia out of its Latin American *barrio* and into the global marketplace.

Betty Grows into a Swan: Global Markets, Local Productions and Trading the Betty Format

Part of the Betty travelogue must at some point include a discussion of the business culture of the international TV market and 'how human agents mediate global television trade' (Havens 2006: 3). Esmeralda, played by the uncredited Salma Hayek, may make bad choices when it comes to men, but *Ugly Betty* exists thanks largely to the business acumen of the Hollywood A-list, Mexican-born actress and her production company Ventanarosa. Hayek optioned the series for US television along with Ben Silverman, who acquired the rights and scripts for *Yo soy Betty, la fea* in 2001. Starting her career in Mexican *telenovelas*, landing the title role in *Teresa* (Televisa, 1989–91), Hayek has first-hand knowledge of Latin American *novelas* (Schneider 2010) and 'cultural proximity' to local Mexican TV culture, but at the same time now observes those trends from a different locale, living as she does in the United States. Personal preferences and tastes, as well as an understanding of how a programme trend might profitably migrate and institutionally translate from one cultural territory to another, guide the acquisition and movement of TV programming.[1] As Hayek said of her choice, 'We've been trying to bring the Latino experience to television for many years. I was a big fan of *Betty, la fea* because it was different – it was very funny. So we thought this would be the perfect bridge where we could bring something that all the Latin community would feel is theirs into American culture' (Wilson 2006: 7).

Similarly, the Dori Media Group (DMG), responsible for distributing, and creating a market for, Latin American *telenovelas* in Israel, introduced the genre into that nation-state. Company founder is Argentine-Israeli businessman, Yair Dori, who grew up in Argentina watching *telenovelas*, before becoming a distributor of the genre in Israel and launching VIVA in 1999, a niche Israeli cable channel devoted to *telenovelas*. It was on VIVA, notes Amit Lavie-Dinur and Yuval Karniel in their contribution on the Israeli Betty, that *Yo soy Betty, la fea* first entered the Israeli media space. What emerge are bi-cultural international TV players able to exert some influence on programming types and the trade and flow of a particular television trend.

Another kind of influence is what Timothy Havens describes as 'local executives [acting] as intermediaries between viewers and exporters, deciding which programmes to purchase and how to schedule them based upon their own understanding of the culture' (ibid.). Havens charts the role of 'international jet-set' (2006: 6) media executives, producers and buyers, who are translating the foreign into local markets and defining national tastes. Jean Chalaby, in this collection, interviews Jeff Ford, the then-director of acquisitions responsible for purchasing *Ugly Betty* for the UK broadcaster, Channel 4. Ford talks about the close-knit international community where TV buyers perennially travel the world and exchange ideas with each other *about* television at various international TV sales markets like MIPTV (MIPTV) and the LA Screenings (LA Screenings. org). Such global experience informs buying decisions, but so do local broadcasting demands, corporate agendas and schedules. Long have we known that high-profile US signature series/serials can help build a reputation for a non-US channel (Rixon 2007; Knox 2007; Goode 2007) – giving it brand recognition (Johnson 2007) and help deliver a particular demographic to advertisers (McCabe 2005).[2] And *Ugly Betty* certainly met those requirements for Channel 4. Any decision about acquisition, Ford also reveals, is often about what is not purchased for a particular television territory and culture. For example, at no point did Channel 4 ever consider purchasing the Colombian original, despite *Ugly Betty* delivering ratings and prestige for the UK broadcaster.

Yo soy Betty, la fea has travelled far beyond its native Colombian borders. The original (canned, sometimes dubbed/subbed) and its local adaptations have migrated to more than 70 countries and speak a variety of foreign languages (Kraul 2006; Hecht 2006). What follows is a series of chapters focusing on questions of acquiring and adapting the Betty format, and in particular how *Yo soy Betty, la fea* was replicated, recycled and/or recreated in different broadcasting territories and cultures around the world. In becoming local, adaptations must hold localized appeal.

This reflects research that shows audiences, given the choice, tend to prefer local programming or that which appeals to cultural similarities or proximities (Straubhaar, 1991: 51; 2007: 25–7; Waisbord 2004: 369). Universal themes combined with discernable local elements that resonate with a national audience (allowing for identification) emerge as a theme in this collection. Interpretation and analysis may differ, but each author deals with the localizing of a universal tale of love and transformation. What unites them is a generic story involving interpretation and limits, possibilities and constraints, transfer and barriers.

This part of the journey begins with a series of interviews conducted by Andrea Esser with TV executives involved in the German adaptation, *Verliebt in Berlin* (*In Love in/with Berlin* [SAT.1, 2005–7]) – Alicia Remirez, head of fiction at SAT.1, Michael Esser, co-creator and scriptwriter of *ViB*, Jonas Baur, story editor, and Vasha Wallace, vice-president of format acquisitions at FremantleMedia. While the interviews highlight several issues discussed elsewhere (more of which later), one of the most significant elements in the adaptation process is choosing a format that has had proven success elsewhere. Tracking what fans in the USA had to say about *Yo soy Betty, la fea,* says Esser, helped them enormously in understanding why the *novela* had initially done well – and demonstrates once again how ideas *about* television are often formed and observed in different locales, Germany looking to Colombia via the Hispanic community in the United States. Prior success is key. It makes good business sense; for, as Albert Moran notes, 'adapting already successful material and content offers some chance of duplicating past and existing successes' (2006: 11).

Offering a comparative analysis of *Verliebt in Berlin* and *Yo soy Betty, la fea,* and incorporating interviews with those involved in the productions, Bianca Lippert focuses on how the central heroines – Colombian/Betty, German/Lisa Penske (Alexandra Neldel) – traverse several different borders in terms of national frontiers and trans-media storytelling. Lippert starts with Roland Robertson's theoretical concept of 'glocalization' (1995). This term, as Robertson explains, refers to how national cultures absorb and localize foreign influences into domestically created products. That process of incorporating foreign ideas into the local is used by Lippert to dissect the cross-cultural appeal of the Betty franchise (see also Lippert 2008; 2011). It enables her to explain how precisely the Colombian format translated into the German *media-* and *ideoscape*, with Latino passion metamorphosing into Protestant virginity, Latin American social melodrama transforming to German romantic fairytales while retaining a *telenovela* structure. Lippert considers further how the franchise was customized for the German television environment, tailored for its scheduling demands, and perpetuated across different media platforms (Jenkins 2006), and why, despite huge success, no attempt has since been made to adapt another Latin American *telenovela* format in Germany.

Finding the universal and adapting it to the local is also explored in Alexander Dhoest and Manon Mertens's study of the Flemish version, *Sara* (VTM, 2007–8). Drawing on interviews with writers and producers, as well as reflecting on its reception, and adopting theories of genre, this chapter seeks to understand how *Sara* was positioned in the Flemish television landscape. Formats are a way of keeping costs down and can make good financial sense for small markets like Belgium. The proven popularity of *Yo soy Betty, la fea* and its success in a similar market (the phenomenal popularity of the German adaptation),[3] helped persuade Flemish executives to take a chance on *Sara*. Never before had a *telenovela* successfully played on Belgian television. It was a risk. But in domesticating the genre, as Dhoest and Mertens argue, *Sara* represented something new and something different, while at the same time retaining 'national' flavours rooted 'in the mundane details of everyday life' – the 'everyday nationalism' of Flemish TV fiction (see Dhoest 2007). As *Sara's* producer, Reinhilde Dewit, succinctly put it: 'The large story was kept entirely, but you have to make the details local. That's really important, otherwise people don't recognise themselves, and you always have to show people a mirror, otherwise it doesn't work' (interview with Dhoest and Mertens in this anthology).

Both the above adaptations were made possible because of one of the global leaders in creating, producing and distributing entertainment brands FremantleMedia. Vasha Wallace, in the Esser interviews, says that 'FremantleMedia did a multi-territory deal for the rights' to *Yo soy Betty, la fea*. Owned by RTL, the leading European entertainment network, FremantleMedia held the European franchise to the Colombian *telenovela*, with local adaptations entrusted to affiliated studios. Drawing on an exclusive interview with Roberto Sessa, one-time general executive manager at Grundy Italia (and another part of RTL), Stefania Carini charts how the Italian-based content provider was responsible for adapting the Spanish, *Yo soy Bea* (Telecino, 2006–9), with know-how originating from Australia, which itself developed a style shaped by British social-realist traditions. This rather tangled transnational web of production knowledge, industrial practice and licensing agreements allows Carini to talk about the trade in television formats, the role of large global media conglomerates and their impact on producing local content.

At its most basic, a format is a concept, a programme idea (Moran 2006: 20). It may contain narrative elements, scripts and character dialogue (21); it perhaps includes suggestions for staging (camera angles, musical arrangements). Another aspect is ideas for distribution (promotion, auxiliary markets), creating a format package. What is provided, in other words, is a 'system of knowledge' (30). And it is this 'system of knowledge' that Carini seeks to disentangle as she explains why an Italian-based studio provided content for Spanish television, but not for its own domestic market. What her work also underlines is how a global media conglomerate like FremantleMedia may sell production expertise and know-how, but also reassurance, as well as a strong market brand. It is important, in turn, for the company to exert what Wallace calls 'brand guardianship', protecting the brand while endlessly promoting and talking confidently about what exactly that might mean. Illustrated in the above – German, Flemish, Italian/Spanish – is how a proven format somehow reduces a sense of risk; or, as Jade L. Miller puts it, 'executives optioning formats for development prefer the sense of security obtained through formats having been "proven" in a market with similar tastes' (2010: 203).

Content is not always what is most wanted from a TV format. In licensing a format it has long been known that producers want as much flexibility as possible when it comes to selecting the components they use for adaptation. As Albert Moran comments, 'There is a recognition that the original set of knowledges and their organization may have to be varied to fit production resources, channel image, buyer preference and so on' (2006: 68). Xiaolu Ma and Moran advance such thinking in their chapter on the Chinese adaptation, *Chou Nu (Nv) Wu Di* (*The Ugly Girl Is Matchless* [Hunan TV, 2008–10]). Emergent television territories like China have only recently entered the global TV marketplace, and so what is required from a TV format is not necessarily the same as what the

Germans or Spaniards want. Rather than purchase the original Colombian format, the Chinese opted instead for the Mexican version. PRC purchased the format of Televisa's *La fea más bella*, which was based on, and licensed from, the Colombian original. The reason for such a choice was because the programme franchise element suited Chinese needs much better. They were buying not only content, but also, and more importantly, a business strategy. What they wanted from the format deal was knowledge about financial decisions related to 'product placement, artist packaging services, programme promotion and derivative product arrangements'. In short, they were looking to create a different kind of TV product for the emergent Chinese television market based on (global) commercial interests fused with local cultural preferences and institutional needs.

Another emergent market, India, and its adaptation, *Jassi Jaissi Koi Nahin* (*There's Nobody Quite Like Jassi* [SET, 2003–6]), is the subject of the next chapter by Divya McMillin. Based on extensive ethnographic fieldwork conducted in Bangalore in 2004, and later in 2005, McMillin explores the various 'webs of desire' created in and through this adaptation of the original Colombian format. Like *Chou Nu (Nv) Wu Di* (but for different reasons), *Jassi Jaissi Koi Nahin* announces its global ambitions within its local flavours. While this chapter deals with how the Indian adaption was a product of the new global, synergistic media environment (distribution and satellite platforms, product placement), the fieldwork takes McMillin on a different kind of journey. Her findings on the shifting opinions and attitudes of her respondents reveal how the central heroine emerges 'as a sign of a carefully and artfully manipulated Indian womanhood that sits well with conservative longings for a woman who knows her place, as well as progressive fantasies of a woman who can navigate the public sphere without losing respect'.

Returning to *Ugly Betty*, and the transition from the high melodrama of the spoof *Vidas de Fuego* to the relative realism of the Suarez living room at teatime represents another kind of movement – a relocation from one fantasy space into another imaginary world involving national styles and local preferences. It announces what *Ugly Betty* is leaving behind, as the camera quite literally pulls out of, and away from, the Mexican *telenovela*, and into psychological realism of US TV drama with its more naturalistic performance styles. Enclosed in the fictional world of *Ugly Betty*, the *telenovela* with its hyper-melodramatic storyline, Hayek's camp portrayal of the outlandish heroine, and its tawdry stories of sex, seduction and betrayal is *made strange*; its tales are as out of sync with the heart of the US story that belongs to Betty Suarez as is the dubbing. But *Ugly Betty* reinvigorates and diversifies the serial dramedy form as it absorbs stories, generic codes and narrative conventions from elsewhere. Such transformation is not only startling, but emerges only gradually in its bold visual style, representational types, proliferation of new identity politics and (cultural) values while paradoxically continuing to adhere to prevailing US TV norms (narrative structure, generic format).

McMillin notices similar types of formal and aesthetic movement in *Jassi Jaissi Koi Nahin*. For example, *Jassi Jaissi* metamorphoses into a local Indian idiom through recourse to formal and aesthetic styles commonly associated with Bollywood, while retaining elements of the original that originated elsewhere. Laurence Raw makes a similar argument in terms of how Taner Akvardar, the director of the Turkish adaptation *Sensiz Olmuyor* (*Won't Work Without You* [Show TV and Kanal D, 2005]), consciously produced 'the *telenovela* in the style of *Yeşilçam* melodrama, a low-budget popular cinema that flourished in the Republic of Turkey between the 1950s and the late 1970s'. Questions of local styles and cultural preferences, and how these elements are appropriated to localize specific adaptations, are ones that authors in this collection return to time and again.

Before leaving the question of business strategy and commercial interests behind, and journeying into the myths and fairytale mythology of the Betty story, a few words about trademarks, copyright and the legal protection (or not) of a format are warranted. FremantleMedia may have acquired the European rights to *Yo soy Betty, la fea*, and the Chinese may have purchased the format of the Mexican version, but, along with these official adaptations, unofficial ones also existed – sometimes broadcasting simultaneously in the same television environment. The Betty story was, for example, cloned in Mexico by TV Azteca, as *El amor no es como lo pintan* (*Love Is not as They Depict It* [TV Azteca, 2000–1]). This version inspired by *Yo soy Betty, la fea*, in turn, itself became an international franchise, adapted in Portugal and Israel. *Esti Ha'mechoeret* (*Ugly Esti* [Channel 2, 2003]), the Israeli adaptation, went into production following Darset (a subsidiary of Dori Media Group) acquiring the rights from TV Azteca to adapt the 'Alicia' (rather than Betty) story. In 2005, however, as detailed by Lavie-Dinur and Karniel in their chapter, RCN Television threatened to litigate against Darset for copyright infringement, sensing that the Israeli adaptation shared far too many similarities with *Yo soy Betty, la fea*. *Esti Ha'mechoeret* may have translated the Cinderella myth into a Romeo-and-Juliet tale set in the divided territories, but it also highlights concerns around copyright in a format. In the process of circulating and adaptation, ideas are reworked, added to and reinterpreted. Often the original concept is developed further and an initial idea may even be improved as additional knowledge or experience shape it. (It is a debate charted further in Hilmes's chapter.)

Not So Ugly: (Still) Peddling the Cinderella Myth

At the end of the *Ugly Betty* pilot, following the trials and humiliations of the first 42 minutes, Betty is vindicated and (temporarily) wins out. It is the end of a long working day, and it has been a good one, as Betty helps Daniel save the Fabia account with her smart 'mothers and daughters' campaign, and its simple tagline – 'It's not the big events, but the little events that matter.' Standing on Madison Avenue, at the corner of 25th, Daniel bids Betty 'good night'. She turns to leave as the first 'chugging' guitar-based rhythms of K.T. Tunstall's anthem to female power, 'Suddenly I See', begins. 'Her face is a map of the world/Is a map of the world' cuts to a mid-shot of Betty smiling, almost lost in thought, before slipping off the kerb. Immediately, lyrics and visuals remind us of the global Betty brand. It is a face that has travelled widely, and recently arrived in Manhattan. Only a minor stumble – Betty rights herself, beams (if slightly embarrassed) and continues walking with renewed urgency and confidence: 'You can see that she's a beautiful girl/she's a beautiful girl.' Cut to Daniel. He smiles as he watches her, his gaze pledging loyalty and establishing affection. 'Suddenly I see' announces unconsciously that Daniel recognizes from the beginning our heroine's hidden virtues – a key feature of our best-loved, classic fairytales such as Cinderella. Cut to them both travelling (for now) in different directions. '(Suddenly I see)/This is what I wanna be' and the focus is back on Betty as she crosses the road, almost disappearing in the commuter traffic, and into Madison Square Park. 'Suddenly I see (Suddenly I see). Why the hell it means so much to me.' In this very brief sequence the US Betty, and her take on female aspiration and desire, renew the brand and reaffirm the universal – timeless, possibly – story centring 'on a heroine, on a young woman suffering a prolonged ordeal before her vindication and triumph' (Warner 1995: 202).

No discussion of the global popularity of *Yo soy Betty, la fea/Ugly Betty* with its family dramas, improbable plotlines and happy outcomes, would be complete without understanding the universality of its story. Or, put another way, why do we feel compelled to keep retelling the same old tale, selling it to different markets, consuming it across different territories, adapting it over and over again, and even risking litigation to spin it once more. Why is our modern consumerist culture still so in thrall to the fantasy of fairytale heroines whose beauty remains hidden until found by Prince Charming? Grounded in a Russian Formalist approach to the study of narrative structure, Vladimir Propp (1984) analysed the 'morphology' of folkloric tales, seeking to tabulate and dissect systematically component parts and their relation to one another, common to each story. Studying 100 fairy tales, and analysing the various archetypes and different sorts of action, Propp arrived at a typology of intrinsic plot elements, otherwise known as 'functions'. He listed 31 generic functions constituting '*the fundamental components of the tale*' (21). These are limited, not always the same, but there are specific rules and a consistent logic of how one function develops from another.

This taxonomy provides a list of constituent parts, but it does not quite explain why the same stories shoot up in different locations, skewed differently, with distinct local flavours, and offering renewed pleasure to new generations. It is the persistence of the antique tale of female suffering, survival based on believing in something better and finding redemption (often through love) at the end that has preoccupied scholars such as Marina Warner (1995). Second-wave feminism may have taught women to be suspicious of the Cinderella myth with its 'script for female domestication' (xiv), but still the tale endures. Our latter-day Cinderella is more preoccupied with paying the rent and fetching the coffee than sweeping hearths, but her tale of desire and aspiration remains vividly alive in our cultural imagination – and is in no danger of disappearing any time soon. 'Shape-shifting is one of the fairy tale's dominant and characteristic wonders,' writes Warner (xv), with its 'nomadic' motifs and plotlines, 'travelling the world and the millennia, turning up on parchments ... in an oral form ... in a ballad ... in a fairy story' (xvii) and in its latest incarnation, in a Colombian *telenovela*, a US primetime network series and a Greek one (to name a few). Betty Kaklamanidou, in her contribution on the Greek adaptation, *Maria i Asximi* (*Maria the Ugly One* [Mega Channel, 2007–8]), explores the role of myth and fairytales (Cinderella, The Ugly Duckling, Beauty and the Beast) that resonate in Greek culture. Including interviews with a writer and director of *Maria i Asximi*, the chapter investigates the mythic subtext of the series to explain why Greek audiences felt compelled enough to tune in every day for two years to follow the story of Maria Papasotiriou (Angeliki Daliani). Revealed also in this study of the travelling Cinderella myth made over for a modern Greek audience, and supported in the findings of Giovanna Del Negro (2003), is how the mythic subtext of the Betty story, communicating its common values, seems to find a keener resonance with viewers based in more deeply old-fashioned, patriarchal nations, often with a strongly conservative, religious heritage.

Structures of myth and universal storytelling help explain the programming flow of the *Yo soy Betty, la fea* format into territories as diverse as Russia, the Czech Republic, India, Israel and even China that seem to contradict and even thwart the strict logic of 'cultural proximity' (Straubhaar 1991). Joseph Straubhaar revised his original thesis to include proximities of genre, values and thematics (2007: 197), in an effort to account for this apparent theoretical impasse. He first claims that any discussion must take place 'within the context of an ongoing hybridization of television genres, which implies an underlying hybridization amongst their appeals to their audiences as well' (ibid.). Some genres are more amenable to exchange than others, and, as Straubhaar contends, the *telenovela* has had a long history of being shared across diverse cultures. An essential ingredient in its popularity, adds Miller, is its short run and daily scheduling (five to six nights-a-week format), 'which serves to capture and maintain a steadfast and transfixed audience' (2010: 204).[4] Another is the 'basic rags-to-riches "Cinderella" storyline on which the *telenovela* is based, with protagonists achieving love and success against the odds' (205; see Ortiz de Urbina and López, 1999).

Talking of proximity, Straubhaar speaks of how 'cultural proximity is cultural shareability ... [referring] to common values, images, archetypes and themes across cultures that permit programs to flow across cultural boundaries' (2007: 201). Stories that originate in Latin America but are relevant to audiences in Eastern Europe, for example, are based on this kind of cultural shareability in terms of values and themes. Often migratory tales, of a heroine travelling from a rural to urban area, which weave themes of adjustment and social mobility, of family and romance, of (economic) change and metropolitan living. Focusing on the Czech Republic and its Betty adaptation, Irena Carpentier Reifová and Zdeněk Sloboda argue for how *Ošklivka Katka* (*Ugly Katka* [TV Prima, 2008]) revises the social project of the *telenovela* on contemporary Czech television. Argued here is how the Cinderella storyline was adapted to negotiate the transition from socialism to capitalism in a post-socialist society. Oppositions such as work/unemployment, social inequality/ mobility, private business/large corporations are worked through, with those struggles mapped onto the female body of the Czech Cinders, Kateřina Bertoldová (Kateřina Janečková), who, in turn, mediates and moves between both worlds. Those prominent themes of upward mobility, from (socialist) poverty to (post-socialist) material success, and aspirational images of middle-class life central to most *telenovelas* are adapted anew in the Czech political context, and serve as a site of intense local struggle with political past and globalized future.

That socio-political shift is also common to (if not slightly different from) the Russian adaptation. Exploring how Latin American *telenovelas* have long travelled as far as Russia, Straubhaar contends that these nations' experience of industrialization and urbanization explains the popularity of the genre in the world's largest country. With the collapse of the Soviet Union and ensuing economic and social crises, *telenovelas* have remained as popular as ever in Russia. Elena Prokhorova argues that the international circulation of *Yo soy Betty, la fea* and its Russian version – *Ne Rodis' Krasivoy* (*Be not Born Beautiful* [STS, 2005-6]) – has provided Russian viewers with 'a format to provide positive answers to both questions, "overcoming" class, economic and social conflicts of post-Soviet society via a healthy portion of comedy and a heavy dose of melodrama along the way'. Her approach supports the work of other scholars like Kocihi Iwabuchi (2002), who analysed how US cultural products often denote proximity based not 'on true cultural familiarity but desire or aspiration' (Straubhaar 2007: 201) – and certainly the Latin

American *Yo soy Betty, la fea telenovela* performs a similar function in particular national markets. In its circulation of aspiration and acquisition, like *haute couture* travelling across international borders, the format allows local viewers to see precisely what global mobility looks like (see Featherstone 1990).

This question of travelling narratives is explored in Paul Julian Smith's contribution. Offering a journey (of sorts) from Spain to the United States and back again, Smith examines how movement is defined by geography, metaphor and the social. Focusing on the Spanish, *Yo soy Bea* (*I Am Bea* [Telecino, 2006–9]) and the US, *Ugly Betty*, allows Smith to suggest how the local comes into view in and through comparisons with a national Other. Why particular aesthetic styles and forms function in one national territory but not another, why certain themes preoccupy while another is concerned with something else, and why race and ethnic diversity interweave with transnational identities in the US *Betty*, but not in the Spanish *Bea*. As Betty and Bea travel respectively from local social worlds to others defined by global consumerism and cosmopolitan lives, mobility patterns may remain the same, but the local life strategies needed to negotiate that journey differ. It is in these in-between spaces that Smith reveals what the collection also seeks to give shape and understanding – namely, the trading of television narratives and the movement of cultural storytelling across borders and within local television territories.

Journey's end comes with a chapter by Dana Heller who explores what kinds of stories we are telling ourselves through the different Betties. Global aspirations speaking through a local vernacular, new media technologies profoundly reshaping national broadcasting territories, emergent political economics transforming traditional cultural identities and the sense of belonging – Heller brings together several themes discussed elsewhere in this anthology, but she also offers a perspective on *Ugly Betty* and how it 'affirms the relevance of the American Dream – the nation's perennially beloved makeover mythology'.

Aspiration and social mobility, private desires and global ambitions, travelling tales and local adaptations – it is *in* and *through* the central heroine, and *across* her body in particular, that these narratives are deeply embedded and circulated. It does shed light on what is at stake in the modern fantasy: aspirational surroundings, a hidden beauty revealed through style, designer *couture* and having the perfect body. The

Cinderella/Ugly Duckling story may be popular enough to sell globally, but what is the accompanying language of female beauty, femininity and the feminine that often remains unspoken – and why are unruly eyebrows, heavy stainless steel braces, unkempt hair and thick spectacles ubiquitous signifiers of female ugliness the world over? Central to each of the Betties is a heroine disguised behind calamitous sartorial choices, orthodontic hardware and unstyled bangs. Before the climatic moment of her metamorphosis – her figure trim, her hair groomed, her complexion glowing, her style impeccable – reveals the heroine's true value and she becomes available as a suitable bride. What are we to make of these dominant motifs for representing the worth of the woman? And why is female beauty still deeply entangled with feminine empowerment?

Any casual comparison of the after images of the different Betties indicate similar accepted attitudes and values as to what the correct female body should *look* like. Following the removal of what offends, of anything that troubles the perfect female body as an object of desire – braces, glasses, those few extra pounds, the heroine emerges as the feminine ideal. Always culturally specific, with deeply entrenched ideology internalized (see Bordo 2003), the images of Betty as beautiful swan are compelling enough to entangle us psychically and from which we are not entirely able to free ourselves. Intoxicatingly presented, persuasively offered as being about modern feminine accomplishment, each Betty is embedded in and through prevailing norms of the feminine self, her body (slender, fashionable, attractive), her lifestyle choices (hard work and social mobility, family stability and eligibility for marriage).

Betty as beautiful swan, from Bogotá to Berlin, Mumbai to Moscow, seductively embodies a type of feminine empowerment that is utterly digestible. It is a kind of power that is taken for granted precisely because it exacts a powerful, normalizing hold over us, shaped and inscribed as it is with the imprint of prevailing historical, socio-cultural and political norms that manage and animate our perceptions and experience of what the 'correct' female body *should* look like. In the Chinese version, for example, and with the assistance of Dove Soap, Wu Di quite literally becomes fairer faced with her lightened skin. Paler skin in China has long been regarded as more beautiful, as part of the historicity of the female form, part of a cultural and social mythology defining the ideal of Chinese womanhood – now achievable through consumer purchase.

In the West, as Marina Warner describes, 'the blondness of the fairytale beauty is one of the most potent and recurrent symbols within the genre … a quasi-mystical image of light and vitality' (1995: xxi). And the Betty makeover continues to celebrate (unconsciously) this mythology, as the more discipline our heroine has over her body the more success she has – in business and in love. What is suggested here is that while we *know* that what she represents is a constructed ideal, and while we *understand* what her representation is doing, we nevertheless compulsively *pursue* that ideal as something that truly matters.

One Betty that does more than any other to deconstruct the mythology is the US *Ugly Betty*. Launched in December 2006, the 'Be Ugly' campaign served to promote self-esteem among young women. The drive behind the idea was to end stereotyping in a culture obsessed with celebrities of skeletal proportions and Size 00 models. In the West, we are now routinely invited to look behind the body imaging process – plastic surgery, extreme diet and exercise plans, radical dental work, anti-ageing substances to be applied and/or injected – and *Ugly Betty* may have gently poked fun at and/or critiqued these ideals and ideologies but at the same time never quite stopped believing in them. The face of the campaign was, of course, America Ferrera. But like the other Betties around the world, beneath the soot of bad fashion choices, glasses and dishevelled hair, she scrubbed up rather well, appearing at events in designer dresses, with hair and makeup perfect.

Michel Foucault has maintained that power relations are never seamless, but instead are always producing new forms of culture, identities and subjectivities, new chances for change and transformation. Where power exists, he claims, so does *resistance*. Dominant institutions and values are persistently being infiltrated and reinvented by forms, conventions and values that have developed and gained potency and uniqueness at the periphery. *Yo soy Betty, la fea* may have emerged from the fringes of the international television market, but its globetrotting formula and beloved heroine adaptable to most consumer markets has something important to tell us about contemporary television culture and sexual politics, both locally and internationally. Betty may mean something different to different national territories or regions, but our Betty remains compelling nonetheless.

Works Cited

Appadurai, Arjun, *Modernity at Large: Cultural Dimensions of Globalization*, 7th edn (Minneapolis: University of Minnesota Press, 2005).

Barrera, Vivian, and Biebly, Denise D., 'Places, Faces, and Other Familiar Things: The Cultural Experience of *Telenovela* Viewing among Latinos in the United States', *Journal of Popular Culture*, vol. 34, no. 4 (2001), pp. 1–18.

'Betty la nuestra', *Semana*, 8 July 2000, pp. 24–9.

Bordo, Susan, *Unbearable Weight: Feminism, Western Culture, and the Body* (Berkeley and London: University of California Press, 2003).

De la Fuente, Anna Marie, '*Ugly Betty* Grows into Swan Around Globe', *Variety*, 5 February 2006, online at: http://www.variety.com/article/VR1117937365?refcatid=14&printerfri endly=true (accessed 19 July 2011).

Del Negro, Giovanna, P., 'Gender, Class and Suffering in the Argentinean *Telenovela Milagros*: An Italian Perspective', *Global Media Journal*, vol. 2, no. 2 (Spring 2003), online at: http://lass.calumet.purdue.edu/cca/gmj/OldSiteBackup/SubmittedDocuments/archived papers/spring2003/delnegro.htm (accessed 25 July 2011).

Dhoest, Alexander, 'The National Everyday in Contemporary European Television Fiction: The Flemish Case', *Critical Studies in Television*, vol. 2, no. 2 (Autumn 2007), pp. 60–76.

Donahue, Ann, *Ugly Betty: The Book* (London, 2008).

DMG, Dori Media Group, online at: http://www.dorimedia.com/content.asp?page=history (accessed 21 July 2011).

Featherstone, Mike, 'Global Culture: An Introduction', *Theory, Culture & Society*, vol. 7, no. 2 (June 1990), pp. 1–14.

Goode, Ian, '*CSI: Crime Scene Investigation:* Quality, the Fifth Channel and "America's Finest"', in Janet McCabe and Kim Akass (eds), *Quality TV: American Television and Beyond* (London: I.B.Tauris, 2007), pp. 118–28.

Haven, Timothy, *Global Television Marketplace* (London: Palgrave Macmillan, 2006).

Hecht, John, *Telenovela* Market. *The Hollywood Reporter*, 26 September 2006, online at: http://www.hollywoodreporter.com/news/telenovela-market-138873 (accessed 14 July 2011).

Herman, Edward, and McChesney, Robert, *The Global Media: The New Missionaries of Global Capitalism* (London: Cassell, 1997).

Hernandez, Lee, 'Salma Hayek Adapts Argentine *Telenovela* for ABC', *Latina*, 2 November 2010, online at: http://www.latina.com/entertainment/tv/salma-hayek-adapts-argentine -telenovela-abc (accessed 26 July 2011).

Hernandez, Sandra, 'The Ugly Truth about *Betty la fea*', *Salon.com*, 1 June 2001, online at: http://archive.salon.com/mwt/feature/2001/06/01/betty/ (accessed 11 July 2011).

Hodgson, Martin, '*Ugly Betty* Woos Colombian Viewers Night After Night', *Guardian*, 18 September 2000.

IBOPE Media Information, March 2001, online at: http://www.zonalatina.com/Zldata185. htm (accessed 14 July 2011).

Iwabuchi, Koichi, *Recentring Globalisation: Popular Culture and Japanese Transnationalism* (Durham, NC: Duke University Press, 2002).

Jenkins, Henry, *Convergence Culture. Where Old and New Media Collide* (New York: New York University Press, 2006).

Johnson, Cathy, 'Telebranding in TVIII. The Network as Brand and the Programme as Brand', *New Review of Film and Television Studies*, vol. 5, no. 1 (2007), pp. 11–20.

Knox, Simone, 'Five's Finest: The Import of *CSI* into British Terrestrial Television', in Michael Allen (ed.), *Reading CSI: Television Under the Microscope* (London: I.B.Tauris, 2007), pp. 183–97.

Kraul, Chris, 'Ugly Never Looked So Good', *Los Angeles Times*, 16 September 2006, online at: http://articles.latimes.com/print/2006/sep/16/business/fi-betty16 (accessed 19 July 2011).

LA Screenings.org, online at: http://www.lascreenings.org/LA_Screenings_2011_%40_The_Hyatt_Century_Plaza.html (accessed 21 July 2011).

Lippert, Bianca, 'The Bettyer Way to Success', *Critical Studies in Television*, vol. 3, no. 2 (Autumn 2008), pp. 19–39.

——, *Telenovela Formats – Localized Versions of a Universal Love. Yo soy Betty, la fea and Its Various Adaptations: Successful Remakes ad Infinitum?* (Göttingen: SierkeVerlag, 2011).

Martinez, Margarita, 'Colombians Under the Spell of Ugly Duckling', *The Daily Camera*, 23 April 2001, online at: http://translate.google.co.uk/translate?hl=en&sl=es&u=http://www.pobladores.com/channels/series_tv/betty_la_fea__/area/8&ei=M1IlTtrhH9OFhQfZxczrCQ&sa=X&oi=translate&ct=result&resnum=6&ved=0CC4Q7gEwBQ&prev=/search%3Fq%3DMartinez.%2BMargarita.%2BColombians%2BUnder%2BSpell%2Bof%2BUgly%2BDuckling%26hl%3Den%26client%3Dsafari%26rls%3Den%26prmd%3Divnso (accessed 19 July 2011).

McCabe, Janet, 'Creating "Quality" Audiences for *ER* on Channel 4', in Lucy Mazdon and Michael Hammond (eds), *The Contemporary Television Series* (Edinburgh: Edinburgh University Press, 2005), pp. 207–23.

Miller, Jade, L., '*Ugly Betty* Goes Global: Global Networks of Localized Content in the Telenovela Industry', *Global Media and Communication*, vol. 6, no. 2 (2010), pp. 198–217.

MIPTV, The World's Entertainment Content Market, online at: http://www.mipworld.com/miptv/ (accessed 21 July 2011).

Modleski, Tania, *Old Wives Tales: Feminist Re-Visions of Film and Other Fictions* (London: I.B.Tauris, 1999).

Morales, Magaly, '*Betty la fea* Leaves 80 Million Novela Fans', *South Florida Sun-Sentinel*, 9 May 2001, online at: http://www.accessmylibrary.com/article-1G1-121083234/betty-la-fea-leaves.html (accessed 19 July 2011).

Moran, Albert, with Malbon, Justin, *Understanding the Global TV Format* (Exeter: Intellect, 2006).

Nordenstreng, Kaarle, and Varis, Tapio, *Television Traffic: A One-Way Street?: A Survey and Analysis of the International Flow of Television Programme Material* (UNESCO, 1974), online at: http://unesdoc.unesco.org/images/0000/000075/007560eo.pdf (accessed 20 July 2011).

Ortiz de Urbina, Araceli, and López, Asbel, 'Soaps with a Latin Scent', *The UNESCO Courier*, vol. 52, no. 5 (May 1999), pp. 43–5, online at: http://unesdoc.unesco.org/

images/0011/001158/115858e.pdf#115881 (accessed 21 July 2011).

Paxman, Andrew, 'Hybridized, Glocalized and hecho en México: Foreign Influences on Mexican TV Programming Since the 1950s', *Global Media Journal*, vol. 2, no. 2 (Spring 2003), online at: http://lass.calumet.purdue.edu/cca/gmj/sp03/gmj-sp03-paxman.htm (accessed 20 July 2011).

Propp, Vladimir, *Morphology of the Folktale* (Austin, TX: University of Texas Press, 1984).

Rixon, Paul, 'American Programmes on British Screens: A Revaluation', *Critical Studies in Television*, vol. 2, no. 2 (Autumn 2007), pp. 96–112.

Robertson, Roland, 'Glocalization: Time-Space and Homogeneity-Heterogeneity', in Mike Featherstone, Scott Lash and Roland Robertson (eds), *Global Modernities* (London: Sage, 1995), pp. 25–44.

Schiller, Herbert, *Mass Communications and American Empire* (New York: A.M. Kelley, 1969).

———, 'Not Yet the Post-Imperialist Era', *Critical Studies in Mass Communication*, vol. 8 (1991), pp. 13–28.

Schneider, Michael, 'ABC Buys Salma Hayek's *Telenovela* Adaptation', *Variety*, 2 November 2010, online at: http://www.variety.com/article/VR1118026743?refCatId=4076 (accessed 21 July 2011).

Sinclair, John, *Latin American Television: A Global View* (Oxford: Oxford University Press, 1999).

———, 'The De-Centring of Cultural Flows, Audiences and Their Access to Television', *Critical Studies in Television*, vol. 4, no. 1 (Spring 2009), pp. 26–38.

Straubhaar, Joseph, 'Asymmetrical Interdependence and Cultural Proximity', *Critical Studies in Mass Communication*, vol. 8 (1991), pp. 39–59.

———, *World Television: From Global to Local* (London: Sage, 2007).

Tomlinson, John, 'Globalisation and National Identity', in John Sinclair and Graeme Turn (eds), *Contemporary World Television* (London: BFI Publishing, 2004), pp. 24–7.

'Ugly Is Beautiful for TeleFutura', *RBR.comTVBR.com*, 12 February 2009, online at: http://www.rbr.com/tv-cable/12877.html (accessed 25 July 2011).

Waisbord, Silvio, 'McTV: Understanding the Global Popularity of Television Formats', *Television & New Media*, vol. 5, no. 4 (2004), pp. 359–83.

Warner, Marina, *From the Beast to the Blonde: On Fairy Tales and Their Tellers* (London: Vintage, 1995).

Wilson, Benji, 'Ugly Betty', *Observer* (*Review*), 31 December 2006, p. 7.

Endnotes

1   November 2010 and it was reported that Hayek, along with her producing partner Jose Tamez, had sold an adaptation of *Los Roldan* (2004–5), an Argentine *telenovela* by Telefe, to the ABC network through Ventanarosa (Schneider 2010; Hernandez 2010).

2   No doubt the boost enjoyed by the Bogotá television industry was related to the increase in primetime Latino audiences and US media outlets aimed at them, with the total advertising revenue for the leading Spanish-language US networks – Univision,

Telemundo, TeleFutura and TV Azteca – estimated at $1.8 billion in 2006 alone (Kraul 2006).

3   Michael Esser talks about visits from Dutch and Belgian producers to find out about their production experience in the Esser interviews in this volume.

4   Cost is another factor in its popularity, as Latin American *telenovelas* (because of low production costs, see above) prove inexpensive imports, either as canned product or as a cost-effective format (205).

The Whole World's Unlikely Heroine: *Ugly Betty* as Transnational Phenomenon

Michele Hilmes

The many histories of the *Betty* format presented in this volume demonstrate both something new and something as old as broadcasting itself. The transnational trajectory of this amazingly protean series does indeed mark a unique moment in the globalization of broadcast television, finding remarkable success from nation to nation, from incarnation to incarnation, in more than 33 languages and across virtually every geographical region. No previous television series has provided so vital a palimpsest for creative reworking, cued to each receptive culture, nor attained such prominence on the world stage and in the hearts and minds not only of audiences but of critics and scholars as well.

With the mixture of age-old myth and postmodern playfulness that characterize Betty in all her manifestations, *Betty*'s malleability of form, character and setting marks a new stage in the negotiations between local, regional, national and global cultures that have characterized television since its beginnings: an established fictional series meets the flexible conventions and hyperactive global marketing of the format trade. Her birthplace, not in the major Western centres of TV production but from a geographically peripheral yet regionally significant Latin American site, Colombia, speaks to the newly criss-crossing lines of cultural influence in this global era. *Betty* exemplifies a kind of 'format fiction' that both harks back to older forms of cross-cultural borrowing and heralds an almost dangerous loosening of the structures and understandings that make it possible to talk about unified identities, properties and texts at all.[1] What unites the 33 flavours of *Betty*? Perhaps it is their very differences that hold this text together – or perhaps it is merely marketing.

Yet if *Betty* represents a departure in some ways, it does not take long to perceive that hers is only a particularly resonant, if enigmatic, episode in a long narrative of marketing-driven, text-twisting transnational cultural influence that has been more excoriated than explored. Here I wish to place the *Betty, la fea* phenomenon in the context of historical tensions and practices that have shaped the transnational trade in broadcast culture since the days of radio. Charting a course that cuts between the politically charged accusations of media imperialism and the often vague and sweeping claims of 'globalization' and unspecified flows of hybridity, I want to assert a place for a history of transnational influence and exchange as productive and culturally vital, as old as mediated communication itself. I also wish to indicate a historical trajectory in which the global *Betty* phenomenon can be seen as harking back to some of the earliest forms of transnational adaptation of broadcast properties, even as it shares in the new global era of format commodification. Finally, I consider *Betty* within the dominant modes of television series exchange and adaptation today, and attempt to link this to considerations of text and authorship.

A Little Backstory

Media globalization has a history, one that goes back far beyond the 1980s when the term first emerged in media studies scholarship. One thing worth remembering is that, in order for the 'intrusion' of the global into television culture to cause both enthusiasm and anxiety – a phenomenon that began as early as the 1960s – a condition of strongly defended *nationalism* was a necessary precursor. The idea of broadcasting as an inherently national phenomenon was introduced in the 1920s, as nations and empires uneasily consolidated after the upsets of the First World War (1914–18). Radio provided the ideal means to delineate the cultural boundaries of the twentieth-century nation-state even as empires spread their consolidating communications through the ether, creating a new stage on which the nation was projected and performed. Nations defined themselves against an array of global 'others', both internal and external, and circulated the preferred national culture via radio more broadly and accessibly than ever before possible (see Hilmes and VanCour 2007: 308–22). Some nations set up systems entirely owned and operated by the national government, as in the Soviet Union; others established a state-licensed monopoly to control and guide broadcasting's development, as in Britain; in other nations, most notably the United States, radio emerged as a privately owned, profit-oriented medium but still under the guidance of a national regulatory body. Others combined aspects of all these forms.

As the world's nations became network nations, the United States and Great Britain squared off as the dominant competing models for modern media-centred national cultures, influential across the globe. From Scandinavia to Japan and across the outposts of empire, nations modelled their broadcasting systems after Britain's BBC, sought its advice and emulated its programming, using strategies of centralization, state ownership, regulation, quotas, tax structures, public funding and other methods to pull together the national culture and to resist de-nationalizing threats both internal and external. In the American sphere of influence, especially in Latin America, private ownership and commercial programming were spread by both government and corporate interests, built on the sale of technology, private investments in national broadcasting infrastructures, advertising agencies marketing American consumer goods, and not least, official international policy initiatives. In Latin America, the place of Betty's birth, public and private stations competed for the national attention in most countries, with nationally owned stations drawing primarily on advertising revenues for support and purchasing programmes from a network of independent producers.

During the 1930s, the successful establishment of such national systems, as well as the development of shortwave radio technology, created more opportunities than ever before for the transnational exchange of popular culture. High culture had its established channels of transnational exchange – schools, museums, concert halls, lecture series – but the international flow of popular culture that began with film in the 1920s and carried over to radio in the 1930s was quickly perceived as problematic by national elites. Radio reached into even the poorest homes, far more effectively than print or film. And the fact that radio entered people's homes as a nationalized medium meant that even 'foreign' material took on a culturally legitimated aura once it was included in the local schedule. US radio interests took advantage of this and extended into Latin America (and around the world) via a variety of efforts in the 1930s, from government-sponsored shortwave goodwill broadcasts (Salwen 1997; Cramer 2009) to the more popular commercial programmes disseminated to local stations through advertising agencies such as J. Walter Thompson (McCann 2004).

This era marks the first wave of transnational cultural exchange in broadcasting, much closer to the *Ugly Betty* phenomenon than the later trade in recorded fictions and formats. Mark McCann's book *Hello, Hello Brazil* (2004) describes the process by which US advertising agencies distributed scripts of popular American programmes – not recordings – which were purchased by Brazilian stations, adapted to suit local languages, dialects, customs and circumstances by Brazilian writers, and performed by native actors, using the basic template of characters, setting and narrative trajectory to customize and 'nationalize' the programmes to reflect Brazilian life and suit its audiences (though often to sell US products). This process took place in nations around the world, often creating secondary and tertiary adaptations, as production centres like Cuba and Mexico adapted American programmes and sold them to other countries in the Latin American sphere (Rivero 2009).

Here we see the emergence of a kind of 'format fiction' that resembles the adaptation of literary properties to film, radio or television far more closely than it does the formal trade in broadcast formats that developed later. Often the programmes grew far beyond their original templates and, in some places, sparked an independent indigenous production sphere that rested on the framework of proven popular narratives imported from another country, most often the United States. Quebec provides one example of this. There, the American broadcasts that arrived freely from across the border were used as the inspiration for popular radio programmes adapted into the French language and the Quebec scene, with or without attribution or reference to their originals (and certainly without payment) – just as the creative reinterpretation of familiar literary properties has inspired writers the world over, throughout time, to spin off their own narratives into various media, making interventions that acquire a canonical status of their own.

Though programme producers like J. Walter Thompson might retain some control over their properties, selling their scripts rather than allowing them to simply be used without permission, more often than not transnational exchange in radio programmes took the form of simple but unacknowledged 'stealing' – as Jean Chalaby has argued (2011). In other cases, such profound changes were made that, though original influence might be acknowledged, no attempt was made to put a claim or a price on it, as with the BBC's adaptation of the US radio quiz show *Information, Please* (NBC 1938–51) into the quite distinctly British *The Brains Trust* (BBC/Home Service 1941–9). And even commercial operators like JWT rarely supervised or patrolled the profound variations or deviations from the original that might occur in the new cultural settings.

Television and the Commodity Form

But something happened when the ethereal, aural culture of radio broadcasting met the already globalized commodity culture of film in the second half of the decade, as television emerged. Though the sale of some quiz show formats precedes television – Chalaby discusses the controversy that erupted over the BBC's 'purchase' of *It Pays to Be Ignorant* (Mutual, 1942–4; CBS, 1944–50; NBC, 1951) and *Twenty Questions* (Mutual, 1946–53) on radio in the late 1940s – television made the borrowing of specific structural and visual elements far more obvious (2011). In addition, the arrival of television brought with it a 're-nationalization' of broadcasting culture compared to the international radio excursions of the 1930s and 1940s; until the advent of satellite distribution in the 1980s, television signals were confined by the technological limitations of the medium to relatively limited transmission areas. And television was far more expensive to produce and transmit than radio had been. As nations struggled to find the funding to set up their own television systems in the 1950s and 1960s, most confined their own transmission and distribution well within the boundaries of the country, relying on the low cost of imported programmes to fill up their schedules while directing scarce public funds towards local, live national programmes.

By the mid-1950s, two forms of global television exchange were proliferating rapidly: format sales, usually game and quiz shows, and the sale of filmed television programmes as pre-produced properties, whether as stand-alone productions (single plays, 'specials' or movies) or, increasingly, as series. Formatted game shows such as *Queen for a Day* (Mutual, 1945–57; NBC, 1956–60) and *Double or Nothing* (NBC, 1952–4) were adapted in France, Italy, Spain, German, Sweden and Australia, just to name a few (Chalaby 2011). In Britain, both the BBC and ITV had great success with US quiz show formats like *What's My Line?* (CBS, 1950–67; BBC, 1951–62); *Name That Tune* (NBC, 1952–4) became *Spot The Tune* (BBC, 1956), *Tic Tac Dough* (NBC, 1956–9) turned into *Criss-Cross Quiz* (ITV, 1957–67), and *The $64,000 Question* (CBS, 1955–8) came over as *The 64,000 Question*, with an award of 64,000 sixpences (ITV, 1956–8). The United States, with Hollywood as its epicentre, took an early lead in exporting programmes produced on film (often using the innovative 'three camera film' system developed by Desilu in 1951). The BBC became the world's second largest television exporter with its highly developed system of live production captured on film – called 'kinescopes' in the United States – and sold to television stations and networks around the world.

Film's material, visual form, as opposed to the script-based, ethereal aurality of radio, gave weight and substance to the programme trade, as television formats and programmes now became highly valuable commodities. Television established itself slowly across the globe – not until the late 1960s did the majority of nations possess a national television system – and those nations that developed a broadcasting production infrastructure first found that there were enormous profits to be made, particularly the United States, Britain and Japan. George Beadle, the BBC's director of television, in 1960 envisioned the situation:

> The BBC is an enormous producer of electronic programmes – without a doubt the greatest in the world. Just as Hollywood is the principal world centre for photographic programmes, so the BBC Television Centre is the principal world centre for electronic programmes. Television, for economic reasons, will always be mainly international. Few television stations will be anywhere near self-sufficient in programme material. Most of them will buy heavily from America and Britain. Britain has, or soon will have, the electronic programme ball at her feet (1960).

By the late 1960s, even the BBC had shifted largely to filmed television production, and its Television Enterprises division competed with America's big three networks, film studios and independent production companies in the sale of both formats and filmed series, which began to fill in the schedules of television stations everywhere.

Now, more careful attention to ownership rights prevailed, and systems of licensing and controlling intellectual property shaped the transnational flow of television culture. An international infrastructure began to emerge, organizing the haphazard avenues of exchange of the earlier period into a worldwide system (Havens 2006). A new spate of worries about the Americanization of culture began to generate the strand of media scholarship associated with theories of 'media imperialism' and of cultural imperialism more generally (Schiller 1976; Tunstall 1977; Mattelart 1979).

Terms like 'cocacolonization' and, later, 'Dallasification' mark the tenor of these times, sparked by the much-cited 1974 UNESCO report by Kaarle Nordenstreng and Tapio Varis, *Television Traffic: A One-Way Street?* which, in turn, contributed to the explosive 1980 UNESCO-sponsored MacBride Report (actually entitled *Many Voices One World: Towards a New More Just and More Efficient World Information and Communication Order*) that led to the New World Information and Communication Order controversies and eventually prompted both the United States and Britain to withdraw from UNESCO for the better part of two decades.

Most fingers were pointed at the United States, but Britain, France and Germany figured as dominant world suppliers as well despite a wide gap between the volume of their exports and those of America. The US share of world imports, estimated at between 100,000 and 200,000 hours annually, amounted to between two and three times that of the BBC's Television Enterprises division. It was divided between several hundred distributing organizations, the largest of which were Viacom (formerly owned by CBS),[2] Worldvision (formerly owned by ABC), National Telefilm Associates (formerly part of NBC), Screen Gems (Columbia), MCA and 20th Century Fox.[3]

Into the Global Spin

By the late 1980s, this period of relatively strong national broadcasters selectively introducing and adapting imported programmes began to give way to the era of global exchange. The advent of satellite distribution, cable television and the videocassette recorder took control of the national television culture out of the hands of traditional providers and placed it into the hands of private individuals and transnational corporations. Public service and regulated commercial broadcasters, squeezed by competition and under mandate to broaden and democratize their audience base, moved more aggressively into the global television market and also into lower-cost, reality-based programme forms. In the United States, the expiration of the fin/syn rules brought a new wave of mergers between the film and television industries and the formation of new, vertically integrated, over-the-air networks: Rupert Murdoch's FOX, the WB (Warners) and UPN (Paramount), heightening the competition for television audiences and putting pressure on production costs.

One result was the introduction of a new wave of reality-based formats that the 1990s began to circulate around the world, reversing some of the old patterns of programme flow (Moran 1998; Steemers 2004). These included not only traditional documentary formats, now seen on such channels as Discovery, National Geographic and The History Channel, not only in the United States but worldwide – but game shows (*Who Wants to be a Millionaire?*, *The Weakest Link*), cooking programmes (*Top Chef, Iron Chef*), makeover shows (*What not to Wear, Extreme Makeover: Home Edition*), talent competitions (*Pop Idol/American Idol, America's Next Top Model*), and the structured and staged situational reality shows that became particular hits, such as the globally successful *Big Brother* and *Survivor* franchises. These transnational format programmes – relatively inexpensive to produce, easy to 'nationalize' by encouraging local participation, and blamelessly focused on 'fact' – might pop up anywhere on the new expanded digital cable and satellite universe, or they might have an entire channel devoted to the genre (e.g. The Food Channel, Home and Garden Network).

The second wave of globalization discourse, in the late 1980s and early 1990s, reacted to the advent of these technological and political changes, theorized through anxieties over the erosion of the public sphere and the shift of emphasis in broadcasting's address from citizen to consumer. The globalization and heightened commercialization of national television were discussed in highly negative terms (Garnham 1983; Curran 1991; Blumler 1991). Commercial media were contrasted to public service media in cautionary tones, fed by fears that the global market spearheaded by Hollywood might decisively win out over publicly financed national culture. This period is also marked by some of the first scholarly analyses of the actual dimensions of imports, exports and co-productions (Collins 1986; Schlesinger 1986) and by the beginning of consideration of the ways that audiences understood and used such media (Ang 1996; Morley and Robins 1995).

By the late 1990s, however, some of these second-wave fears had begun to seem almost quaint as the digital revolution swept across the globe, multiplying the number of available channels in each nation exponentially while the Internet provided a virtually stateless new cultural domain. A third wave of scholarship continues to develop, less certain of the basic assumptions of the nation-based frameworks that preceded it and crossing media boundaries as well as national ones. The advent of the European Union and its transnationalizing cultural initiatives helped to reframe the terms of the debate, as did the increase during the 1990s in migration of populations from the outposts of empire and from the margins of wealthier regions, creating new levels of cultural diversity within national boundaries. National identities and national cultures became more highly contested grounds, less firmly held by elites. A new, permeable form of national culture became the norm, with immigrant populations able to tune into channels from home via satellite even as they switched between domestic and other imported offerings. As new media capitals rose (Bombay, Hong Kong, Lagos), fresh ways of theorizing global cultural flows began to appear (Appadurai 1990; Bhabha 1994; Garcia Canclini 2001; Ong 1999) and with them considerations of media culture willing to reconsider the old oppositions and to analyse ever more complex circuits of exchange (Bielby and Harrington 2008; Havens 2006; Kumar 2008). Along with transnational intersections came a growing number of trans-media studies, looking particularly at the ways in which digital media have transformed the forms and formats of film, television, music and added entirely new media venues, such as video games and online worlds, and created a new digital world of intertextuality and expanding global franchises (Gray 2010; Johnson 2009; Jenkins 2006).

And Now Betty

Into this global fray wandered a nice girl with big ambitions, the ugly duckling who not only married some species of prince but won recognition of her abilities and talents as well. Another strand of television history leading to *Betty* would discuss the significant rise in the number and centrality of female characters and woman-centred narratives on schedules worldwide (see Lotz 2006). *Telenovelas*, of course, have always had strong female characters, and the Colombian original that sparked *Betty*'s global journey, *Yo soy Betty, la fea* (RCN, 1999–2001), arose at a time in which the *telenovela* had achieved worldwide circulation, and the importance of Spanish language television had risen sharply in the North American and European markets. So, besides its Colombian origins, what made *Betty* so unique as a global phenomenon?

For television in the 2000s, it is possible to conceive of four distinct types of transnational productions, differing in the way that they make the transition from one context to another and also related, in the way that text and authorship are conceived.[4] An unusual characteristic of *Betty* is its ability to fit into several of these categories simultaneously, depending on the particular manifestation. Roughly, in my highly provisional nomenclature, they are: *imported series, adapted series, format fiction* and *reality formats*. The edges of these categories blur considerably at their margins, so that this is not meant as a set of tight and exclusionary pigeonholes, but simply as a structured way to think through differences.

At one extreme there is the *imported series*, the programme sold internationally as a filmed commodity: produced in one national context and broadcast 'as is' in a new national context. This happened in places where *Yo soy Betty, la fea* aired in its original Colombian version, in its original language, subtitled or dubbed – and a long list of places it is: most of Latin America, plus Spain, Bulgaria, China, the Czech Republic, Georgia, Hungary, India, Italy, Japan, Lithuania, Malaysia, the Philippines, Poland, Romania and Turkey, as well as in the United States on the Spanish-language satellite channel TeleFutura, part of Univision, two years before its adapted version, *Ugly Betty* (ABC, 2006–10), emerged. Though the title often changed in different national contexts – becoming *Betty, the Secretarial Office of Love and Betrayal* (*Betty, Ai to uragiri no hishojitsu*) in Japan, for instance – this was the version written by Fernando Gaitán and first broadcast on RCN-TV, Colombia, sold as a filmed series and aired very much in its original state.

Though changed subtly (or not-so-subtly; see Bucaria 2009) by dubbing and translation, as well as by practices like scheduling, promotion and extra-textual framing, a programme imported whole declares itself openly to be the product of one particular national context (though the fact that *Betty*'s particular original context was Colombia may have escaped many viewers, under a cover of general Latin American-ness). Though its circulation is transnational, its production is national. Thus *Betty* joins a long historical line-up of programmes bought and sold transnationally since the 1950s, viewed sometimes as disruptive and de-nationalizing, as in the Hollywood-dominated 'cultural imperialism' period of the 1970s and 1980s, and sometimes as educational and stimulating, as in the long history of British imports on US television (Miller 2000; Tankel 1984). Some of the adaptations of *Betty* also achieved this status (a second-generation imported series? An imported series once removed?), as in the case of the US version, *Ugly Betty*, which itself was purchased for broadcast in a list of countries almost as long as the original series, including many in Latin America (though in Colombia the series received criticism as a 'pale imitation' of the original version). This sort of global circulation relies upon a highly traditional sense of what a text is (it remains fixed), and what an author does (owns the rights to the text). Even though television as a form produces highly permeable texts, created by many authors and lacking many of the unities on which print-based copyright law relies, the television industry creates and maintains its own kind of legal fictions to hold these elements firmly in place. Profits are allocated according to binding agreements and definitions that make it so.

At the other extreme is the transnational *reality format* programme: quiz shows, game shows, makeover shows, contests of various kinds, from *What's My Line?* and *Pop Idol* to *Survivor*. These programmes are specifically designed to be adapted in such a way as to change virtually every element of the show except for the central organizing concept, and they have received much scholarly attention as the new kid on the global block. Though they rest on a central concept, as Albert Moran points out, more than just a concept is at stake (since an idea cannot be copyrighted); a format is: 'an interconnected parcel of particular knowledges that will be galvanized in the production, financing, marketing and broadcasting of a TV programme' (1998: 25). Here, notions of authorship and text in the classic sense are largely irrelevant; these reality-based programmes exist as a collection of legal attributes and aggregated practices – though, of course, once produced and preserved on film (or digitally) as a season-long text, their status changes. Currently, the market in already-produced past seasons of reality format programming is something that remains confined to the DVD market and to occasional cable TV marathons and clip fests. But surely they will increasingly appear as imported series in the future.

Between these two extremes comes the *adapted series*, which as I will argue here has two types, 'creative' and 'controlled', and *format fiction*, a label I am reserving, for now, for *Betty* as a harbinger of things to come. These are closer to being points on a sliding scale than separate forms, but all three share one determining characteristic: they are not game or quiz or reality formats, but fictional narrative series, whether comedy or drama or something in between. Thus they legally, and pragmatically, adhere to the conventions of the traditional text (the unified expression of an author/owner). But sold as an adaptable property they morph into something different, so that a number of recognizably variant texts emerge (and indeed, over time, some series can stray very far from their originals – a special property of television). This kind of adaptation has long taken place from medium to medium, or platform to platform – a novel becomes a film becomes a television series becomes a videogame – but when it is done transnationally, it falls into a grey area that has been little theorized, and television's unity-defying seriality and permeability pushes it even further into boundary-testing realms. We are all familiar with film remakes, and increasingly with television remakes as well[5] (though 'literary remakes' had better display the authorized characteristics of parody if they want to be legal), but adaptation of a text, especially a serial text, into another national context, though occurring frequently, is likely to receive more popular attention than scholarly. Far more scholarship exists on adapting novels or films into television (forms exhibiting more traditional conventions of text and authorship) than on the transnational adaptation of television series.

The category of 'creative adaptation' includes many programmes whose secondary version becomes more famous than the original (arguably the case, for instance, with *All In the Family*'s [CBS, 1971–9] translation of British television's *Till Death Us Do Part* [BBC, 1965–8; 1970; 1972–5], others that succeeded equally across the national divide (for instance, *The Office* [BBC, 2001–3; NBC, 2005–present] in its US and original British versions), and many more that attempted to capture something of a highly successful show for another national context and failed – this list would be lengthy indeed. But all have the basic system adopted in the 1960s in common: the adapting company pays for the rights to a programme originated in another national context, then changes what it needs to in order to effect a version that will, it hopes, do better than the original would in the home market. Sometimes the adaptation differs so substantially that it is hard to perceive what was drawn from the original, other than a few details of character and situation; at other times the adapted version stays fairly close to the original, for better or worse. Most of the time the series' transnational roots remain unmarked in the text itself, and often in the discourse surrounding it as well, though it may emerge in critical and fan discussions. In the case of the US *Ugly Betty*, more attention than usual was drawn to the fact that its source was a Colombian *telenovela* that had been wildly successful globally – possibly because that original version would have been familiar to many US viewers through Telemundo, possibly because its celebrated roots were seen as good marketing at this moment of heightened Spanish culture consciousness in the United States.

Another variant on the adapted series, what I am calling 'controlled adaptation', is emerging in the 2000s, led by television impresario Dick Wolf and his *Law & Order* franchise (originally screened on NBC, 1990–2010). Aware of the considerable demand for national adaptation of his popular series, above and beyond simple sale as an export, Wolf did not want to expose his valuable 'brand' to cheapening on the world market through poor reworkings or variants that diverged too far from the original property. Instead, his company plays a strong role in overseeing each subsequent national version, working with local production companies to shape the new version along the lines approved by Wolf.

The first controlled adaptation, *Paris Enquêtes Criminelles* (*Paris Criminal Investigations*), debuted in 2007 on TF1 as a version of *Law & Order: Criminal Intent* (NBC, 2001–7; USA Network, 2007–11) specifically shaped to fit the French legal system (no reading of Miranda rights) and French cultural sensibilities. Produced by Alma Productions, a French company based in Paris, it was overseen with obsessive care by its creator, especially regarding the use of the trademark 'ca-ching' sound (which 'should never be used more than two times per act, and should be used to signal a shift in the storytelling, not just a change in location' [Barnes 2007: 1]). A British version, *Law & Order: UK*, debuted on ITV in 2009, produced by Kudos Film and Television and set in London but again held tightly to the original. Two different iterations of the franchise have also been adapted for Russian television, set in Moscow; their translated titles are *Law & Order: Division of Field Investigation* (NTV, 2007–present) (patterned on *Special Victims Unit* [NBC, 1999–present]) and *Law & Order: Criminal Intent* (NTV, 2007–9).

Such a controlled adaptation is not quite a co-production, since control and ownership are retained by Wolf Films, but it is highly transnational in its production circumstances – not just the title and concept move over from one national context to another, but authorial supervision as well – and thus one might expect that its transnationality would leave a strong mark on the text.

It may be possible to watch *Law & Order: UK* without being aware that it stems from a US original, but so many specific elements – the monotone voiceover at the beginning, the use of the 'ca-ching', the two-part structure – mark it out as unique, at least, and stamp something resembling an author's 'voice' on the text. On the other hand, perhaps the integration of these textual elements with the specificity of national legal systems and topical criminal plotlines will work to erase its transnational origins. Its relevance here is that it is an attempt to impose a new form of transnational authorship onto the practice of adaptation, one that has not been the norm for the adapted series in the global television trade up till now. While reality formats might in fact, behind the scenes, erode national trade boundaries and spread certain kinds of cultural forms around the world as effectively as the Hollywood film in the 1930s (Kretschmer, Singh and Wardle 2009), their textual openness, demanding a high level of localization, obscures the transnational influences actually at work.

Yet with the controlled adaptation, the actual presence of authors (and contributors of all kinds) from different national backgrounds at least presents a chance of a more collaborative, culturally dialogic text than either the direct import or the reality format.[6]

What about something in between the adapted series and the reality format? Arguably, *Betty* has found a new role here: in the variety and the disparity of her many manifestations resembling a format, but in a way that only an authored fiction can. Though directly imported into many markets, the show escaped the bounds of authorial control early in the process, as Yeidy Rivero explains in this volume, and was subjected to a far wider scope of adaptation, uncontrolled by its original authors, than that experienced by most programmes. It became a kind of *format fiction*, lending discrete parts of its textual universe to creative reworkings in an astonishing variety of settings, while still maintaining a celebrated attachment to the parent series. Thus, if 'controlled adaptation' represents a move closer to the authorial and textual closure of the imported series, format fiction edges closer to the textual openness of the reality format. Its wide variations from the original text still retain key elements of the original, yet almost every single element has been changed in one context or another, creating a palimpsest of forms and meanings.

In some places *Betty* retained its serial *telenovela* form in adaptation, as in Spain and Mexico; in others, including the USA, it was transformed into a comedy/drama series – which then itself was not only sold worldwide but received its own adaptations. It might be broadcast during the daytime, with correspondingly lower production values, or as part of a primetime line-up; it might add to its original focus on beauty and the importance of appearance themes of ethnicity, class, morality, sexuality, regionality, gender and family relations. Paul Julian Smith, in his comparison of *Betty* in Spain and the United States, describes the diverse writing and production team that produced *Ugly Betty,* a version that focused on ethnic diversity and incorporated elements of transnational identity, especially the Latin American context, far more than other national versions did; this version itself has now found adaptation in Georgia, adjusted, one assumes, to the ethnic and class specificities of that nation (a second-generation adaptation). The German version, *Verliebt in Berlin,* went so far as to dispose of its heroine and introduce a male lead character in the second season. Though in all cases certain elements remain – notably, a heroine characterized as 'ugly' – her type and degree of ugliness shifted, too, until in some cases it became less a matter of physical appearance than of class position or personality. Thus the fictional narrative supplies something more closely resembling a format than a traditional text – a skeletal framework on which all manner of fleshing out might occur.

What does it take to hold such a de-centred and nebulous text together? First of all, a legal structure for asserting rights, into which all parties must enter even if they are relatively powerless on the global scene. For *Betty*, sheer success as an import helped to patrol its borders as an adaptation, even if its creators could not hold it as closely together as they might have wished. A large part of the appeal of formats, on which their price and value is based, is their marketing apparatus, sold along with the other rights. And once a few big players on the scene have purchased rights, they too have a vested interest in making sure that the licensing process continues in an orderly fashion, within a global structure of markets, contracts and legal agreements. This was the missing factor in the earlier period of radio adaptation, when anyone could copy down script ideas and plotlines, thus producing their own version outside the scrutiny of agencies and networks. But with the flexibility of 'format fiction' like *Betty*, certain unities are preserved and a web of textual relationships maintained even as versions vary and proliferate and are celebrated for their proliferation and variance.

We must conclude, then, that *Betty* is indeed special. Other programmes may share in a similar transnational malleability, but none have risen to such prominence on the global stage. Simultaneously an imported series, an adaptation and a format, *Betty* is the protean girl of the moment, speaking across cultures in meaningful ways, displaying the creativity and artistry of writers and producers around the globe, seamlessly slipping into the national cultural consciousness – even provoking scholars to imagine a volume such as this one. Will she remain unique or will she multiply? We will have to stay tuned, but her storyline indicates growth.

Works Cited

Ang, Ien, *Living Room Wars: Rethinking Media Audiences for a Postmodern World* (London: Routledge, 1996).

Appadurai, Arjun, 'Disjuncture and Difference in the Global Economy', *Public Culture*, vol. 2, no. 2 (1990), pp. 1–24.

——, *Modernity at Large: Cultural Dimensions of Globalization* (Minneapolis: University of Minnesota Press, 1996).

Brooks, Barnes, 'NBC Faces Trials Bringing *Law&Order* to France', *Wall Street Journal* (1 March 2007), p. 1.

Beadle, George, 'World's Biggest TV Program Centre Opens June 29', BBC press release, 8B/3/5 (National Educational Television archive, Wisconsin Historical Society, 22 June 1960).

Bhabha, Homi K., *The Location of Culture* (New York: Routledge, 1994).

Bielby, Denise, and Harrington, Lee, *Global TV: Exporting Television and Culture in the World Market* (New York: New York University Press, 2008).

Blumler, Jay, 'The New Television Marketplace: Imperatives. Implications. Issues', in James Curran and Michael Gurevich (eds), *Mass Media and Society* (London: Arnold, 1991), pp. 194–215.

Bucaria, Chiara, *Dark Humour as a Culture-Specific Phenomenon. A Study in Audiovisual Translation* (Saarbrücken: VDM Publishing, 2009).

Chalaby, Jean, 'At Its Origins: The Nascent TV Format Trade (1949–1962)', Presentation at the Broadcasting in the 1950s Conference, Gregynog Hall/ University of Aberystwyth, 20–22 July 2011.

Collins, Richard, 'Wall-To-Wall *Dallas?* The US-UK Trade in Television', *Screen*, vol. 27, no. 5 (1986), pp. 66–76.

Curran, James, 'Mass Media and Democracy: A Reappraisal', in James Curran and Michael Gurevich (eds), *Mass Media and Society* (London: Arnold, 1991), pp. 82–117.

Cramer, Gisella, 'The Rockefeller Foundation and Pan-American Radio', in William Buxton (ed.), *Patronizing the Public* (Lanham, MD: Rowman and Littlefield, 2009), pp. 77–100.

García Canclini, Néstor, *Consumers and Citizens: Globalization and Multicultural Conflict* (Minneapolis: University of Minnesota Press, 2001).

Garnham, Nicholas, 'Public Service Versus the Market: Nicholas Garnham Considers the Impact of New Information Technologies on the Future of British Broadcasting', *Screen*, vol. 24, no. 1 (1983), pp. 6–27.

Gray, Jonathan, *Show Sold Separately: Promos, Spoilers, and other Media Paratexts* (New York: New York University Press, 2010).

Havens, Timothy, *Global Television Marketplace* (London: BFI Publishing, 2006).

Hilmes, Michele, *Network Nations: A Transnational History of British and American Broadcasting* (New York: Routledge, 2011).

——, and VanCour, Shawn, 'Network Nation: Writing Broadcasting History as Cultural History', in Michele Hilmes (ed.), *NBC: America's Network* (Berkeley: University of California Press, 2007), pp. 308–22.

Jenkins, Henry, *Convergence Culture: Where Old and New Media Collide* (New York: New York University Press, 2006).

Johnson, Derek, *Franchising Media Worlds: Content Networks and the Collaborative Production of Culture* (Unpublished PhD dissertation, University of Wisconsin-Madison, 2006).

Kretschmer, Martin, Singh, Sukhpreet, and Wardle, Jonathan, 'The Exploitation of Television Formats,' ESRC Digital Resource, Bournemouth University, 2009, online at: http://tvformats.bournemouth.ac.uk/overview.html (accessed 25 July 2011).

Kumar, Shanti, *Gandhi Meets Primetime: Globalization and Nationalism in Indian Television* (Urbana: University of Illinois Press, 2008).

Lotz, Amanda D., *Redesigning Women: Television After the Network Era* (Urbana: University of Illinois Press 2006).

Mattelart, Armand, *Multinational Corporations and the Control of Culture: the Ideological Apparatuses of Imperialism* (Brighton: Harvester Press, 1979).

McCann, Bryan, *Hello. Hello Brazil: Popular Music in the Making of Modern Brazil* (Durham: Duke University Press, 2004).

Miller, Jeffrey S., *Something Completely Different: British Television and American Culture* (Minneapolis: University of Minnesota Press, 2000).

Moran, Albert, *Copycat Television: Globalization, Programme Formats, and Cultural Identity* (Luton: University of Luton Press, 1998).

——, with Malbon, Justin, *Understanding the Global TV Format* (Exeter: Intellect, 2006).

Morley, David, and Robins, Kevin, *Spaces of Identity* (London: Routledge, 1995).

Nordenstreng, Kaarle, and Varis, Tapio, 'Television Traffic: A One-Way Street?' *UNESCO Reports and Papers on Mass Communication*, vol. 70 (Paris: UNESCO, 1974).

Ong, Aihwa, *Flexible Citizenship: The Cultural Logics of Transnationality* (Durham: Duke University Press, 1999).

Rivero, Yeidy, 'Havana as a 1940s–1950s Latin American Media Capital', *Critical Studies in Media Communication,* vol. 26, no. 3 (August 2009), pp. 275–93.

Salwen, Michael B., 'Broadcasting to Latin America: Reconciling Industry-Government Functions in the Pre-Voice of America Era', *Historical Journal of Film, Radio and Television*, vol. 17, no. 1 (1997), pp. 67–89.

Schiller, Herbert, *Communication and Cultural Domination* (New York: International Arts and Sciences Press, 1976).

Schlesinger, Philip, 'Trading in Fictions: What Do We Know about British Television Imports and Exports?', *European Journal of Communication*, vol. 1, no. 3 (1986), pp. 263–87.

Steemers, Jeanette, *Selling Television: British Television in the Global Marketplace* (London: BFI Publishing, 2004).

Tankel, Jonathan, 'The ITV Thriller: The Interaction of Media Systems and Popular Culture' (Unpublished PhD dissertation, University of Wisconsin-Madison, 1984).

Tinic, Serra, *On Location: Canada's Television Industry in a Global Market* (Toronto: University of Toronto Press, 2005).

Tunstall, Jeremy, *The Media Are American* (New York: Columbia University Press, 1977).

Weissmann, Elke, 'Paying for Fewer Imports: The BBC License Fee 1975–1981 and Attitudes Towards American Imports', *Television & New Media*, vol. 10, no. 6 (2009), pp. 482–500.

Endnotes

1 Yeidy Rivero reveals some of these dangers: loss of authorial rights and control, pressures that can impede the professionalization of television writing and production.

2 With the implementation of the fin/syn rules, all three major networks had spun off their distribution arms.

3 The BBC remained the world's single largest exporter of programmes, however, given this dispersal of sites of production and distribution in the USA.

4 I focus here on the series form, since it has provided the basis for the international trade in television since the 1960s.

5 Generally speaking, a 'remake' is a version of a programme that is reconceptualized across temporal boundaries (a redo of an older show) rather than national.

6 One might also term this the 'franchised adaptation', since it partakes of many of the legal and creative negotiations found in franchised properties such as those associated with comics and sci-fi genres. See the work of Derek Johnson (2009) for a discussion of the franchise, both historically and in the contemporary era.

Our *Betty*: The Legacy of *Yo soy Betty, la fea*'s Success in Colombia

Yeidy M. Rivero

In the autumn of 2000, I received a phone call from my good friend, Colombian communications scholar Clemencia Rodríguez. The main purpose of her call was not to discuss the trials and tribulations of academia but instead to share her enthusiasm for a Colombian *telenovela* that was being broadcast on the US Spanish-language network, Telemundo. Her excitement for this show was so contagious that I decided to tune in. The programme in question was *Yo soy Betty, la fea* (*I Am Betty, the Ugly One*, 1999–2001), a *telenovela* produced by the Colombian network, RCN, which at the time was being broadcast in Colombia, the United States and many Latin American countries. Needless to say, like my friend and millions of viewers across the Americas, I was hooked. I cried with and for Beatriz, I laughed with her funny friends (*El cuartel de las feas* [The Ugly Women Club]) and, like some fans, I was quite disappointed by the very traditional *telenovela* marriage ending. Let me go back to the original story, though. After witnessing the bizarre regional frenzy of *Yo soy Betty, la fea*, a television furore not seen in Latin America since the early 1970s' Peruvian *telenovela* hit, *Simplemente María* (*Simply Maria*, Panamericana TV, 1969), Clemencia decided to put together a group to write a book about the *telenovela*'s production and reception. To cut a long story short, the book never materialized but I did write an essay about *Yo soy Betty, la fea*, and just as I was waiting for the essay to be published, news about an Indian adaptation appeared in trade magazines. At the time, none of the people involved in the book project knew that *Betty* was about to explode onto the global scene. We were not the only ones caught by surprise.

Ten years after RCN began to broadcast Fernando Gaitán's story about an ugly, highly intelligent, competent and decent woman who worked in the fashion industry, Colombian television professionals and scholars who specialize in the *telenovela* genre continued to be mesmerized by a format that has not only been sold globally but has also originated new formats. As one Colombian media professional mentioned to me, 'in 1999 [when the *telenovela* began to air in Colombia], no one had a clue about what would become of *Yo soy Betty, la fea*'. On the other hand, in his analysis of television production and exportation across Latin America, the United States and Spain, communication scholar Lorenzo Vilches writes, 'It may be that a phenomenon the same as *Betty, la fea* may not be repeated ... but there is no doubt that other scripts with similar effects will arise' (2008: 46). While it is not clear when, where, or if we might see the emergence of another global media product such as Betty, at least up to this point in television history, the global adaptation of one particular fictionalized television product is, indeed, exceptional. Furthermore, the fact that this artefact originated in a small-regional television market adds to the uniqueness of the Betty craze. Whether it was due to the well-developed narrative and character structure, or the insidiously global patriarchal beauty culture, or perhaps a result of today's industrial television practices, the Betty concept has travelled and continues to travel. The publication of this anthology and the inclusion of articles addressing various, multilingual and multicultural Betties is a testament to the uniqueness of *Yo soy Betty, la fea* as a global television product.

In this piece I return to what I deem as my Betty, that is, the Colombian version. Drawing from personal interviews with Colombian television professionals, I present a brief history of the internationalization of the Colombia *telenovela* and Fernando Gaitán's role in that history. I then analyse the ways in which the success of Betty is transforming Bogotá's network television industry.[1] My primary objective is to contextualize the genesis of this very special *telenovela* and to call attention to a less publicized side of the global Betty phenomenon: the suctioning of profits, talent and creativity out of Colombia. As Silvio Waisbord contends in relation to format exporting, the 'global television industry is becoming a giant cultural vacuum cleaner that constantly sucks in ideas from around the world and turns them into commodities' (2004: 378). In a non-unionized television system such as Colombia's, the *Yo soy Betty, la fea* case presents a different side of the global television 'giant vacuum cleaner' trend. As I explain below, in an industry that remained local for many years, it was not until the selling of the Betty format that questions about labour, authors' rights and profits began to concern many media professionals working in Colombia. Therefore, while the siphoning of profits, talent and creativity did not originate with the *Yo soy Betty, la fea* production, these labour concerns are another 'ugly' element associated with Betty.

Colombian Television: From the Local to the Regional Market

In the world of Latin American television exportations, Colombia can be categorized as a new and rather contained exporter, especially when compared to Mexico and Brazil, which are, according to Rafael Roncagliolo, 'net exporters' (1995: 335–42).[2] Contrary to, for example, Mexico, which has dominated the Latin American television market since the late 1970s, Colombian *telenovela* scripts and *lata* (canned programming) only began to be sold in the early 1990s. To be sure, there is no correlation between Colombia's limited market integration and the quality of its products. In fact, in the *telenovela* and television series' hierarchical structure (primarily developed by academics and industry people), the Colombian product has prestige. As an interviewee observed regarding what are considered the 'best' Latin American *telenovelas* and series, '"the Brazilian" [productions] are aesthetically and dramatically superior. Then we have the Argentineans' which are psychoanalytical, urban, and fast. Then we have the Colombians'" (media professional, 2008). Thus, even though many Colombian media professionals did not anticipate the tremendous global success of Betty, they – as well as others familiar with the flow of programming in Latin America – were not surprised by the Colombian origins of this media-changing cultural product. As a relatively new *telenovela* producer (in relation to other countries in the region) the Colombian television industry has done quite well.

Colombia's belated arrival to the *telenovela* export business is tied to the politics of an earlier era in which the State, which controlled the industry, expressed little interest in the genre (Rey 2002: 117–62). Whereas a country such as Cuba had been selling *radionovela* scripts since the 1940s and had produced its first *telenovela* in 1952, and while Mexico and Brazil had also initiated *telenovela* production in the 1950s, Colombia aired its first *telenovela* in 1963. According to media professionals who began their television careers in the 1950s, the Colombian government and many involved in television production did not deem the *telenovelas* appropriate programming for the Colombian citizen (Rodríguez and Tellez 1989).

As a medium institutionalized by a military dictatorship in 1954 and run by the government until 1995, the State delineated the types of programmes that would be televized. Throughout its first three decades, but particularly in its first 10 years, the primary purpose of Colombia's television was to educate the people through its broadcasting of high culture programming. Theatre, opera, classical music and adaptations of literary classics filled Colombia's television schedule. 'The State institutionalized a high culture and enlightened type of programming. The fiction produced for television had a pedagogical and cultural objective,' observed Colombian media scholar Omar Rincón (2008). Even after the government began auctioning programming time-slots and genres first to advertising agencies (after 1956) and later to independent production companies (during the early 1960s), the State continued its interest in 'high culture' programming. Of the different high-culture genres aired on Colombian television, the live-broadcast *teleteatros* (tele-theatres) are considered a pivotal preamble for the gestation of the Colombian *telenovela*. As Jesús Martín-Barbero and Germán Rey's research has documented, the *teleteatros* formed a cadre of performers, writers and directors who, although formally trained in theatre, initiated the transition to the technical, aesthetic and narrative particularities of television production in general and the *telenovela* in particular (Rey 2002: 144–5; Martín-Barbero 1999).

A combination of economic and industrial factors during the early 1960s opened the space for the *telenovela* genre within Colombia's television programming fare. The state reduction of the television budget, the establishment of new independent production companies, the national expansion of the television signal and the advertisers' interest in reaching a broader Colombian audience (especially housewives), instigated the production of *telenovelas* (Vizcaino Gutierrez 1994; Carmen Julia and Tatiana 1999). Notwithstanding the fact that the first Colombian *telenovelas* were adaptations of Cuban *radionovela* scripts, the Bogotá-based professionals rapidly indigenized the genre. As Martín-Barbero and Rey note, starting in the mid-1960s, 'fictional characters talked to social characters, both of which experienced similar questions and apprehension' (1999: 122). By adapting Colombian literary classics, the *Colombianness* of the genre began to emerge.

The state's emphasis on education and culture, according to some interviewees, influenced what is known as the Colombian style of television fiction. In other words, the restrictions set by the state in terms of culturally oriented programming, the emphasis on adaptations of literary/theatrical pieces, and the independent production companies' goal of obtaining television contracts, pushed Colombian media professionals to be innovative and to create new techniques for televising literary-theatrical works. Furthermore, the lack of a financially sustainable film and theatre industry provided an opportunity for independent production companies to hire highly educated individuals with literary and theatre backgrounds. All of the aforementioned factors, in addition to the need to address Colombia's embattled social, cultural and political realities, served (and continue to serve) as important ingredients in Colombia's television fiction (Rincón 2008; Martín-Barbero and Rey 1999).

Four primary characteristics differentiate the Colombian *telenovela* and series model from that of other Latin American products: an urban context, strong and forceful women who 'control their destiny', a mixture of comedy and drama, and a 'playful take on melodrama's values' (Rincón 2007: 133-58). Of these elements, the representation of strong female characters and the incorporation of comedy, according to some interviewees, have been most responsible for the buying of Colombian scripts across Latin America, a process that, as I previously mentioned, began in the early 1990s.

Before the *Yo soy Betty, la fea* format export boom, Colombia's strongest television influence in the region was in Mexico. In the mid-1990s the newly instituted Mexican network, TV Azteca, bought the rights to Bernardo Romero Pereiro and Mónica Agudelo's Colombian hit *Señora Isabel* (Canal A, 1993–4). The story of a love affair between a middle-aged woman and a younger man was adapted to a Mexican context and produced by the Mexican Production Company, Argos, for TV Azteca. The Colombian *Señora Isabel* became the highly successful Mexican *telenovela Mirada de mujer* (*The Gaze of a Woman* [TV Azteca, 1997–8]). After capturing audiences in Mexico and across the region and becoming a legitimate competitor of Mexico's powerful network, Televisa, Argos/TV Azteca bought the rights to other Colombian titles (for example, *La otra mitad del sol* [*The Other Half of the Sun* (Canal A, 1995–6)] and *Pecado santo* [*Holy Sin* (Tevecine, 1995)]). Despite the fact that subsequent adaptations of Colombian scripts were not as successful as *Mirada de mujer*, TV Azteca, according to one interviewee, 'initially competed with Televisa by appropriating the Colombian *telenovela* model' (media professional, 2008). Today, Mexican networks Televisa and TV Azteca have Colombian *telenovela* and series formats in their libraries and have adapted and produced Colombian concepts, including most recently, *Yo amo a Juan Querendón* (*I Love Juan Querendón* [El Canal de las estrellas, 2007–8]), from the Colombian *Pedro, el escamoso* (*Pedro the Scaly* [Caracol Televisión, 2001–3]) and *Destilando amor* (*Essence of Love* [El Canal de las estrellas, 2007]), from Colombia's *Café con aroma de mujer* (*Coffee, with the Scent of a Woman* [Canal A, 1994–5]).

Fernando Gaitán's *Café con aroma de mujer* was the most famous Colombian *telenovela* export in the early 1990s. Other 1990s Colombian products, such as *La otra mitad del sol* (*The Other Half of the Sun* [Canal A, 1995–6]), *Las Juanas* (*The Juanas* [Canal RCN, 1997–8]) and *Perro amor* (*Dog Love* [Canal Uno, 1998–9]), also caught the attention of audiences in different parts of Latin America. Nonetheless, it was with *Café* that Latin American producers and distributors began to pay closer attention to Bogotá's productions. Additionally, after witnessing *Café's* success, independent Colombian production companies and the commercial networks Caracol and RCN – established in 1997 – opened themselves up to the possibilities of conquering the Latin American market (Sullivan 1997; López González 2006).

In a 1998 interview, Gaitán addressed the impact that *Café* had on his life. 'For me, the success of *Café* is horrible because that success came when I was beginning my career rather than at the middle or the end of it. For me, *Café* is an amazing *novela*, I loved it, but I do not want to repeat it, that is my battle. I do not want to pigeonhole myself' (Carmen Julia and Tatiana 1999: 87). As we know today, he did not.

Fernando Gaitán: The Showrunner of *Yo soy Betty, la fea*

In today's US television world, the term showrunner is generally used to describe the individual behind all aspects of producing high-budget, 'quality' programming. As *Los Angeles Times* writer Scott Collins observes, showrunners are 'a curious hybrid of starry-eyed artists and tough-as-nails operational managers. They're not just writers; they're not just producers. They hire and fire writers and crew members, develop story lines, write scripts, cast actors, mind budgets and run interference with studio and network bosses' (Collins 2007). Even though award-winning and critically acclaimed series are in the hands of hundreds of people, showrunners have been depicted by the industry as TV 'auteurs', the architects and sole figures in charge of producing quality programming (Mann 2009: 99–114).

In Colombia, probably as a result of the high-culture, theatre and literary traditions that defined the television industry for many years, scriptwriters are seen as *auteurs*. 'We do not sell stars, we sell stories,' remarked media scholar Omar Rincón (2008) in reference to the centrality of the author in Colombian television. Nonetheless, while scriptwriters are at the top of Colombia's television hierarchical structure, only a few have the power to control different aspects of television production. In other words, just a handful of writers could be categorized as showrunners. Fernando Gaitán is one of those select few. As a scriptwriter who has spent most of his professional career working for RCN and who has provided the company with various hits, Gaitán has the network's trust.

Highly protective of his creative work, Gaitán took over the executive and creative aspects of the *Yo soy Betty, la fea* production. As he responded when I asked about his involvement with *Betty*,

I selected the director, the technical crew, the actors, and the editor. I did the budget, dealt with the press, selected my research team who, in addition to performing research for the *telenovela*, was in charge of the Bible. I took over the control of the filming of exteriors and interiors. I became involved in the selection of food and hotels. I also took the technical and artistic crew to *rumbear* [party] at my bar every 15 days. (2008)

To be sure, this is not the first time Gaitán has immersed himself in his creations. For instance, when preparing for *Café*, the only *telenovela* script to date that he has been commissioned to write (RCN asked him to author a script that would focus on Colombian coffee production), he conducted extensive background research before initiating the writing process. As he observed in a 1998 interview, 'all stories need investigation, I mean, every story has a context. ... Basically, one applies a journalistic technique, thus, first one relies on the books, biographies, everything that one encounters. But the most important thing that the writer needs to do is what I call *reportería* – interviews and reportage' (Carmen Julia and Tatiana 1999). Characterized by a writing style that combines facts, fiction, drama and humour, his scripts have been defined as 'literary journalism' (Colombian scholar, 2008).

Gaitán's journalistic approach to creative writing, together with his interest in re-enacting Bogotá's quotidianity, served as the starting point for *Yo soy Betty, la fea*.

The idea came up at the channel [RCN]. I used to work a lot at the channel. There one can observe two drastically distinct worlds. One is the world of a typical industry and the other one is the world of the big divas of the country. These two worlds overlap. Naturally, I used to listen to the secretaries talking. These ladies used to go to their barrios and everybody used to ask them about the actors, how they behave, etc. ... And there were a bunch of secretaries that were amazing. A very audacious cartel! On the other hand, there was a secretary of a big shot executive, who was *feita* [ugly] and who was treated horribly by her boss. One day the secretary left and the boss did not know what to do with his life. He could not find anything. ... On the other hand, here in Colombia, there is an obsession with plastic surgery... people take away ribs, they change their faces, have breast implants ... So, that is how all of *Betty*'s themes began to develop (Gaitán 2008).

The story of the ugly, clumsy, working-class, brilliant and hard-working Beatriz Pinzón Solano, a secretary at the high-fashion company EcoModa, was, in fact, the story of an unknown, hard-working, efficient and not very attractive RCN secretary. The seven 'I do not give a damn about what you think of me' women of *El cuartel de las feas* originated from a group of apparently 'kick-ass' secretaries at RCN. It is unclear who served as the muse for the other characters, but they might have been a collage of people, social actors who are part of Bogotá's world.

Trained in literature and a big admirer and follower of the 'gringo sitcom', Gaitán is a self-taught television scriptwriter who learned the craft through books and instructional pamphlets. Today, after more than 20 years in the business, Gaitán is considered one of the best (and for some *the* best) Colombian television authors. According to several interviewees, Gaitán's winning scriptwriting formula comes from his character development, his vivid portrayal of aspects of Colombia's cultural and social environments and his mastership of comedy.

For Gaitán (as well as for several Colombian media professionals I interviewed), humour is a key ingredient in the Colombian *telenovela*. 'We are killing ourselves so much that we need to live the day-to-day with a good vibe' (Colombian scholar, 2008), one interviewee satirically remarked in reference to the comedic elements in the Colombian television fiction. Regardless of the actual social and industrial conditions that pushed comedy into the Colombian *telenovelas* and series, humour has defined Gaitán's creations, especially *Yo soy Betty, la fea*.

Gaitán classified *Yo soy Betty, la fea* as a programme more attuned to the US sitcom than to the *telenovela*. 'Schematically, in terms of script, set, filming, and episodic duration [in Colombia, the original episodes were 30 minutes long], *Yo soy Betty, la fea* is very similar to a US situation comedy' (Gaitán 2008). This structural proximity to the situation comedy mentioned by Gaitán may have accounted for the migration of the *Yo soy Betty, la fea* format to places familiar with the sitcom genre but which, at the same time, were not conversant with the *telenovela* genre conventions. As communication scholars Antonio La Pastina and Joseph Straubhaar observe, genre codes are important factors in audiences' selection of particular types of programming (2005: 271–88). Even as many global Betties are relatively loose adaptations of the Colombian version, those who transformed the concept in countries where audiences are not familiar with *telenovelas* probably diluted the melodramatic component of the format and exalted the situation comedy elements. Yet, regardless of the diverse translation and adaptation processes, something intriguing about Gaitán's conceptualization of *Yo soy Betty, la fea* as comparable to a US sitcom is the malleability of genres and generic categorizations. As Jason Mittell argues, genres are 'historically situated cultural products constituted by media practices and subject to ongoing change and redefinition' (2004: 3). In the Colombian case, Gaitán's appropriation and reconfiguration of the US sitcom seems to be part of two distinct processes: (1) a manifestation of his own creative formula as a writer and (2) an industry trend within Bogotá's network television.

Colombian communication scholar Germán Rey observes that in Gaitán's work 'there is a dialogue with the traditions of the melodrama but, at the same time, there is an introduction of innovations' (2002: 151). In the particular example of *Yo soy Betty, la fea* and its genre's amalgamation, the story of an impossible love and the suffering of the protagonist for being 'ugly' fit into the *telenovela's* melodramatic structure. On the other hand, the incorporation of comedic moments and characters, as well as the episodic structure and filming, represent innovations borrowed from the sitcom genre. In terms of the industry, Gaitán's use of the sitcom can also be seen as part of an industrial formula wherein all external influences are 'devoured' and incorporated into the *telenovela* genre (Rincón 2008). This ongoing consumption and transfiguration of foreign influences has kept the Colombian *telenovela* and series fresh and original, a factor that has impacted the current popularity of Colombian formats. However, while the 'devouring' of external ideas, formats and genres has helped sell Colombian television products, it was the international success of *Betty* that opened the global television market for Colombia. 'Betty provided us the access to present other types of products on the market. ... The market now demands the Colombian product,' a Caracol network executive remarked (2008). Today, and thanks to Gaitán's creation, Colombia is an active player in the global television world.

Selling Colombian Formats/Producing Global Television

In the early 2000s, the story of an ugly woman opened the door to the global selling of Colombian formats. In the late 2000s, a young woman's obsession with enlarging her breasts (*Sin tetas no hay paraíso/Without Tits there is no Paradise* [Caracol TV, 2006]) became the second most successful format export to emerge from Bogotá. Even though, at first glance, women's painful struggles with their bodies seem to be the central theme of these two format hits, what connects *Yo soy Betty, la fea* and *Sin tetas no hay paraíso* is more than beauty and ugliness. In these two stories, a woman's rejection of her body becomes an instrument for exploring class stratification and poverty, societal and political corruption, and violence – physical and psychological. This thematic richness that permeates many Colombian *telenovelas* and series is most likely facilitating global adaptations of Colombian formats.

Authored by Gustavo Bolivar and produced by Caracol, the format of the series *Sin tetas no hay paraíso* has been sold to the United States (for English- and Spanish-language versions), Spain, Italy, Russia and Mexico. Learning from the apparent mistakes related to the selling of the *Yo soy Betty, la fea* format, Caracol prepared itself for the possibility of a television hit with *Sin tetas* (through conversations I surmised that, because of inexperience, RCN executives lost opportunities to maximize their profits, particularly in terms of creating new formats based on the 'original' *Betty* and the selling of the product through different platforms). As a Caracol network executive explained,

> *Sin tetas* is the first Colombian television production where the creative team and the sales team worked together. … The market is changing. With *Sin tetas* we began by selling the Bible instead of the *lata*. We also protected the corporations that bought the format. For example, in a period of two years, the adaptation made in Spain can only be broadcast in Spain and can be sold only to other territories that did not buy the product. Thus, Spain's version of *Sin tetas* cannot enter the US Spanish-language television market for a period of two years after the show began broadcasting in Spain. Nor can the US Spanish-language version enter Spain, Russia, or Italy. The five countries that bought the format have their

respective territories protected. Now, there also will be five versions competing with each other in the global market. ... Also, Caracol will obtain royalties from all of these productions. Furthermore, if they produce DVDs, merchandise, etc., Caracol will obtain fifty percent of the profits (Media professional, 2008).

After setting up an internal business structure for selling formats, Caracol forcefully entered the global market. For example, in 2008, Caracol sold several formats which included the *telenovelas La ex* (*The Ex* [Caracol TV, 2006–7]), about a woman who seeks revenge on her ex-husband, and *Nuevo rico/Nuevo pobre* (*Newly Rich/Newly Poor* [Caracol TV, 2007–8]), about two newborns switched at birth. Caracol also established a programming business agreement with Reveille Productions to sell both scripted and unscripted formats to the US market (Scheneider 2008). Following Caracol's initiative, Sí Hay Ideas/Teleset Production Company sold the format of the dating show *La ruleta del amor* (*The Rules of Love*), a concept developed specifically for international audiences (Fuente 2008).

But the growing exportation of Colombian television formats is not the only industrial change in the post-*Yo soy Betty, la fea* era. Bogotá is also becoming an important television production centre in Latin America.

Although Colombia is still considered by many to be a country at war, a sense of socio-political stability and security has apparently eased the concerns of foreign television investors. The Fox TeleColombia studios, which are the home of Fox productions for the United States, European and Asian markets, the Telemundo-RTI Bogotá facilities where the filming of *telenovelas* for the US and global markets takes place, and the presence of Sony Pictures Television International, which in 2009 bought 50 per cent of the Colombian production company, Teleset, are three examples of Colombia's broadening participation in the web of global television production (*Semana*, 2008: 91; *TV Mas*, 2009). The commercial success of local programming, the Colombian creative and technical staff know-how, and a large, cheap, talented, non-unionized labour force are major factors in these recent transformations. Of these factors, the 'no one will ever stop a filming' mantra associated with the absence of unions has been quite appealing for transnational media corporations. As one interviewee observed, 'we are a *maquila*', hinting at a form of labour exploitation defined by border-crossing corporations and centre-periphery relations of power. Even though the Colombian networks and production companies have been able to protect themselves financially from shady business deals, television creators are still at a disadvantage. Gaitán's business arrangement for *Yo soy Betty, la fea* is an example of the power disparities between Colombian corporations and creators in today's global television sphere.

When I asked Gaitán about the global Betties, his possible involvement as a creative consultant and, indirectly, his potential revenues, he simply replied, 'I do not have any rights. RCN has all the rights' (2008). I also received a similar response when inquiring about the business arrangements for Gustavo Bolívar, the author of *Sin tetas no hay paraíso*. In Bolívar's case, however, the situation was more complex, given that he had sold the rights of his book to publisher Oveja Negro y Quintero, who subsequently sold them to Caracol. The fact that Bolívar was hired to write the script for the television series was an 'unexpected bonus', said another scriptwriter.

In Bogotá's television industry, the cases of Gaitán and Bolivar are not the exception but the norm. Colombian scriptwriters sell their scripts to television networks and, with this transaction, they give away all of their rights as authors. Certainly, someone such as Gaitán, who has had enormous commercial success and who has prestige locally and regionally, has been financially rewarded. But, as someone close to Gaitán expressed, '[The RCN network executives] have been very generous but they have not been just. In the case of *Betty* it has not been fair' (Media professional, 2008).

Whereas local business arrangements between scriptwriters and networks are highly unfavourable for the authors, particularly if the sold *telenovela* or series script becomes a hit locally and regionally, the present intersection of Colombian cultural workers' labour with global market forces increases the level of 'unfairness' described by one of the interviewees. As the authors of *Global Hollywood 2* observe, in the New International Division of Cultural Labor, 'core and periphery are blurred, the spatial mobility of capital is enhanced, the strategic strength of labour is undermined, and the power of the state is circumscribed by the ability of capital to move across borders' (Miller et al. 2005: 109). In a television industry such as Colombia's, which is progressively becoming more integrated into global television market exchanges, the absence of unions is producing a paradox. On the one hand, as I previously implied, the lack of labour organizing has provided more jobs for local television professionals. In the case of the scriptwriters, several are currently in demand to author original scripts and to adapt formats from other countries. For instance, as part of RCN's business partnership with Disney Media Networks Latin America, Gaitán was hired to adapt *Desperate Housewives* (ABC, 2004–present) and *Grey's Anatomy* (ABC, 2005–present) for the Colombian market. Whereas, as I explain below, in the end, Gaitán worked only as the creative consultant for *A corazón abierto* (*With Open Heart*, the Colombian adaptation of *Grey's Anatomy*, which began airing in April 2010), local-global television arrangements have opened up more spaces for both renowned and new scriptwriters.

On the other hand, the new local-global Colombian television structure is exacerbating the financial exploitation of television's creative and technical workforce. For example, even though *A corazón abierto* was produced for the Colombian market, the series is being exported to other countries in the region. At the same time, the *A corazón abierto* set will be used to film TV Azteca's version of *Grey's Anatomy* for the Mexican market. Neither the scriptwriters in charge of writing *A corazón abierto* nor the designer who created the set received extra remuneration for the sale and use of their creative product beyond the national-local borders. Globalization, as the authors of *Global Hollywood 2* argue, 'does not offer an end to centre-periphery inequalities, competition between states or macro-decision-making by corporations; it just reduces the capacity of the state system to control such transactions, and relegates responsibility for the protection and well-being of the cultural workforce to multinational corporate entities and financial institutions' (Miller et al. 2005: 56). In the Colombian case, we are not seeing an exclusive centre-periphery level of labour exploitation, but rather, an interconnected local, regional and global structure wherein the transnational media machinery nomadically moves in search of cheaper labour, industrial resources, and new markets. Today, Bogotá and Miami – another non-unionized city, are centres of production for the geo-linguistic region and the global markets. In 15 years, it might be Havana or some other place that offers the best financial, legal and creative resources void of unions and state intervention.

When asking Colombian media professionals about the possibility of a scriptwriters' union or any type of labour movement in the television industry, no one I spoke with believed a union would ever be created. Most professionals were also hesitant about that possibility. However, one person who hoped for the development of labour organizing was Gloria de la Pava, Gaitán's lawyer and agent. 'I firmly believe that the scriptwriters have to create coalitions but that is very difficult. I tried to organize the scriptwriters about five years ago but no one wanted to join me. Here individualism prevails. Most of them [scriptwriters] fail to think about the future' (2008). What seems to be the scriptwriters' lack of interest in unionizing (particularly those scriptwriters who have been financially successful), together with the increase in employment opportunities, appears to be the main problem facing labour organizing in Colombian television. In addition, in an author-oriented industry, being a producer of *telenovela* hits provides the scriptwriter with an array of creative and managerial opportunities. Gaitán, for example, had the chance to work as the showrunner for *Yo soy Betty, la fea* and, more recently (in 2009), he was named vice-president of production for RCN. Today, Gaitán is in charge of supervising all RCN productions, keeping the network at the top of the ratings, and protecting the network's image (*El Universal*, 7 June 2010).

The Colombian scriptwriters' (and television professionals') present labour situation has left me wondering whether local unions would be sufficient for creating better working conditions. For instance, although in a different labour context, Aviva Chomsky's (2008) research on the history of Colombia's labour movement in the textile industry presents a bleak picture of Colombian unions' lack of power, particularly when dealing with multinational and US corporations. In the specific case of Colombian television and global television business practices, one of the main problems facing authors is piracy. Many of the interviewees mentioned the Mexican television industry's ongoing practice of copying Colombian *telenovela* ideas and scripts without paying royalties. The most recent example cited by the interviewees was *Yo amo a Juan Querendón* (*I Love Juan Querendón* [Televisa, 2007–8]) from the Colombian *Pedro, el escamoso* (Caracol TV, 2001). In each of the alleged piracy cases, neither the Colombian networks nor the authors have had the power to fight the Mexican networks. Whereas Mexico's television networks do not have the clout of the multinational textile corporations studied by Chomsky, the absence of Colombian television unions and of transnational union coalitions has limited the profits for Colombian scriptwriters.

Nonetheless, what appeared to be the main point of distress for Gaitán and for his lawyer/agent regarding *Yo soy Betty, la fea*, was Gaitán's absence of power in the business negotiations for the global Betties. Due to what was described as the 'openness of the RCN contract', foreign corporations that have purchased the format can do whatever they please with *Betty*. According to Gloria de la Pava, in one case, the essence of *Yo soy Betty, la fea* was lost, resulting in a 'shameful adaptation'. In the example provided by de la Pava, the network in charge of the adaptation destroyed the concept and the principal character. The spirit of Betty vanished.

Of course, Gaitán's control over the *Yo soy Betty, la fea* sales and format adaptations might be different today due to his managerial position at RCN. Then again, his situation is unique. He might be able to protect the spirit of future Betties and his other cultural creations, but other Colombian authors seem to be in a Catch-22 situation. Those I spoke to are fully aware of their lack of rights regarding their scripts and their limited financial remuneration, but at the same time, they are also grateful for the employment opportunity that, while unstable, allows them to do what they love.

Conclusion

The principal decorative item in Gaitán's home office was an enormous photograph of Beatriz Pinzón Solano, the Colombian Betty. The centrality of this photograph in Gaitán's office could be seen as a symbol of the ways in which *Yo soy Betty, la fea* impacted his career as a scriptwriter and television professional. Betty has taken Gaitán around the world and has also provided him with an array of professional opportunities. Yet, the success of Betty, as I discussed in this piece, transcends Gaitán's career – it has transformed the Colombian television industry. All of the media professionals I talked to were very proud of *Yo soy Betty, la fea*, 'nuestra Betty' [our *Betty*] as some of them called it.

The *Yo soy Betty, la fea* phenomenon, its impact on Bogotá's television industry and what I categorize as the suctioning of profits, talent and creativity throughout the selling of the Betty format bring us to an important aspect of global television studies: unions and labour relations. As Rosalind Gill and Andy Pratt note regarding creative work, 'The lack of trade unionization and labour organization in many areas of cultural work is striking, and is both cause and outcome of industries that are individualized, deregulated and reliant upon cheap or even free labour ...' (2008: 19–20). In the case of Colombia, the key question then, is how the Colombian government, commercial networks and media professionals will negotiate the country's new position in the global television environment. What will it mean for Colombian media creators when the next *Fea*, or *La ex* finds a new *Paraíso* in Miami, Mexico City, Tel Aviv or Beijing? The answer for the Colombian television industry and for other industries in countries or cities where labour organizing is absent might be in the hands of the state. The *Yo soy Betty, la fea* case, then, should be considered not only in terms of the popularity of format exporting or the existence of a patriarchal beauty system around the world, but also as an example of how contemporary global television trades may activate a local, regional and global labour exploitation trend.

Acknowledgements

Thanks to Clemencia Rodríguez and Omar Rincón for obtaining access for me to Colombian television professionals and for co-ordinating my interviews in Bogotá. Special thanks to Cecilia Percy who served as my personal guide and provided valuable information about the industry. *Mil gracias* to all the television professionals who welcomed me into the privacy of their homes, shared information, and made me feel at home.

Works Cited

[Anon.], 'Made in Colombia', *Semana*, 19–26 May 2008, p. 91.

———, 'Negociaciones, compra y venta de productoras y formatos', *TV Mas Magazine*, January–February 2009, online at: http://www.tvmasmagazine.com/paginas_edicion Actual/enero-febrero2009/informe_especial1.html (accessed 20 July 2011).

———, 'Fernando Gaitán responde a líderes afrocolombianos', *El Universal*, 26 July 2009, on-line at: http://www.eluniversal.com.co/cartagena/actualidad/fernando-gaitan-responde -lideres-afrocolombianos (accessed 20 July 2011).

Carmen Julia and Tatiana, 'Como así ... para toda la vida: Análisis de la telenovela colombiana y los factores que permitieron su penetración en el mercado venezolano' (Unpublished thesis, Universidad Católica Andres Bello, Venezuela, 1999).

Chomsky, Aviva, *Linked Labor Histories: New England, Colombia, and the Making of a Global Working Class, American Encounters/Global Interactions* (Durham, NC: Duke University Press, 2008).

Collins, Scott, 'Who Really Runs Things: Show Runners Are Shaping up to Be the Most Influential Players in the TV Industry', *Los Angeles Times*, 23 November 2007, online at: http://articles.latimes.com/2007/nov/23/entertainment/et-channel23 (accessed 20 July 2011).

Gill, Rosalind, and Pratt, Andy, 'In the Social Factory?: Immaterial Labour, Precariousness and Cultural Work', *Theory Culture Society*, vols 7–8, no. 25 (2008), pp. 1–30, 19–20.

De la Fuente, Anne Marie, 'Sony Plays 'Roulette' Dating Show', *Variety*, 9 October 2008, online at: http://www.variety.com/article/VR1117993738?refCatId=14 (accessed 20 July 2011).

López González, Santiago, 'De Colombia para el mundo: Investigación sobre la venta y distribución de la telenovela colombiana en el mundo' (Unpublished thesis, Pontificia Universidad Javeriana, Bogotá, Colombia, 2006).

Mann, Denise, 'It's not TV, It's Brand Management TV: The Collective Author(s) of the *Lost* Franchise', in Vicki Mayer, Miranda J. Banks and John T. Caldwell (eds), *Production Studies: Cultural Studies of Media Industries* (London: Routledge, 2009), pp. 99–114.

Martín-Barbero, Jesús, and Rey, Germán, *Los ejercicios de ver: Hegemonía audiovisual y ficción televisiva* (Barcelona: Gedisa, 1999).

Miller, Toby, Govil, Nitin, McMurria, John, et al., *Global Hollywood 2*, (London: BFI Publishing, 2005).

Mittel, Jason, *Genre and Television: From Cop Shows to Cartoons in American Culture* (London: Routledge, 2004).

La Pastina, Antonio C., and Straubhaar, Joseph D., 'Multiple Proximities between Television Genres and Audiences', *Gazette: The International Journal for Communication Studies*, vol. 67, no. 3 (2005), pp. 271–88.

Rey, Germán, 'La Televisión en Colombia', in Guillermo Orozco, ed, *Historias de la televisión en América Latina* (Barcelona: Gedisa, 2002), pp. 117–62.

Rincón, Omar, 'Colombia: Cuando la ficción cuenta más que los informativos', in Lorenzo Vilches (ed.), *Culturas y mercados de la ficción en Iberoamérica, Anuario OBITEL 2007* (Barcelona: Gedisa, 2007), pp. 133–58.

Rodríguez, Clemencia, and Tellez, Patricia, (1989) *La telenovela en Colombia: mucho más que amor y lágrimas* (Bogotá: CINEP, 1989).

Roncagliolo, Rafael, (1995) 'Trade Integration and Communication Networks in Latin America', *Canadian Journal of Communication*, vol. 20, no. 3 (1995), pp. 335–42.

Scheneider, Michael, 'Reveille Pacts with Caracol', *Variety*, 24 October 2008, online at: http://www.variety.com/article/VR1117979772?refCatId=19 (accessed 20 July 2011).

'Sí Hay Ideas firma un "world wide deal" con SPTI', online at: http://www.teleset.com.co/Espanol/Noticias/Si_Hay_Ideas_firma_un_World_Wide_Deal_con_SPTI/ (accessed 20 July 2011).

Sullivan, Maureen, 'Colombia Begins New TV Era', *Variety*, 1 December 1997, online at: http://www.variety.com/article/VR1116677574.html?categoryid=19&cs=1 (accessed 20 July 2011).

Vilches, Lorenzo, 'Compared Synthesis of the Obitel Countries', in Maria Immacolata Vasallo de Lopes and Lorenzo Vilches (eds), *Global Markets, Local Stories, Obitel Yearbook 2008* (Rio de Janeiro: Globo Universidade, 2008), pp. 23–51.

Vizcaino Gutierrez, Milcíades, *Historia de una travesía: 40 años de la televisión en Colombia* (Bogotá: Inravisión, 1994).

Waisbord, Silvio, 'McTV: Understanding the Global Popularity of Television Formats', *Television and New Media*, vol. 5, no. 4 (2004), pp. 359–83.

Interviews

Caracol executive, May 2008, personal communication.
Colombian scholar, May 2008, personal communication.
Media professional, May 2008, personal communication.
Omar Rincón, May 2008, personal communication.
Fernando Gaitán, May 2008, personal communication.
Gloria de la Pava, May 2008, personal communication.

Endnotes

1   Colombia has both regional channels and national networks.   In this article I am exclusively focusing on Colombia's national television networks.

2   Net exporters, according to Roncagliolo, are countries that are centres of media productions and that, by way of their cultural products, are part of global economic trades.

Acquiring *Ugly Betty* for Channel 4: Interview with Jeff Ford

Jean Chalaby

Before talking about why you acquired Ugly Betty (ABC, 2006–10), *can you say a few words about the purchasing process?*

The whole year is a market. I mean there are always shows coming up from cable or broadcast throughout the year, and there are a number of markets throughout the year that … highlight these … feeding frenzies as buyers are encouraged to bid higher than they should do. And those markets are things like MIP in April and MIPCOM in October. But there is one big market, which is the most important … of the year, and that is the Los Angeles screenings. And the LA screenings happen in May, when … the [US] networks have made their decision on what shows they're going to put onto the fall and into the winter schedules.

They may have 500 programme ideas across the studios and networks, which end up as 50 or 60 pilots. And then these are viewed by the network heads, and from those they make a decision about which new shows they're going to have in their schedule, which programmes they're going to axe, and which shows will replace other shows that fail to work in the fall.

The LA screenings is the time when we go over to America, to LA, to see the fruits of their labours and discuss the decisions they've made during the previous few weeks.

So for us, although there's a buying process throughout the whole year, this is really the most important part of the calendar when you [watch] every single pilot from every single studio and network. You spend Sunday through to the following Friday sitting in a darkened room basically watching every single new show and trying to work out will this show fit our schedule, where is this show going, is the talent attached for the whole series or just the pilot? Try to work this out … and by questioning, you question yourself, you question the people you're with and the people buying it from the networks. [How] exactly does a particular programme fit with the brand that is your channel, and what the studios are saying [about it]? Will they follow through their promises of how the production's going to look and how it's going to feel and who's going to be in it, and who's going to be creating it.

Now at least that's better than some of the commissions that we do here. Obviously, because you commission from a piece of paper, and that's what they're doing, they're commissioning from pieces of paper in the States. But at least there we get a full episode to watch. The difference that we in the UK have is that once we've sort of said we're going to buy that show, we're then committed to 22 hours. And if the 22 hours aren't very good or they don't follow through on what they're saying, you've got 22 times your problem. Over here if we commission it, or if they commission it in the States, you've got control. You can actually say 'well, we want to go this way, we want to go that way'. So you can influence the commissioner or the programme. But obviously here we're just buying it complete. It's like anything, if you buy something you pays your money and you takes your chance.

And that's how you came across Ugly Betty?

That's absolutely correct. ABC at that time was having a fantastic run. A few years before that they had *Lost* (2004–10), *Desperate Housewives* (2004–12), *Grey's Anatomy* (2005–present), all in one year. They were doing some really smart commissioning, and *Ugly Betty* was another one of those shows … But they were having a superb run, and they really had found their … commissioning mojo and were really making smart, interesting and different TV. At that time I was working for Channel 4, and the whole thing that attracted us about *Ugly Betty* was that it was different. It was very colourful and bright, it was escapist: it absolutely fitted with what Channel 4 was always looking for – something different, out of the ordinary and not traditional drama. Because at Channel 4 we did pick *Lost* and also *Desperate Housewives* as well, so it suited our style of programme at that time.

I remember there being quite a huge debate about should or shouldn't we pick it up. It wasn't everybody's favourite: ... was it a bit boring, ... a bit juvenile. I certainly recognized ... [that it had] something, it was engaging and you could feel that it had potential. And the [brilliant] cast, ... and it actually got better and it really did grow. But at the time I remember it wasn't as straightforward as it could have been. But that's the point. I think you can't just go 'oh, we're going to buy that programme'; it's a real intellectual debate about why does this show work, how can it work, and why will it work, because it is a huge financial risk for the company, [and you don't want] 22 weeks of pain. You want 22 weeks of glory. That's what you want.

Did you have a conversation with the commissioning team at Channel 4?

Kevin Lygo was the director of programmes, and it was also the scheduling team as well, because they came out to LA. So it's only a small team, and it was about trying to work out where and how it would fit. ... you don't just say 'oh, that show's great, we must buy it'. You've got to work out where you're going to put it, how it builds in the schedule, what is its relationship with the other programmes. So again, it's not just about saying it's a great show, because there are a lot of great shows ... Each channel has its own identity and it has to fit within that identity. But it also has to fit in with the needs of the schedule, and [the] gaps within [it]. Okay you can create a hole, but at the end of the day, it all has to come together.

Do you remember the terms of the discussion?

At that time there was a deal in place with Disney and ABC, which meant we had a first look; and so in that way it was an easy decision ... because if we wanted the show, then that was the show we could get. And so, in terms of negotiation, it was probably one of the more simple ones. The discussion about should we buy it was the hard part, and the negotiation was the easy part. Usually it is the other way around. If you see a programme that you really want and you think 'oh, we've got to have that', it is the negotiation that's the difficult part, because usually if it's a show that you think is pretty good, then there's probably somebody else who's almost certain to want it as well. I think acquisitions, changing channels, or prices being paid is well documented.

… And if you're talking £500,000, which is a huge amount of money, we just don't have that amount, we're not built that way, and that's sort of getting on for almost a commissioned drama price. That's very expensive. So in terms of negotiation it was very simple, as I say, usually … that that's the tricky part, trying to work out what you can give … what we want and financially where can we go in, and the risk involved [in] that negotiation.

So in terms of programming, did you think Ugly Betty *matched the core values of the Channel 4 brand?*

Yeah.

Was it the quirkiness?

I think so, the quirkiness, the freshness. It was very young and it was always going to [have] a young appeal. And its use of music and production techniques, its use of colour … it was a very different sort of show. I think in many ways it … related to *Desperate Housewives* in its brightness and colour, but in a much more comic book approach. And I think it was again that different view on production that made me think … it sits more with what Channel 4 does in [terms of] taking risks and being different … what Channel 4 has always been known for. And I think that the show did have that, that … difference and risk taking. And again it split our team …

Was it a great success for Channel 4?

Huge success. Obviously [*Yo soy Betty, la fea*] had been a huge success following its original launch in South America and then internationally. And I think Germany had a version of it before. So the format had sort of travelled, but I think the very heart of [*Ugly Betty*] may well be very similar to the South American, but its production was very different.

Was the Channel 4 acquisition important in terms of the international roll out of Ugly Betty?

Yes.

I think we purchased it quite quickly after LA. I think studios always like to shout when a show has gone to the UK. It's … English language, so culturally similar, and I think the UK has always been good for having the best TV in the world. So to bring an American show to its heart and … [say] 'yes we're putting this in the same vein as all our other great shows that have been commissioned', I think it is a real positive for the Americans.

Plus, if the American market were to say we've sold *Ugly Betty*, it's gone to Channel 4 in the UK, or … to the BBC, … to 5 or … to ITV, it does mean something. Because on the main channels, there isn't a huge amount of American drama or American shows. I mean if you look at BBC, there probably aren't that many in primetime. BBC2 has *The Tudors* (2007–10) and *Nurse Jackie* (2009–present), but that's it. ITV has none, and we're not talking about digital channels at the moment. Channel 4 does. I mean it had all those [shows] we were talking about, and probably *The Event* (2010)… was the last one.

But that didn't work for them.

No?

No, it didn't work in the States and they've had to now move it. I think they're playing it about 11.00, 11.30, so it didn't move then. For us of course, we're exactly the opposite; we have the *CSIs* (*CSI: Crime Scene Investigation* [CBS, 2000–present], *CSI: Miami* [2002–12] *CSI: NY* [2004–present]), *NCIS* (CBS, 2003–present), *Mentalist* (CBS, 2008), *Walking Dead* (AMC, 2010–present), to name half a dozen. So I think obviously the terrestrial channels are different. But the thing is Channel 4 is always looking for something. ITV did put one in a few years ago called *Pushing Daisies* (ABC, 2007–9). They played it in primetime, but it really wasn't an ITV show. It was a Channel 4 show. But [ITV] was trying. They tried to move into a different area and it didn't work. They are always looking for a show, because at the end of the day if you can buy a show that costs £100,000 an hour, and you don't have to commission something that's £600,000 or £700,000 an hour, and you can get repeats out of it, it makes economic sense. But of course at the end of the day good drama has to stand up. There's no point in buying something that is not going to work in terms of just being a pure drama, because it's a false economy.

So I think they're always looking for stuff, but we want to put it on the main channel and in primetime. Of course on the digital side, the pay side, it's very different, and everybody has to utilize acquired shows because they are generally cheaper. Saying that though, the *Glee*s (Fox, 2009–present) of this world, the *Lost*s, the *Desperate Housewives*, the *Family Guy*s (Fox, 1999–present), the *24*s (Fox, 2001–10), the *Simpsons* (Fox, 1989–present), … *Vampire Diaries* (CW, 2009–present), they're not going to be cheap, particularly when they become successful.

In terms of rights, I suppose you acquired the UK terrestrial licence plus the cable and satellite licence?

Yeah, we had all the rights that we needed for all the channels. Obviously VoD as well I think, we probably got VoD, can't remember how long ago it was now when VoD may have been a twinkle in somebody's eye at that time. But certainly we would have acquired those rights, and we acquire those rights going forward. Now VoD is just part of broadcast rights. It's just another way of people sort of consuming it, and we have to have that so people can catch up because it helps them get to the second episode if they've missed the first. So yeah, we would have got all the rights we could have had … to transmit the show and support it.

Did you pick up the format rights …?

No, we're not interested in format rights. I think on drama – in the UK it's such a mature market – we don't. It's very rare. I'm not saying we don't, but it's very rare for anybody to take an American show … we talking about scripted here.

Did you have an audience in mind for Ugly Betty?

Yes, I think the key was it was continuing in the vein that we are well known for, which is top American quality drama.

Ugly Betty ... fit that mould of quality drama, and for the most part what Channel 4 is known for ... young audiences. We knew *Ugly Betty* would attract that young audience. It chimed in with the brand values of the channel, and in that way it was an easy one for us to do. Eventually when we intellectualized the whole debate, (and Channel 4 had *Friends* (NBC, 1994–2004) and all these shows that were very young), we knew it would sit perfectly in the schedule. I think it started Friday at nine, if memory serves me right.

About scheduling, how was the decision reached about the Friday night slot?

It is what we're traditionally known for. Channel 4 Fridays, 9–10 o'clock, always used to be quiet (because of the way US acquisitions were used years ago with ... *Cheers* (NBC, 1982–93). American programmes were a bit of a USP [unique selling proposition] for Channel 4. We were proud of them because ... we absolutely know these are the best quality shows from the States, and we're bringing them to the UK. [*Ugly Betty*] brought those values with it; it immediately says 'we're Channel 4, we're proud of this show and we think it's going to appeal to 16 to 34s and here it is'. We then put it in the slot where traditionally we put our attractive 16 to 34 shows. [The viewers] came because they trust us: there was a great trust between the audience and Channel 4 at that time.

Were you surprised by the success of the show?

Probably I think we were all a little bit surprised at how well it did. I can't actually remember the full numbers, but we were very pleased the next morning when the ratings came in, and ... for the next four years or so. The ratings in the end, like most shows, tend to ... die off ... [and] you're very lucky to get five or six seasons out of these shows. But at the end it really did extremely well. ... It was a really good acquisition, and it did, and for all the reasons I said earlier, absolutely reinforce what the channel was about and ... held up as a prime example of what Channel 4 stood for.

Regarding the buying process, did you look at the ratings elsewhere?

No because the decision was made before it had aired in the States.

Oh really?

… This is the one thing about the LA screenings, because it happens in May for the autumn launches … [which] used to be September, now they're … in October, sometimes November. … Of course … it's about risk isn't it, and you see the first episode and say we'll buy it from that, and hope and believe that it's going to be correct. Or you go … don't know about that, not quite keen, [and] wait and see the second and third episode. But of course somebody might make the decision in between times and say 'no, we think it's right for us and we're going to buy it'.

So you have to either make a decision, or you say 'no, we're not going to buy it, we'll wait and see the second and third episodes', but it may well have gone by then. … It's like buying anything. If you leave it, then you can either think 'gosh, that was a good decision', or 'oh, sugar, we should have actually picked that up'. And that decision happens all the time, … sometimes it's not about the things you pick up, it's also about the things you don't pick up. But nobody knows that because that's the boring bit.

Did you ever consider picking up the original Yo soy Betty, la fea?

No, Channel 4 did have some *telenovelas* at one point. Earlier in its life, at six o'clock, [the channel] played dubbed *telenovelas*, which is one of those strange things that it did. But again, the maturity of the market and the maturity of Channel 4, because it was 180, 160 episodes, whatever it was. And the American one was good enough and it did what it did for us and that's what we wanted it for.

Thank you very much for your time.

Interviews with TV Executives Involved in the German Adaptation, *Verliebt in Berlin*

Andrea Esser

Interested in the transnationalization of television, I started researching formatted content in 1995. Since then the trade in formats has become more systematized and franchised, programming has become an important driving force in the internationalization and commodification of audiovisual content. From a business perspective, formats are a sensible solution: whilst allowing for a necessary localization, they also speak to the benefits of a global TV trade. Analysis of trade literature and some statistical research I conducted into German and US primetime schedules between 2007 and 2009 (Esser 2010) revealed both the extent to which formatted programming had come to dominate television schedules and the increased emphasis the industry now places on formats. Furthermore, it revealed new patterns and flows: more and more genres were coming to be formatted and flows became increasingly multi-directional and global. *Yo soy Betty, la fea* (RCN, 1999–2001) exemplifies these trends; and it is in this context that I carried out a range of interviews with TV executives in Berlin and London in 2008 and 2009.

The interviews with producers involved in the Betty adaptations, and from which the extracts below are drawn, were part of a broader project aimed at illuminating formats' global-local nexus. I wanted to understand how much know-how is shared across borders, and how much and in which aspects did local adaptations change. One key factor is genre: fiction is usually more localized than game shows, for instance. Other important factors include the experience and financial strength of the production market where the adaptation takes place. Brand power of a particular format as well as the market power of the licensing company are also crucial in determining to what degree adaptations are, and can be, localized. The reasons for local variations are even more multifaceted, where a complex matrix of cultural, economic and circumstantial motives spawned variations. Bianca Lippert's account of the male lead in the German adaptation, *Verliebt in Berlin* (*In Love in/with Berlin* [SAT.1, 2005–7]), taking paternity leave necessitating a narrative detour, or the perceived need to write three young people into the *novela* to boost its appeal amongst the primetime target group are two interesting examples.

Three of my interviewees were directly involved in *Verliebt in Berlin* (*ViB*): Alicia Remirez was head of fiction at SAT.1 when the channel produced the *telenovela*, between 2004 and 2007. SAT.1, together with RTL, is Germany's oldest commercial channel, and today ranks third in terms of audience share for the advertiser relevant target group of 14–49-year-olds. Both channels are part of the two rival groups that dominate the German commercial free-to-air market, the ProSiebenSAT.1 Group and the RTL Group. It is interesting to note that RTL's German production powerhouse Grundy UFA produced *ViB*, despite the show being commissioned and screened on SAT.1. The second interviewee, Dr Michael Esser, had joint responsibility for the *ViB* script department together with co-head writer Peter Schlesselmann. Esser is managing director of screenwriting agency Dramaworks GmbH and teaches at the Technische Universität Berlin. Jonas Baur worked as story editor on *ViB*. He is now creative producer for the German soap *Verbotene Liebe* (*Forbidden Love* [Das Erste, 1995–present]).

Like the three German producers, my final interviewee, Vasha Wallace, vice-president of format acquisitions at FremantleMedia, provided valuable insight into the adaptation process and the workings of the format business more generally. FremantleMedia is one of, if not, the largest format producer and distributor globally. The RTL subsidiary owns production offices in over 20 countries as well as most of the European adaptation rights to the *Yo soy Betty, la fea* format. Wallace, along with her team, works with the global production network (including the various Grundy UFA production houses), keeps a watchful eye on all international entertainment shows and trends, and acquires formats around the world.[1]

With the exception of the last, the interviews were conducted in German and are reprinted here in translation.

Andrea Esser: How was Yo soy Betty, la fea *acquired for the German market?*

Alicia Remirez: Haim Saban [US media mogul and owner of the ProSiebenSAT.1 Group at the time] had heard of the enormous success of *Betty, la fea* in America's Spanish-speaking community and in Israel. He did not know the *telenovela* personally but decided, on the basis of the high audience ratings in these two countries, that SAT.1 staff should look into this. He was a huge fan of adaptations. In fact, he established a format department in the ProSiebenSAT.1 Group.

Roger Schawinski [then managing director of SAT.1] and myself were the only people who spoke Spanish. We both looked at the tapes Haim had given us. I only watched the first episode, though. The quality of the tapes was bad, and the Colombian version didn't impress us. We knew it wouldn't work in Germany as it was. We read the storylines and that's what we asked the producers to work with. The producers never saw the [*Yo soy Betty, la fea*] tapes or any of the scripts.

The basic story was very strong and that's why we bought the rights. But apart from that basic story, the Colombian original had no relevance for us.

I knew I wanted someone for the female lead who was beautiful and possessed comic talent. I did everything I could to get Alexandra Neldel to take the role [of Lisa, the German Betty], which she loved.

AE: How was the original adapted for the German market, and in what ways?

Michael Esser: The tapes we received from Haim Saban did not play a great role. We did extensive Internet research and the Fremantle department, responsible for market observation, provided us with further information. We used summaries from fans in America who watched [*Yo soy Betty, la fea*] and we knew about the success of the series in America.[2]

Jonas Baur: We never really built on the original. Only the characters were copied and the A-plot, i.e. Betty's story; all the B-plots were developed by the German scriptwriters. The Colombian version would never have worked in Germany.

AR: In the Colombian version Betty's boss and love interest is married and he has an affair with Betty to ensure her loyalty and help. In a conservative, Protestant country like Germany, the audience would have found this unacceptable. Betty's boss is thus single and, even though he exploits her by suggesting he loves her, he never goes as far as to sleep with her. For Catholic countries, although conservative, the deceit is acceptable. Sins are forgiven as long as the sinner repents.

Also, in the German version Lisa does not change her looks completely. She is still very recognizable, clearly her old self. Alexandra Neldel did not want her character to change into a completely new person.

ME: I think our perspective is more female. It is about 'finding one's place'. The Colombian point of view is more male; the Latin American machismo and sexism is very much at the heart of the *telenovela*. Maybe this is different because we based our scripts on summaries and comments made by female fans watching the Colombian version.[3]

Moreover, our characters are less stereotypical. The humour is not as obvious – the slapstick, heavily employed in the Colombian version, for instance, would not have worked in Germany – and characters are given more time to develop. They are also more credible.

AE: You mentioned to Bianca Lippert that the main reason for changes was to 'localize the story according to our needs' (2011: C). Could you define 'our needs' a bit more? Are you talking about 'national needs', economic ones, or the commissioning channel's?

ME: I'd like to point out that producers do not consciously think of national characteristics and we do not have discussions about what we could add to a format that is 'German'. Most important in the adaptation process is to find and define the universal needs in the format. Localization comes afterwards. It means thinking about what has worked in Germany in the past. It is the knowledge of production successes and flops in Germany that creates and determines 'localization'.

The needs of a particular channel – including time slot – don't have much significance in the case of daily series [which in Germany are usually screened in access primetime, i.e. 5–8pm]. All channels have very similar profiles here. The target groups are the same and they are quite homogeneous, too. A primetime programme for a big channel, on the other hand, not only has to attract women but men also. Making *Germany's Next Top Model* for Pro7 (2006–present) at primetime is more difficult. Channel differentiation is important in primetime, but not so much in the afternoon and access primetime slots.

AE: Who had the most influence on how the telenovela developed?

AR: The writers, in particular Peter Schlesselmann,[4] had the greatest influence on the outcome. In the 1990s, when more TV movies and miniseries were made, the channels' commissioning editors had a lot more impact on the production. Today, producers are mostly left to do the job. In the case of daily series, it is producers only who destine production. But there are many, many more people of course who contribute to the making of a TV series.

AE: Did SAT.1 carry out research to find out what the audience wanted?

ME: I don't think research was very important in this case, as the audience share was very good. There was, however, a big study by Rheingold[5] towards the end of the first season to determine the success factors for the second [featuring a new A-plot, with Lisa's brother Bruno as the main protagonist].

The second season was not as successful as the first. But it still had an audience share twice that achieved by RTL afterwards. I think giving up the *ViB* brand was a huge mistake.[6]

AE: According to Roger Schawinski (2007), two versions of the wedding were produced. Did SAT.1 conduct research to find out which ending the audience would prefer?

JB: I don't know whether or how much audience research SAT.1 carried out. Results are usually only passed on to producers if audience figures are deemed unsatisfactory and changes necessary. For the producers it was always clear that Lisa would marry David.

What we knew, though, was that viewers were extremely eager to know when Lisa would turn into a beautiful swan. As a result, we decided to wait until the very end. The more suspense, the more likely viewers are to stay tuned in.

AE: Not only a second season was developed for the German market, but the number of episodes in the first season of ViB was also increased because of the enormous success of the series. Is this common practice, and common for Latin American telenovelas?

ME: I think so. In Latin America producers react very strongly to audiences and they are known for being flexible. I can't imagine them not changing the number of episodes as required. In Germany, the *telenovela*, *Alles was zählt* (*All that Matters* [RTL, 2006–present]), was turned into a soap, and the number of episodes for *Sturm der Liebe* (*Storm of Love* [Das Erste, 2005–present]) was also increased. If the focus is on one love story, as in *Sturm der Liebe* or *ViB*, there are only so many episodes one can add, though.

AE: Why was the second season of ViB accredited to Yo soy Betty, la fea, *even though the A-plot was new?*

JB: I am not really familiar with the rights situation. But I believe an additional contract needed to be drawn up because many of the characters were still the same and it was a continuation of the *Betty* story after all. There is no standardization for such incidents. The format trade is not yet sufficiently developed for this.

AE: The US version, Ugly Betty, *was broadcast as* Alles Betty *on SAT.1 in April 2007. Due to low ratings it came off air after only two weeks.*[7] *Why do you think the US version did not work in Germany?*

ME: It was broadcast too closely in time to *ViB.* I also think it wasn't a good idea, psychologically, to ask Alexandra Neldel to promote *Alles Betty.* It's like saying to your fans: I'm no longer here for you but try my replacement; which is like saying try the second best. They tried, saw something completely different and didn't like it. So yes, the timing was bad, and the marketing addressed the wrong target group.

JB: The biggest mistake was the (near) simultaneous broadcasting and the 'me-too' factor.

AE: Do you think it might have worked on another channel, in another time-slot?

JB: No, I don't think so.

AE: Who owns the rights for the German adaptation, Verliebt in Berlin?

JB: The German rights are with ProSiebenSAT.1. They bought [them] directly from RCN. Fremantle was involved, though.

AE: Who owns the other European adaptation rights to Yo soy Betty, la fea? *Local producers or the commissioning TV channels? And who sold the German adaptation,* ViB, *to France, Canada, Hungary, etc.? Was it SevenOne International?*

Vasha Wallace: It depends on the production country and the local broadcaster. SevenOne International [the sales arm of the ProSiebenSAT.1 group] sold the German adaptation.

AE: What was the relationship between RCN and Fremantle if the contract was between local producers and RCN?

VW: FremantleMedia did a multi-territory deal for the rights to *Ugly Betty*. Germany initially did their own deal.

AE: Was Grundy UFA involved in other European Betty, la fea *adaptations?*

ME: Dutch and Belgian producers and others (from another country I can't remember now) came to see us to find out about our production experience. There were long talks, but I don't know whether they received scripts from us. The meetings, as far as I know, were organized via Fremantle.

AE: Was there much co-operation between [Fremantle] producing countries in the case of the local Betty *adaptations? If so, who organized it? Is transnational co-operation something Fremantle tries to push?*

VW: There is some degree of co-operation between the Fremantle drama production companies. Senior creative personnel meet regularly for workshops.

The various drama productions submit selections of their current output to a process of peer review. This process encourages honest reflection and constructive criticism. Ideas are exchanged in a process of collectively beneficial inspiration and reflection. The various *Betty* adaptations have been included in this process. The process also builds up friendship and trust between the key creative personnel from the different territories. This enhanced trust and familiarity leads naturally to more contact and exchange of ideas throughout the year.

In addition to this, specific exchanges of information and other learnings from the various *Betty* productions are encouraged and facilitated by FremantleMedia's Worldwide Drama department, based in London.

As with all FremantleMedia drama, creative control for each territory is in the hands of the specific production company in that [region]. They know their market and broadcaster client better than anyone else. But it is the responsibility of the Worldwide Drama department to ensure that these productions get all the information and help necessary to make the best creative and commercial judgements possible. In that sense Brand Guardianship is shared across the group.

AE: Do you know whether any European country used the German (or any other country's) scripts for their Betty adaptation? [German producers apparently based their scripts on plot summaries written by fans. They received the storylines from RCN much later.]

VW: None of our production companies used the German scripts as source material. The original Columbian story is always the starting point for any adaptation. Creative decisions about how best to adapt the material are then made independently by each production company in keeping with the cultural specifics and commercial imperatives of their respective territories. The best adaptations are always the most authentically local ones.

Having said that, our various production companies were, and are, very aware of the German adaptation. As the first European adaptation, the German production is an extremely high quality, hugely successful series that served as an inspiration and benchmark for all other FremantleMedia adaptations.

Works Cited

Baur, Jonas, Interview with author, 7 October 2008 (Berlin).

Downey, Kevin, 'Univision Steals Away Telemundo's Top Shows', *Media Life*, 19 June 2001, online at: http://www.medialifemagazine.com/news2001/june01/june18/2_tues/news3 tuesday.html (accessed 6 June 2011).

Esser, Andrea, 'Television Formats: Primetime Staple, Global Market', *Popular Communication: The International Journal of Media and Culture*, vol. 8, no. 4 (2010), pp. 273–92.

——, 'Format'iertes Fernsehen – Die Bedeutung von Formaten für Fernsehsender und Produktionsmärkte', *Media Perspektiven* (November 2010), pp. 502–14.

Esser, Michael, Interview with author, 9 October 2008 (Berlin).

Henz, Christian, 'Mal wieder: SAT.1 wirft *Ugly Betty* raus', *Medienmagazin*, 5 November 2010, online at: http://www.dwdl.de/nachrichten/28685/mal_wieder_sat1_wirft_ugly_ betty_raus/ (accessed 10 June 2011).

IP (2008) I-Punkt Gesamtjahr 2007: Fakten – Wirkungen – Argumente. Leistungswerte für Fernsehen, Teletext und Internet. 4. Quartal und Gesamtjahr 2007, report, online at: http://tinyurl.com/6jrxaq6 (accessed 6 June 2011).

Lippert, Bianca, *Telenovela Formats. Localized Versions of a Universal Love* (Göttingen: Sierke Verlag, 2011).

Mantel, Uwe, '*Alles was zählt* erstmals vor *Verliebt in Berlin*', *Medienmagazin*, 18 October 2006, online at: http://www.dwdl.de/zahlenzentrale/8123/alles_was_zhlt_erstmals_vor_verliebt_in_berlin/ (accessed 18 October 2006).

Remirez, Alicia, Interview with author, 7 October 2008 (Berlin).

Riedner, Fabian, 'Erfolg für letzte *Verliebt in Berlin* Episode', *Quotenmeter* (2006), online at: http://www.quotenmeter.de/cms/?p1=n&p2=22827&p3= (accessed 10 June 2011).

Ruoff, Markus, 'SAT.1 schmeißt *Alles Betty!* aus dem Programm', *Quotenmeter* (2007), online at: http://www.quotenmeter.de/cms/?p1=n&p2=20040&p3= (accessed 6 June 2011).

Schawinski, Roger, *Die TV Falle* (Munich: Kein & Aber, 2007).

Spiegel Online, '*Verliebt in Berlin* droht baldiges Ende, *Spiegel Online*, 10 June 2007, online at: http://www.spiegel.de/kultur/gesellschaft/0,1518,487727,00.html (accessed 6 June 2011).

Univision Communications Inc., 'Telefutura, America's Newest Broadcast Network Announces 2002–2003 Programming Lineup', press release, 15 May 2002, online at: http://www.univision.net/corp/en/pr/New_York_15052002-2.html#null (accessed 10 June 2011).

Wallace, Vasha, Interview with author, 22 June 2009 (London).

Endnotes

1   Scripted formats were only added to her portfolio in 2008, so Wallace was not directly involved with 'Betty'. She very kindly collated answers to my *Betty*-specific questions from colleagues.

2   *Yo soy Betty, la fea* had its US premiere on 8 August 2000 on Miami-based Spanish-language network Telemundo, where it proved an enormous, unexpected success. During the 2001 February sweeps, the *telenovela* was watched by about 1.4 million viewers per night and was largely responsible for increasing Telemundo's share of the commercially relevant (18–49), Spanish-speaking audience from 22 per cent the year before to 28 per cent. The final episode of *Yo soy Betty, la fea* was screened on 11 May 2001, one day after the *novela* ended in Colombia. Telemundo lost the series a month later to its larger competitor Univision, which had entered a five-year exclusive deal with RCN, including rerun rights to *Yo soy Betty, la fea* and rights to the sequel. In the 2002–3 programming season, a rerun of if was screened during daytime on TeleFutura, Univision's second Spanish-language channel, launched in 2002 (Downey 2001; Univision 2002).

3   It is interesting to note that Esser said he was not conscious of this at the time of writing the German scripts. It was only after a conference he had attended with *Yo soy Betty, la fea* creator Fernando Gaitán that Esser realized the gender difference in perspective between the Colombian original and *Verliebt in Berlin*.

4   Peter Schlesselmann joined Grundy UFA in 2001, working as a storyliner, editor and consultant. After his job as head writer for *ViB* ended, he became producer for the German soap *Verbotene Liebe*. Schlesselmann has a background in theatre.

5   Rheingold is a renowned German market research institute, based in Cologne. The
     company specializes in morphological market and media research and conducts in-
     depth psychological studies internationally.

6   *Verliebt in Berlin* premiered on SAT.1 on 28 February 2005. The *telenovela* was aired
     Mondays to Fridays 7.15–7.45pm. The first season ended with Lisa and David's wedding
     on 1 September 2006 after 364 episodes (increased from the originally planned 225).
     The second season, following on without break, introduced a new A-plot, centring
     on Lisa's brother Bruno and his love interest Hannah. They, too, marry in the final
     episode, screened on 12 October 2007. The audience shares of the two final episodes
     provide insight into both the enormous success of the German adaptation and the
     lesser popularity of the second season. The wedding of Lisa and David, a 90-minute
     special screened at 8.15pm (the common start time in Germany for primetime fiction),
     achieved a sensational audience share of 38.6 per cent amongst the advertising relevant
     target group of 14–49-year-olds. (For comparison, the average SAT.1 audience share for
     this target group during primetime in 2007 was 10.4 per cent [IP 2008: 29].) Bruno and
     Hannah's wedding achieved an audience share of 14.1 per cent amongst 14–49-year-
     olds. The second season had started with a market share of 21.8 per cent but six weeks
     later had dropped to 13.4 per cent. The reappearance of Neldel (Lisa) for 16 episodes
     temporarily revived ratings, with an average audience share of 14.9 per cent (Mantel
     2006; Riedner 2006; Spiegel Online 2007).

7   The US adaptation, *Ugly Betty*, premiered in Germany six months before the second
     season of *ViB* ended. It was launched under the German title *Alles Betty* on 27 April
     2007 as a primetime programme (screened at 8.15pm). Like *ViB*, *Alles Betty* was shown
     on SAT.1, and was dubbed like all foreign imports on German channels. SAT.1 hoped
     the weekly series would improve the channel's Friday night audience share. But with
     disappointing ratings *Alles Betty* was taken off air after only two weeks. The first episode
     achieved a market share of 9.1 per cent amongst 14–49-year-olds, dropping to 5.8 per
     cent in the second week (Ruoff 2007). In August 2010, SAT.1 relaunched *Ugly Betty*
     under a new name, *Betty – Allein unter Models (Betty – Alone Amongst Models)*. It was
     screened on Sunday afternoons, then moved to Saturday afternoons. Again, the market
     shares were disappointing and the show was discontinued in November 2010 (Henz
     2010). Since May 2010, *Ugly Betty* has also been broadcast by Sixx, a ProSiebenSAT.1
     cable and satellite channel for women, launched in the same month.

Betty and Lisa:
Alternating Between Sameness and Uniqueness

Bianca Lippert

A big smile, an even bigger heart, thick-rimmed glasses and braces on the teeth. These physical characteristics have become the global trademark of Betty and her national alter egos. While none of the various country-specific heroines are exactly the same, what the German Betty, Lisa Plenske (Alexandra Neldel), shares with the others are the multi-directional paths of import, export and adaptation. Not only does the story of the industrious, honest heroine transcend national borders, but also the different types of media (for example, cross-media storytelling through web-based applications). Yet these various forms of globalization exemplified by the Betty franchise do not override locality, as explained by Roland Robertson, 'what is called local is in large degree constructed on a trans- or super-local basis' (1995: 26). Robertson elaborates on the concept of 'glocalization' – internationally oriented strategies adapted to localized markets – to identify the simultaneity of both homogenization and heterogenization and their complementary and interpenetrative character (ibid.). It is exactly the integration of global and local elements, in contrast to oppositional pairings such as global versus local that makes Betty and Lisa at the same time unique *and* similar.

The aim of this chapter is to elaborate further on the heroines' person-ality and character development in relationship to the multiple factors influencing it: or, to put it another way, to analyse the interdependence of the heroines' interpersonal movements and international flows and TV flavours. How Betty morphs into Lisa makes visible this transition from a global TV phenomenon to a localized hit television serial. Lisa succeeded in the German TV market partly because of her characterization and partly because of the economic context, which, in turn, influenced Lisa's personality. What role the format trade played in the transformation from the Colombian Betty to the German Lisa also sheds light on the interrelated influences that built the glocal phenomenon of a modern ugly duckling conquering the fashion world and winning the heart of her boss as well as millions of viewers around the world.

Of particular interest are the similarities and differences of the heroines in the Colombian original and the German adaptation: what are the specific characteristics of Betty and her German counterpart Lisa? How far do these personal features affect the overall orientation and story development? What is the shared foundation on which both heroines mature and find happiness? And accordingly, what are the differences? Above all, how do specific market orientations determine those differences?

One of a Kind ...

Commenting on the viewing figures for the finale of the German adaptation, *Verliebt in Berlin* (*In Love in/with Berlin* [SAT.1, 2005–7]), former head of the private channel SAT.1, Roger Schawinski (2007: 64), compared its enormous rating success to the world football championship two months earlier. Just as the sporting event had attracted a huge male audience, *Verliebt in Berlin* did the same with a female one, climbing to 76 per cent in the relevant 14–29-year-old target group. But high ratings were not the only thing Betty and Lisa had in common.

The humorous approach taken in the Betty franchise distinguishes it from other classic *telenovela* productions, which are deeply rooted in the melodramatic tradition and tell of a decent but beautiful heroine meeting the (rich) man of her dreams and, after many trials and tribulations, marrying him. The same is true for Betty and Lisa, except that neither is beautiful at the start. The humorous tone is immediately reflected in the heroine's attention-grabbing appearance, including a metallic smile and huge, horn-rimmed glasses that seem to impede her vision, or how else, one might ask, can one explain her outdated hairstyle and unflattering fashion sense. Overturning the physical convention of the *telenovela* leading lady is relative, as both actresses, Colombian Ana-María Orozco and German Alexandra Neldel, are known in their respective countries as beautiful women.[1] Instead of hiding her slender appearance under tent-like clothes, as Orozco had done in *Yo soy Betty, la fea*, Neldel wore a specially tailored fat-suit that made her look at least three sizes bigger. It is precisely this contrast between the natural beauty of the actress and the highly stylized, manufactured ugliness of her character that adds humour. The common setting furthers the theme of beauty and ugliness, with the stories set in or around the fashion industry where a high premium is placed on physical attractiveness. The dramaturgical incursion of anti-fashionista Betty/Lisa conquering the fashion world provides, through this oppositional character, a source of comic relief while simultaneously speaking about other issues like social ostracism (though presented in a humorous but touching way).

Related to the generic *telenovela* convention mentioned above (the poor but beautiful heroine), the question has to be asked: does the use of an ugly protagonist demand a humorous approach for an audience to accept them and, if so, to what extent? Do we really want to see the 'ugly side of life'? And if so, does humour help us to cope with it?

Fernando Gaitán, the literal father of the original Betty, explained that the object of a *telenovela* is to fulfil 'un sueño collectivo' (Lippert 2011: 157), a common dream, that can hardly be reconciled with existing reality, but which is expected to stand out in comparison to everyday life. With regard to Betty and her alter egos, this common dream is the triumph of the underdog, which fosters identification processes with the non-conventional heroine. It is exactly the exaggerated setting of beauty and ugliness in the Betty franchise that is the driving force for emotional proximity as Oswald Hugo Benavides explains for the Colombian Betty: 'It is clear to all viewers that *las feas* (Betty included) are not real people – nobody is that ugly or campy. ... Yet it is this "realistic" distance which affords a "real" proximity to the emotional identification with the characters that most viewers feel, an emotional proximity that has to be consciously denied but that allowed *Betty la fea*'s economic success ...'

(2008: 57). Thus, even though Betty's appearance is exaggerated (as is Lisa's), they nevertheless reflect fears and desires of women that have to face competition or unfair treatment, be it in their professional or private life. And though in real life not every challenge is won, the 'sueño collectivo', the common dream, is fulfilled in the *telenovela*, in most cases consisting of the heroine's social advancement and the marriage with the man of her dreams.

Indeed, common to all Betties worldwide is the desire for a happy ending. The decisive question here is two-fold: what do we expect of this ending and how do we define happiness? Does anybody really want to see the ugly duckling *not* developing into the swan? Don't we still long for the fairytale fantasy, where the beautiful princess is rescued and marries her Prince Charming? Looking, however, at the US adaptation, *Ugly Betty* (ABC, 2006–10), one might be tempted to say no. Along with the second season slogan, 'bigger, bolder, Bettyer', the US *Betty* starring America Ferrera promoted the idea that self-esteem carries more weight than physical appearance.[2] In the US version (which was different from the Colombian and German ones), Betty's romantic quest with Daniel Meade (Eric Mabius) has not (yet) ended in the traditional 'I do' wedding formula. Instead, the finale kept open the possibility for the fairy tale to come true – though maybe bigger in a double sense (with a cinematic ceremony as Carrie Bradshaw [Sarah Jessica Parker] had in the movie, *Sex and the City*, Michael Patrick King, 2008).

Thinking further about the universal appeal of the Betty franchise, one essential part is the comedic approach predicated on oppositions, for example, ugliness versus beauty, which is similar to mythic narration. As Roger Silverstone (1981: 149) emphasizes, there are a number of binary codes at work within a (televisual) text, such as the locations of a particular story, the movement of the characters from one location to another, their clothes, their way of articulation, the acoustic components, etc. Prominent locations in all Betty versions and the movement from one to another are, for example, the private and the business environment. These different places can be differentiated between, respectively, a position of domestic security and relative inactivity at the heroine's home, and one of extrinsic insecurity and action at the office. Claude Lévi-Strauss regards these binary categories as fundamental human thought processes as an inherent part of mythic narration and which can also be found in the basic plot development common to all Betty versions (1955: 428–44). Betty, Lisa and all the other national alter egos cross on a daily basis the boundaries of home and workplace, incorporating and finally balancing the oppositional pairings described by Roger Silverstone (for a detailed analysis of the different codes, see Lippert 2011: 69–114).

However, though humour is part of every national Betty version, the use of it is very specific. Contrasting Betty with Lisa, the Colombian version is where parody meets passion, while in the German one it is toned down following primarily a romantic storyline injected with some humour: for while the Betty character is comically exaggerated with her quirky voice, strange laugh and slapstick performance (together with her male counterpart and best friend Nicolas Mora [Mario Duarte]), Lisa, in *Verliebt in Berlin*, is known for her witty voice-over, as she questions and critiques her surroundings with self-irony and critical asides. The voice-over is also used to emphasize the romance of the story, similar to the diary entries of the Colombian Betty, and of the dream sequences in both versions, which either supports the specific humour of each national version, or serves as a direct connection to the heroine's desires, thus fostering further identification with the audience.

Virginity Versus Passion

There are some differences that go beyond physical and behavioural characteristics but relate instead to specific cultural preoccupations (for example, submissiveness to authority, machismo, intergenerational discourse). The passion of the Colombian version is defined by the sexual relationship between Betty and her boss Amando Mendoza (Jorge Enrique Abello), whereas the German fairytale approach is related to the heroine's virginity. Whereas in both versions the main conflict in the love story concerns abuse of trust, the (geographical) distance between the heroine and the man of her dreams is created differently, relating to cultural as well as production-related reasons. Interviews I conducted with the Colombian and German scriptwriter, Fernando Gaitán and Michael Esser respectively, explain why. Gaitán, for example, describes how the *telenovela* speaks of the social struggles in Latin America, tapping into the collective dreams of the poor oppressed by the rich. These struggles are mapped onto those of the suffering heroine, who eventually overcomes misfortune to triumph over her antagonists and finally marry her one true love. Basal feelings like revenge and justice, delayed gratification of the poor and the punishment of rich oppressors are key components of an inherent Latin American collective fantasy. *Telenovelas* are told from the perspective of the socially downtrodden, or as Ingrid Delgadillo put it:

> Este sentimiento es propio de muchas historias afectivas de las mujeres de nuestro medio social, en donde actuando en posición de víctimas se sufren abandonos, maltratos, heridas afectivas que reducen y marcan ... luego se espera en la telenovela (y en la vida, aunque no siempre se resuelva) la revancha, la venganza, las cargas que se equilibran y cada cual recibe un merecido castigo y escarmiento. (63)

> (This feeling is closely connected to many love stories embracing women of our social environment, in which the protagonists play the victim who is abandoned, ill-treated, with emotional wounds ... subsequently is expected by the *telenovela* (and in real life, although this does not always come true) that it fulfills the longing for revenge, vengeance and the burden that balances [the injustice] and that anyone receives a come-uppance and a lesson to learn.)

Such conventions are at work in *Yo soy Betty, la fea*, as when Betty leaves her job in disgrace and travels to Cartagena following Armando's sexual betrayal. Humiliated and treated badly, Betty puts as much distance between herself and her boss. But her trip also becomes a personal journey of self-discovery and self-regard; it allows her inner beauty to flourish, made complete with her physical makeover. Her transformation into beautiful swan is accompanied by a change of attitude, with her return to the company as the new CEO emerging as a strong statement about justice. Betty's formidable comeback, challenging her jealous rivals, speaks to the collective Latin American dream of the poor fighting back – at least in the fictitious world of the *telenovela* as Delgadillo defines it above.

If class conflict, exploitation of the downtrodden, social elevation, revenge and justice shape the transformation of the Colombian Betty, these issues are toned down in the German version with its virtuous-romantic, fairytale approach. The passionate relationship between Betty and Armando is replaced with a chaste love story that resembles Goethe's Werther-like dedication to the unreturned affection for the love of one's life. The romantically idealized virginity of Lisa and her non-sexual relationship with David Seidel supports the sentimental tone of *Verliebt in Berlin*, and underlines Lisa's innocent, naive and uncorrupted character. Such a dramaturgical approach thus does not require Lisa to quit her job and journey far away from her love.

However, distance is created by the absence of the male protagonist, which also facilitates the love detour with a second admirer for Lisa. (This is similar to the Colombian version, although the German rival, Rokko Kowalski [Manuel Cortez], plays a major role unlike his Latin American counterpart, Michel Doinel [Patrick Delmas].) This distance, interestingly, evolved not only out of narrative concerns but was also a production necessity when the actor who plays David, Mathis Künzler, took paternity leave. To solve the problem and fill the void, the creative team came up with a kidnapping plot, with David abducted by his enemy Richard von Brahmberg (Karim Köster). This narrative reworking also impacted on Lisa's transformation and stands in stark contrast to Betty's public humiliation, her transformation (both mental and physical) away from home, and her dramatic return that overwhelms rivals and friends. Lisa's transformation differs, in that she does not leave the working environment in disgrace, with her journey of self-discovery taking place at home. Instead, her transformation is carried out more slowly and without heightened melodrama. Of course Lisa, like Betty, matures, grows and gains experience through the challenges she faces, but her physical makeover occurs simultaneously with her wedding preparation. Transformation thus plays a different, less pronounced role than in the original version, in which the makeover becomes intimately interwoven with social struggle roots of the *telenovela*.

The Market Rules

Just as cultural differences, production-related necessities and the creative power of the scriptwriters affected the transformation of the heroine in both the Colombian and German versions, market specificities also influenced the storyline. In the German adaptation, for example, it was not only the actor's paternity leave but also the broadcast schedule that prompted the story of David's kidnapping. The 2006 Soccer World Cup, held in Germany, interrupted the daily broadcast. Schedules were given over to live games, and *Verliebt in Berlin* was temporarily interrupted at a crucial narrative moment: following David's kidnapping, Lisa finds him in a precarious state and tension is created around if, and how, he will survive.

During the hiatus for the World Cup, specials were produced centring on one of the *telenovela* protagonists, summarizing his/her point of view via extracted scenes from already broadcast episodes. This kind of narrative summation has several advantages. First, for those who had missed episodes it offered an opportunity to catch up; and secondly, for those who were already up-to-date, it provided an interesting new angle on the plot presented through the eyes of alternating protagonists. And thirdly, no one missed the further continuation of the story because of the simultaneous live football coverage. Shortly before the World Cup finished, the last three episodes before the break were rebroadcast to facilitate re-entry into the story. Directly after the World Cup, the story continued with the last 40 episodes, culminating in Lisa's marriage to David.

Another example that vividly illustrates differing approaches of the Colombian and German versions is the composition of cast members. In the Colombian version, the so-called '*cuartel de las feas*' ('Ugly Women Club') comprises company secretaries and assistants of different ages and from disparate ethnic groups, while the German equivalent presents a younger cast, including apprentices and trainees, to attract a young demographic. In fact, the different cast can be explained by cultural as well as economic factors. The cultural dimension includes the term '*cuartel de las feas*' and its signification as it relates to how society is partitioned into rich and poor, beautiful and ugly. Though the expression is not explicitly explained in the show, it refers to the divide between the working class and management. However, members of the '*cuartel*' use these different labels in a self-assured way, as it indicates a special team spirit following its own rules and behavioural patterns. This cultural connotation is toned down in the German version, though the differentiation between working class and management also exists. As explained above, another reason for 'rejuvenating' the cast was to attract a young demographic. Considering the timeslot, as well as the broadcasters of *Verliebt in Berlin*, this decision becomes clearer. Given that the show was produced for the private channel SAT.1, which in contrast to public broadcasters, is dependent on advertising revenues, it was important for it to attract the lucrative 18–49-year-old demographic. The early evening timeslot is highly competitive, as this target group is imagined to be watching. Thus, instead of differently aged secretaries (from young to retirement age) as in the Colombian version, the German cast includes three teenagers exploring business-related challenges as well as the ups and downs of a classical love triangle between them.

Expanding the Experience

Watching television initiates a panopticon of possibilities to enhance the viewing experience through other forms of communication. Though transmedia storytelling is not an invention of modern times, digital media offers new ways of interaction. The messages are sent 'through multiple channels that reinforce each other' (Castells 2009: 121). The *Betty* franchise is a prime example of the global orientation built around consumerism in a customized way (ibid.). For example, a closer look at Lisa's finale makes clear what Manuel Castells described above as concerning the reinforcement of different communication channels. The decisive question in the last weeks was: David or Rokko? The two suitors vying to marry Lisa were promoted in numerous ways, including traditional media such as print and television, as well as digital media (enhancing interactivity) and live events (with direct communication with viewers). Beyond the dramaturgical suspense of the love triangle David–Lisa–Rokko, various incentives promoted the feature-length finale of *Verliebt in Berlin* and encouraged viewers to vote for either David or Rokko as the perfect partner for Lisa. Two endings were recorded, but it was ultimately the fans who decided which one would be broadcast during a live event attended by 2,000 people at the drive-in theatre, Berlin-Friedrichshain. Not only could those in Berlin choose an ending, but anyone else could call in or participate, via the Internet, and vote for their preferred denouement.[3]

Furthermore, the live event included a huge pre-show programme, which built further anticipation for the finale, with commentaries and serial highlights. After the finale aired, in an atmosphere of euphoria, the cast and crew thanked fans for their commitment and the new protagonist of the second season was introduced. Remarkably, all communication channels were interlinked. They provided a coherent message and offered feedback opportunities through web-based tools as well as offline media (for example, call-in events, opinion polls, raffles). These efforts must be seen in the broader context of marketing strategies, or as Henry Jenkins puts it, 'there are strong economic motives behind transmedia storytelling' (2006: 104). The reason that content is presented via multiple channels does not lie in the story itself, but to establish a brand around the original content (in this case, the *telenovela*) and create long-term relationships with the audience-cum-consumer.

This is also true for the following specific form of merchandising, the so-called 'reversed product placement' (Edery 2006; Gutnik 2010). This marketing strategy relies on expanding audience experience by linking the fictional world of *Verliebt in Berlin* with the real one via a brand that can be purchased at certain retailer shops. The B.Style label originates from the homonymous company managed by Lisa Plenske that offers modern, affordable fashions. In John Fiske's sense, the intertextuality created by elements of the fictional world that are integrated into the audience's everyday requirements (1989: 70), such as clothing and accessories, blurs the boundaries with real life and provides what I called 'prolonged pleasures'. The audience, or consumer, is invited to share parts of the fictional world with their private one supported by personal income. To this end, *Verliebt in Berlin* is a successful example of the integration of online, video on demand, mobile, teletext, call-TV, fashion, music and merchandising platforms; and this combining of various communication strategies is also central to other national versions. Besides content-related similarities, the communicative possibility beyond the television screen and, driven by economic forces, is another common feature of the *Betty* franchise that, analogue to the content, adapts to national requirements.

Boone or Bane: The Format Trade

The song 'Home Sweet Home' describes the feeling of belonging to a particular place with certain customs and conditions, but it can also be applied to how audiovisual productions are adapted and consumed at a local level, or so-called, 'cultural proximity'. That local programmes are preferred over imported ones has been well documented in various studies (Lantzsch 2008: 170f, Moran 1998: 5f, 19f). Advantages such as a proven record of success, minimal development costs and support of the local industry (Esser 2009) have been reported alongside the fact that imported programmes remain less expensive (even though a successful format cannot always guarantee success elsewhere [Moran 19f]). For example, the Brazilian *Betty* did not do as well as was initially expected. Rede Record, the TV station together with Mexican Televisa that produced the Brazilian version, initiated some research to investigate why *Bela, a Feia* (*Bela, the Ugly* [Rede Record, 2009–10]) only achieved moderate ratings ('Outro Canal', 2009). The findings led to the show being rescheduled in a later time slot. The strategy worked and *Bela, a Feia* led the ratings, peaking with its broadcast of Bela's transformation into a beautiful girl with 25 points at IBOPE, the Brazilian Institute of Public Opinion and Statistics ('Bela, a Feia', 2011)

Still, critical voices against the format trade might be eased if adaptations as the epitome of cultural homogenization fail. Is the TV format business as a form of standardization really a reduction of cultural variety? Does Ritzer's well-known principle of 'McDonaldization' apply to the TV format trade pursuing a 'one size fits all' credo? As the *Betty* franchise impressively illustrates, there are multiple ways of localizing the universal appeal of the story. Yet, as *Verliebt in Berlin* head writer Esser commented, the challenge to adapt a format is not 'das eigene Lokale in ein Format einzubauen, sondern vielmehr die Aufgabe, das Universelle an einem Format zu erkennen, denn nur das garantiert einem den Zugang zum eigenen Publikum' ('to include the local specificities of a given market into the format, but the important task is to recognize the universal within the format as this is the only way to achieve the national audience') ('Rückfragen', 2008). As Esser explains further, only three video clips of the original show were available before the localization in Germany started, together with weekly plot synopses written by fans.

'Wir haben die Charaktere verstanden, wir haben die Grundgeschichte verstanden, und von hier aus machen wir uns auf unsere eigene Reise' ('We understood the characters and the basic story and from there we went on our personal journey [with Lisa]') ('Interview', 2008). This approach turned out to be successful given the market conditions and circumstances highlighted above.

However, since the first season of *Verliebt in Berlin* in 2006, there has been no other attempt to adapt another Latin American *telenovela* format for the German market – that is, until recently. The reason for this might be that producers saw no need for formats or just did not find an adequate format to fit their requirements. Thus, there were various trials to establish a genuine German love story in the style of the *telenovela* genre for different market segments. Examples include *Sophie – Braut wider Willen* (*Sophie – The Unwilling Bride* [Grundy UFA, 2005–6]), which took place in the nineteenth century with ostentatious costumes and sets, *Lotta in Love* (Rat Pack Filmproduktion, 2006) and *Schmetterlinge im Bauch* (*Love Is in the Air* [Producers at Work, 2006]), both of which were targeted at a younger audience. There were also *telenovelas* that included elements of crime such as *Das Geheimnis meines Vaters* (*Forbidden Love* [Studio Hamburg Produktion, 2006]). None of these attempts convinced the audience. There is much speculation as to why this is so, but as Torsten Dewi, head author of *Lotta in Love*, said in his blog: sometimes the audience is just not willing to take a chance on a new show.

However, other daily German productions did establish a loyal audience base. Beside long-running, almost traditional daily soap operas such as *Gute Zeiten, Schlechte Zeiten* (*Good Times, Bad Times* [Grundy UFA, 1992]) or *Marienhof* (Bavaria Film, 1992), some productions were able to conquer a certain time slot and quickly built up a constant viewership. For example, the first (genuine) German *telenovela Bianca – Wege zum Glück* (*Bianca – Paths to Happiness* [Grundy UFA/teamWorx, 2004]) gradually constructed a narrative basis on which the main couple could be replaced by a new one as soon as the former found their way to happiness, ending in marriage. Along with Bianca Berger (Tanja Wedhorn) and Oliver Wellinghoff (Patrik Fichte), five different couples fought for love until the finale of *Wege zum Glück* in 2009. Another successful example of a German *telenovela* is *Sturm der Liebe* (*Storm of*

Love [Bavaria Fernsehproduktion, 2005–present]), based on a similar concept using the existing story background and including a new central couple with its focus on the female protagonist. True to the motto 'never change a running system', *Sturm der Liebe* constantly achieves a high market share in its afternoon slot, broadcasting far more than 1,000 episodes with no end in sight.

The public channel ZDF initiated another approach in the 2010 autumn season. With its new telenovela *Lena – Liebe meines Lebens* (*Lena – Love of My Life* [Wiedemann & Berg Television (member of the Endemol group), 2010–present]), it brought a different tone to the romantic afternoon timeslot. Adapted from the Argentinean *telenovela Don Juan y su Bella Dama* (*Don Juan and His Beautiful Lady* [Telefe, 2008]), the second adaptation of a Latin American original for the German market (after *Yo soy Betty, la fea*), it mixes traditional and modern elements of the genre. This new approach to character constellation, narrative perspective and pace is different from what the German audience has come to expect from ZDF in the afternoon, and includes the risk of rejection, a topic already discussed on the official *Lena* Internet bulletin on the ZDF website ('Lena – Liebe meines Lebens', 2011). Ignoring the general characteristics of the German audience as 'creatures of habit', meaning that it takes time to establish a loyal (and measurable) fan base, the ZDF lost faith in the local adaptation Lena, which could not, in due time, tie in with the success of its Argentinean original story Don Juan.

Conclusion

Questions remain as to what makes a format like Betty and her various international alter egos universally appealing. To clarify the relationship between 'universal' and 'local', Tony Garnett offered the following delineation:

> In drama, some themes are universal. Themes around family, blood and generations. Themes around sex, greed, jealousy and God. Great drama always is – it appeals to important things in each of us, however culturally different we seem. But the paradox is that

these generalities always come best out of the closely observed, the culturally specific, the unique and the precise and particular. If you want to achieve the universal, be local. (Garnett, 2008)

The examples of *Lisa* and *Lena* illustrate that adapting a TV format is far more than changing actors and backdrops. Beside the challenge of finding the universal and applying it via local elements, there are also business-related success factors, such as programme scheduling and the runtime of a serial. Thus the recipe for success consists of many different ingredients – and to make it even more complicated – for each adaptation the mix of these ingredients is individual.

Works Cited

Breitbach, Sybille (ed.), 'Alexandra Neldel', *Wasted Management*, 8 March 2010, online at: http://wasted-management.de/alexandraneldel/alexandra_neldel_biografie.html.

Benavides, Oswald Hugo, *Drugs, Thugs and Divas: Telenovelas and Narco-Dramas in Latin America* (Texas: University of Texas Press, 2008).

'Bela, a Feia' bate recorde de audiência com transformação de protagonista', *Contigo! Blog Chiado*, 8 April 2010, online at: http://contigo.abril.com.br/blog/chiado/2010/04/08/bela-a-feia-bate-recorde-de-audiencia-com-transformacao-de-protagonista/.

Castells, Manuel, *Communication Power* (New York: Oxford University Press, 2009).

Chavez, Guillermo, 'Passion Travels', *Worldscreen.com*, April 2007, online at: http://www.worldscreen.com/featurescurrent.php? filename=novelas0407.htm.

Delgadillo, Ingrid, 'Consumo Televisivo Femenino. El Caso de *Betty, la fea* (unpublished MA thesis, Bogotá: University de Colombia, 2002).

Dempsey, John, 'Soaps not Sudsy for MyNetwork TV. Network Revamps Its Schedule', *Variety.com*, 1 February 2007, online at: http://www.variety.com/article/VR1117958532.html.

Dewi, Torsten, 'Lotta in Love – Eine Story mit Folgen V', *Online Post*, 16 August 2007: http://wortvogel.de/2007/08/lotta-in-love-eine-story-mit-folgen-v/.

Edery, David, 'Reverse Product Placement in Virtual World', *Harvard Business Review*, December 2006, online at: http://hbr.org/2006/12/reverse-product-placement-in-virtual-worlds/ar/1.

Esser, Andrea, 'Audio-Visual Content in the EU: Production and Scheduling', in Richard Rooke (ed.), *European Media in the Digital Age. Analysis and Approaches* (London: Pearson Education, 2009), pp. 182–215.

Esser, Michael, telephone interview, 16 January and 16 December 2008.

——, 'RE: Rückfragen zum Interview', email to the author, 17 September 2008.

Fiske, John, 'Moments of Television: Neither the Text nor the Audience', in Ellen Seiter, Hans Borchers, Gabriele Kreutzner et al. (eds), *Remote Control. Television, Audiences, and Cultural Power* (London: Routledge, 1989), pp. 56–78.

'Lena – Liebe meines Lebens', Bulletin Board, *Zweites Deutsches Fernsehen*, 15 April 2011, online at: http://lena.zdf.de/ZDFforum/ZDFde/inhalt/15/0,1872,8096879,00/.

Gaitán, Fernando, personal interview, 31 March 2008.

Garnett, Tony, Lecture at the Conf. Television without Borders: Transfers, Translations and Transnational Exchange. University of Reading, Reading, 29 June 2008.

Gutnik, Lilia, Huang, Tom, Blue Lin, Jill et al., 'Strategic Computing and Communications Technology: New Trends in Product Placement', *UC Berkeley School of Information*, Spring 2007, online at: http://people.ischool.berkeley.edu/~hal/Courses/StratTech09/Tech/Preso/ D-placement.doc.

Jenkins, Henry, *Convergence Culture. Where Old and New Media Collide* (New York: New York University Press, 2006).

Lantzsch, Katja, *Der internationale Fernsehformathandel. Akteure, Strategien, Strukturen, Organizationsformen* (unpublished dissertation, The Business of Entertainment, Medien, Märkte, Management. Wiesbaden: VS, 2008).

Lippert, Bianca, 'Telenovela Foramts. Localized Versions of a Universal Love. *"Yo soy Betty, la fea"* and Its Various Adaptations: Successful Remakes ad Infinitum?' (unpublished dissertation, Göttingen: Sierke, 2011).

López, Elena M., and Ruiz, Norma G., 'Ana María Orozco', August 2003, online at: http://www.anamaria-orozco.com.

Lévis-Strauss, Claude, 'The Structural Study of Myth', *Journal of American Folklore*, vol. 68 (1955), pp. 428–44.

Lewontin, Richard C., Rose, Steven, and Kamin, Leon J., (1984) *Not in Our Genes. Biology, Ideology, and Human Nature* (New York: Pantheon, 1984).

Mikos, Lothar, and Perrotta, Marta, 'An Analysis of National Adaptations of *Yo Soy Betty, La Fea*' (paper presented at the Annual Meeting of the International Communication Association, Marriott Hotel, Chicago, 20 May 2009), online at: http://www.allacademic.com/meta/p296869_index.html.

Moran, Albert, *Copycat TV. Globalization, Program Formats and Cultural Identity* (Luton: University of Luton Press, 1998).

———, with Malbon, Justin, *Understanding the Global TV Format* (Exeter: Intellect, 2006).

'Outro Canal: Record faz pesquisa para decifrar fracasso de Bela, a Feia', *Folha Online*, 2 September 2009, online at: http://www1.folha.uol.com.br/folha/ilustrada/ult90u618378.shtml.

Quiroga, Marisa, 'Don Juan y su Bella Dama' (lecture, Endemol, Cologne, 22–3 January 2010).

Ritzer, George, *The McDonaldization of Society* (Thousand Oaks: Pin Forge, 2004).

Robertson, Roland, 'Glocalization: Time-Space and Homogeneity-Heterogeneity', in Mike Featherstone, Scott Lash and Roland Robertson (eds), *Global Modernities* (London: Sage, 1995), pp. 25–44.

Schawinski, Roger, *Die TV-Falle. Vom Sendungsbewusstsein zum Fernsehgeschäft* (Zürich: Kein und Aber, 2007).

Silverstone, Roger, *The Message of Television. Myth and Narrative in Contemporary Culture* (London: Heinemann Educational, 1981).

Straubhaar, Joseph D., *World Television: From Global to Local* (Thousand Oaks, CA: Sage, 2007).

Weis, Manuel, 'ZDF-*Lena* – im Internet ein Hit', *Quotenmeter*, 30 December 2011, online at: http://www.quotenmeter.de/cms/?p1=n&p2=46437&p3.

Weis, Manuel, '"Es liegt an der formalen Umsetzung" – Wie geht's weiter mit "Lena"?' *Quotenmeter*, 10 December 2010, online at: http://www.quotenmeter.de/cms/?p1= n&p2=46367&p3.

Zabel, Christian, 'Zeitwettbewerb deutscher Free-TV-Anbieter', *Medien und Kommunikationswissenschaft*, vol. 52, no. 3 (2004), pp. 412–31.

Endnotes

1   Orozco had started her television career already as a child, starring in the children's show *Pequeños Gigantes* (*Small* Giants, López and Ruiz). Neldel began her acting career in the long-running, successful daily soap, *Gute Zeiten, Schlechte Zeiten* (since 1992, Grundy UFA) (Breitbach).

2   Retracing Ferrera's career since her early screen appearances, it is evident that she underwent weight loss, but she is still an exception regarding her full-figured shape by Hollywood standards (e.g. *Real Women have Curves*, HBO, 2002).

3   Schawinski revealed that the actual decision concerning which ending would be broadcast had already been made on the basis of a recent market analysis (64). However, both endings can be found on the DVD, which comprise both David and Rokko respectively as fiancés.

Ugly Betty, Flemish Sara: *Telenovela* Adaptation and Generic Expectations

Alexander Dhoest and Manon Mertens

In a globalizing television market characterized by intensified format trade, the Colombian *telenovela Yo soy Betty, la fea* (*I Am Betty, the Ugly One* [RCN, 1999–2001]) was adapted in Flanders (Dutch-language Belgium) into *Sara* (VTM). In the 2007–8 season, this serial conquered the hearts of Flemish viewers. This paper investigates the success of *Sara*, through an analysis of its discursive context, which explores how *Sara* was positioned and made sense of in the Flemish television landscape. First, it takes a closer look at the production side, interviewing the writer and producers of the show to understand their intentions and why they think *Sara* worked so well. Next, there is an analysis of the critical response, identifying evaluations and explanations in the press. Finally, we interviewed 25 viewers (of different age and gender), to ask them why they watched and liked *Sara*.[1] In this way, the chapter builds a 'holistic' picture of the discursive framework that surrounded this 'domesticated' Flemish *telenovela*, aiming in particular to understand its success in terms of 'global', generic and 'local' Flemish elements.

Although a few *telenovelas* were imported to Flanders in the 1980s, and a domestic one (*Emma*) was broadcast but failed on the public channel Eén in 2007, the genre was largely new at the time *Sara* first aired. Unlike soaps, sitcoms and crime series, it was not one of the genres Flemish viewers were used to. Therefore, it is interesting to consider how such a 'new' and 'foreign' genre was conceived and received. Beside producers/filmmakers, audiences are considered a key element in the 'genre triangle'. Tom Ryall (1975) influentially defined genres as follows: 'Genres may be defined as patterns/forms/styles/ structures which transcend individual films, and which supervise both their construction by the film maker, and their reading by an audience.' Genres create expectations among audiences (Neale 1990), 'horizons of expectation' leading to recognition (Altman 1999), but what happens when a genre with a long international history is introduced into a new local market? Following Jason Mittell (2001; 2004), genres are considered as cultural, discursive practices in which texts, industries and audiences interact in a specific historical and cultural context. This chapter will investigate these interactions and the emergence of a cultural discourse surrounding *Sara* as well as the *telenovela* in Flanders.

Given the importance of cultural context, the issue of adaptation begs attention, as this is one of the first Flemish serials to have been so closely based on an imported format. In the mid-1990s, one of the most important Flemish soaps, *Wittekerke* (Vlaamse Televisie Maatschappij [VTM], 1993–2008), was based on an Australian format (*E-Street*, Ten, 1989–93); but this was an exception, and after the initial episodes, most of its material was original to Flanders. *Sara*, by contrast, was entirely based on an existing serial and part of an international wave of adaptations in a global television market where format trade abounds (Moran 1998; 2000).

The success of the Flemish version makes one wonder what exactly determined its appeal: the 'global', generic and formatted characteristics of the show or the variable elements added to create national, 'local' flavour? Could one attribute the success of *Sara* to its 'Flemishness' and therefore cultural specificity, even if it was an adaptation? Or did 'universal' generic elements play a more important role, even if the *telenovela* genre as such was not well known? If, as noted by Joseph Straubhaar (2007: 195–7), the broad genre of melodrama travels well internationally and creates a sense of worldwide recognition, then does that explain the success of *Sara*?

The Producers' Vision

Sara was broadcast on commercial channel VTM, where it attracted unprecedented audience shares in access prime time (6.30–7 pm). This is a key time slot in the schedules, preceding the evening news, in which the main public channel Eén has been scheduling a successful quiz show (*Blokken,* based on the video game Tetris) for over 15 years. VTM, its main commercial competitor, had never found a good opener for its evening, a crucial moment to attract viewers for the news. *Sara* did appeal to a large and commercially interesting audience in the 18–54 age range, where it reached a market share of about 50 per cent. It was subsequently moved to a more prominent spot in primetime where it attracted up to a million viewers, with a peak for the final episode (24 June 2008) of 1.422.142 viewers (out of a population of about 6 million) and a market share of 59.8 per cent.

Clearly *Sara* was a success, in line with the international appeal of the serial. Nevertheless, it was not a safe bet: it was the first domestic fiction series in this time slot, which is usually reserved for cheaper productions. In a small television marketplace like Flanders it is not easy to recoup the production costs of fiction through advertising, even in a cheaper genre like the *telenovela.* To increase advertising income and to offer maximum possibilities for viewers to follow the serial, all episodes were repeated in an omnibus edition on Sunday evening, where the show reached another 20 per cent of the target audience. Scheduling *Sara* on weekdays at 6.30 pm was also risky because it was a genre largely unfamiliar to the Flemish audiences. If *Sara* had failed, it would have given the commercial broadcaster VMMA many problems. The international success of the format, in particular the German adaptation *Verliebt in Berlin (In Love in/with Berlin* [SAT.1, 2005–7]), helped convince VMMA executives of its viability, but it remained a gamble. For instance, the Dutch adaptation *Lotte* (Tien, 2006) did considerably less well with audiences, so no one was really sure how the Flemish audience would react.

To better understand the way *Sara* was conceived from the industry point of view, we interviewed screenwriter Hugo Van Laere, as well as the producers from both the commercial broadcaster, VMMA (Jan Creuwels and Gitte Nuyens) and the production company, Fremantle Productions (Dieter Debruyn and Reinhilde Dewit). They expressed initial enthusiasm for the project, but also doubts: however much they believed in *Sara*, they could not predict its audience appeal. They embraced the project because of its novelty – which allowed it to attract new, commercially interesting viewers – but they spent a lot of energy positioning this new 'product' in the market. The launch of *Sara* was prepared by a campaign creating curiosity (not showing the actual face of 'ugly duckling' Sara), which led to satisfying audience figures for the pilot episode (in primetime), after which the ratings for the daily episodes in access primetime dropped. Gradually, however, the show started to attract a growing audience of dedicated viewers, which the producers attribute to word-of-mouth publicity. Producer Dewit: 'Everybody was saying: "You have to have seen that", and in the end ... The ones who didn't watch started to watch because you had to have seen it, you see? Success takes care of itself, success attracts success' (2009). Before long, the press started to notice its success and *Sara* became a real story, leading to the phenomenal ratings towards the last episodes. The producers link this growing audience to two complementary characteristics of the show: on the one hand, the clarity of the storylines which allowed new viewers to start watching at any time, and on the other hand, the continuing storyline which kept viewers hooked. The producers regularly refer to this as a soap-like 'addiction': once you start watching, you want to know how it ends. Indeed, formally, there is a likeness to the soap narrative intertwining storylines and spreading them over a long period of time, each episode ending with a cliffhanger.

However, the producers also distinguish *Sara* from the (more familiar) soap form, stressing that *Sara* is really something new. One of the key elements of this difference is the overarching storyline with a clear beginning, middle and end. As explained by screenwriter Hugo Van Laere, this creates a three-act structure with 'plot points' around the evolving relationship between Sara De Roose (Veerle Baetens) and her boss Simon Van Wyck (Gert Winckelmans). From the very first episode, the romantic tension between them is established and it guides the viewer through the entire season, with the 'bedroom scene' in episode 98 providing the 'point of no return'. Several of the producers liken the overall structure and feel of *Sara* to cinema, in particular romantic comedy. While viewers familiar with the rom-com genre know that love will grow, against the odds, in *Sara* this expectation is explicitly established as viewers see the protagonist actually swooning over Simon in the pilot. In this way, strong expectations are set up and a high degree of predictability created. As the producers indicate, the question is never *if* they will get together, but *when* and *how*.

Sara therefore strikes a fine balance between predictability and surprise, which is an important element of any genre, but which in the case of *Sara* depends less on knowledge of generic (*telenovela*) conventions than on broader cultural clichés as well as expectations raised by the show itself. As indicated by producer Creuwels, the show consciously and knowingly exploits clichés, often confirming but also contradicting viewer expectations: 'From time to time you have to prove viewers right and say "You see, I knew it" and at other times you have to say "Oh, I didn't expect that"'(2009). As with the Colombian original, the characters are clearly and strongly typed, so they each create expectations as to how they will act and react. In the case of one secondary character, the flirty, bitchy secretary Britt Van Hove (Sandrine André), this is exploited for comic effect, depicted in part through a consciously slightly over-the-top performance. This is another difference with soap opera, which (at least in Flanders) uses a more natural acting style in line with the more heavy-handed, social-realist narratives. In contrast, *Sara* is consciously light-footed and (moderately) exaggerated, the producers aiming for escapism and a fairytale-like atmosphere. Therefore, beside the key romantic storyline, there is also a heavy emphasis on humour: the characters are larger than life and Sara's clumsiness and awkwardness are comically exaggerated. Although *Sara* is less tongue-in-cheek and hyperbolic than the American *Ugly Betty* (ABC, 2006–10), the Flemish producers do rely on strong comic types and clichés.

Talking about the reasons for the success of *Sara*, the producers mention all of the above, stressing good acting and in particular, Veerle Baetens as Sara. They do not see the show's popularity as an extension of the established success of the soap opera in Flanders (which has two long-running soaps attracting daily audiences of up to 1 million viewers), but rather as an alternative: the stories do not ramble on for ever but move towards a resolution, the tone is lighter and less dramatic, there is room for unabashed romance instead of social issues, and the acting is more exaggerated and therefore more fun to watch. As noted by screenwriter Van Laere, the mode of production is similar to a soap opera, with its high production pace, interior scenes and tight production schedule, but the end product is much more like a (very long) film. In generic terms, then, the success of *Sara* seems less attributable to the familiarity and known appeal of the *telenovela*, but rather to its novelty and differences from the more established soap genre. Instead of building on pre-existing *telenovela* expectations, *Sara* put the genre on the map and created expectations that were capitalized on by several later *telenovelas*. With *Sara*, the Flemish audience first got to know the 'global' strengths of the *telenovela* as a genre.

The producers also note a 'universal' need for romance and escape (contrasting it to the wave of reality TV), which is met by the central love story. Added to that is the focus of the show on an ugly duckling in an age increasingly obsessed with appearance and good looks. According to the producers, this leads to recognition among those viewers who feel unable to meet these ideals of perfection and enjoy watching their insecurities aggrandized on screen. Of this Dewit says, 'It's actually what we're all dealing with. What insecurities do we have? How can we move out of them, what can we do about them?' (2009) Beside these (allegedly) 'universal' elements, the ugly duckling theme and the love story, the producers also refer to local elements, in particular the appeal of the underdog in Flemish culture. The insecure protagonist receives a great deal of sympathy, as humility is perceived to be part of the Flemish character. As Dewit notes, 'Aren't we all a bit too modest sometimes? ... We always think we're not going to do things right, and Sara is someone like that' (Dewit 2009).

More generally, the producers comment on the Flemish elements added to the fixed format to adapt the story to local tastes. Screenwriter Van Laere complains that the German *Verliebt in Berlin* would have been a much easier version to work on, but instead he had to use the original Colombian screenplay which he had to tailor radically to Flemish tastes. For instance, he added numerous side-stories and characters, as he found the original script too poor in dramatic material, too chatty and too slow for Flemish audiences. He notes how the original consisted of endless conversations, mostly between the main protagonists, which he estimates were in 80 per cent of the scenes, while in the Flemish version they were only in 30 per cent of the scenes, other (also romantic) storylines making for more variation. Also, the exaggerations were partly toned down as Flemish audiences are used to a more naturalist acting style and already had to adapt to the quite stereotypical characters. As Reinhilde Dewit says: 'We Flemings have both feet on the ground.' (2009)

Many of the additions are details, but they are important in creating a sense of reality. Van Laere, for example, notes, 'In *Verliebt in Berlin* she takes the metro to work, in *Lotte* in the Netherlands she goes by bike. What does a Flemish person do? She takes a bus. It's in little things like that.' (2009) To Van Laere, it is not about repeating Flemish stereotypes or showing Flemish national character (whatever that may be), but about prompting recognition. For instance, in the original *Yo soy Betty, la fea* the protagonist is a country girl who moves to the big city for work, thus leaving her parents to worry constantly about her safety; but in the highly urbanized Flanders with medium-sized cities such a fear of the metropolis would simply sound false. Producer Reinhilde Dewit confirms this, commenting on the universality of the underlying 'fairytale' storyline: 'The large story was kept entirely, but you have to make the details local. That's really important, otherwise people don't recognize themselves, and you always have to show people a mirror, otherwise it doesn't work.' (2009) To Dewit, despite the seemingly strong similarities between different versions of the show (for instance in the appearance of the female lead), little national details make an enormous difference. This is in line with Albert Moran's observation that national adaptations of a soap (in his case *The Restless Years*, Grundy Productions, 1977–82) vary mostly in terms of accents, locations, cultural associations and 'a plethora of physical objects, social behaviours and routines drawn from everyday life' (2000: 87), thus contributing to a national imaginary:

> Although seemingly trivial and everyday, they form or can form part of a much larger repertoire of images and practices generated in the media, popular culture, education, religion and elsewhere, out of which social groups can fashion various identities, including national identities. (92)

This clearly illustrates the more general tendency of 'everyday nationalism' in Flemish TV fiction (Dhoest 2007). *Sara* is not 'about' Flanders in any explicit way, but like Flemish soaps (and indeed most contemporary drama), it refers to the Flemish context in manifold taken-for-granted, unremarkable ways which, taken together, have the powerful effect of making this show seem quintessentially Flemish.

The Critical and Popular Reception

In reviewing press criticism, it is clear that Flemish journalists were not enthusiastic about *Sara* from the start. For instance, the respected news magazine *Knack* wrote: 'After 200 episodes *Sara* is over. We look forward to it.' (3 October 2007) The press duly announced the new show, commenting on the 'ugly duckling' premise and the difficult timeslot. After *Sara* began, there were some comments about the acting being slightly over the top, but Veerle Baetens was generally considered as a strong Sara. The very critical 'Dwarskijker' in TV magazine *Humo* put it this way: 'There is one point of light: main actress Veerle Baetens, who craftily slaloms through the improbable plot turns and even gives depth to her cardboard character.' (25 January 2008) The quality press in particular was dismissive of the genre, lamenting the predictability and implausibility of the plotlines. The popular newspapers were more positive and gradually started to speculate on when and how Sara and Simon would get together.

When the show turned out to be a success, many journalists started looking for explanations. For instance, quality paper *De Standaard* interviewed Fernando Gaitán, the screenwriter of the original *Yo soy Betty, la fea*, who attributes its success to three factors: female viewers recognizing themselves in the protagonist with her insecurities and love troubles, humour and the fact that Betty remains positive, and her innocence and good nature, which raise a lot of sympathy (*De Standaard*, 5 May 2008). Elsewhere, the critics repeated the same reasons mentioned by the producers and writers above: humour, romance and the recognizability of the central character, in particular her underdog status. However, the show's huge success remained somewhat mystifying, leading one journalist to add: 'Someone urgently has to do a nice research project on *Sara*' (*Het Volk*, 12/03/2008). The critical response shows interesting parallels to the producers' account: first, insecurity (is it going to work?), then bewilderment (why does it work so well?), leading to a host of explanations (or rather speculations) about the show's success.

With the critics turning to the producers for explanations and the producers reading press reviews, a self-referential discourse on *Sara* and the *telenovela* genre gradually grew, in which the Flemish character of the show was a recurring theme.

In our interviews with viewers, many of the elements mentioned above returned and were confirmed, including the mixture of 'global' and 'local' elements conspiring to make *Sara* irresistible. To start with, the 'mystery' of why *Sara* was such a success also emerges in the interviews with viewers. Many do not quite know why they watched and loved it so much, often referring to its enticing, 'addicting' nature, calling it hypnotic and magical. They confirm speculation of word-of-mouth publicity previously mentioned by the producers, as many started to tune in because of friends or family members. Bernadette (60), a teacher, says: 'A lot of my pupils watched it and I also wanted to see what it was all about and whether it was really that fantastic.'

Echoing the literature on soaps, *Sara* became an important topic of conversation and speculation for others. 'We were sitting here together thinking "What is going to happen now? Sara will do this, or that, or that's going to happen, or he's going to run off with another woman again ..." That's fun, thinking ahead what will happen,' responds Lisa (48), a kindergarten teacher. Many other interviewees make similar comments, mentioning the social pressure to watch and the social function of discussing past and future events, in particular the eventual metamorphosis of Sara.

The novelty of the format also appealed to many respondents, who were curious to watch the show because of the advertising campaign. 'It was announced as a new TV format made by VTM and then you're inclined to watch to know what it actually was,' says Katrien (30). Her comment confirms the point made above about generic expectations: viewers did not quite know what to expect and they were drawn to the show because of its novelty. Indeed, the lower ratings for the two subsequent domestic *telenovelas* seem to be at least in part due to the novelty wearing off for Flemish audiences.

Contrary to the mixed newspaper criticism, the viewers we interviewed were predominantly positive about *Sara*. This was to be expected, as we selected only people who regularly watched the show, but their responses offer insight into the reasons why they liked it. What transpires from the interviews is that they cannot quite place *Sara* generically. They liken it to 'a film cut into pieces' or a romantic novel, but less to soap operas. *Sara* is seen as entertaining, feel-good viewing, like the romantic comedy: 'That's just pure entertainment and I can get that sort of entertainment just as well from watching a film, a romantic comedy or the like,' Katrien (30) says. Indeed, the entertainment value of *Sara* was a key reason to keep watching – its clichés and accessibility, its fairytale structure that allowed for escape: 'That's escaping a little from reality. I think that's why it was such a success. The large audience doesn't live in a fairytale where all ends well. It's nice to see that on TV, it creates a feel-good atmosphere,' says Heleen (30). Interestingly, many respondents claim not to watch soaps (any more), complaining about their interminable nature. The fact that the *telenovela* has an actual climax and resolution was liked by many: 'Now you have a nicely finished whole, everybody is happy and there are no conflicts or problems that have to be further thought about' (Philippe, 21).

The fact that its ending was predictable does not seem to have deterred viewers. 'In the end she becomes beautiful and he falls for her and they marry: happy end. Yes that was beautiful and it was the confirmation that you actually always wanted to see, because that's what it was all about: will they get together or not?' said Sandy (22). Such a comment confirms the key drive to watch as indicated by both the producers and press: not 'will they do it' but 'when do they do it' (*Het Nieuwsblad*, 26 September 2007). The same is true for the transformation of Sara: when will she change and how will she look? What clothes will she wear? How will she evolve? For instance, when asked why she kept on watching the show, Martine (18) replied, 'Just out of curiosity [to see] how she would actually look in the end.' Taken together, these responses indicate that *Sara* became a success, firstly, thanks to the (global) strength of the *telenovela* genre (working towards an ending), its likeness to the romantic comedy and its welcome difference from the more established soap genre.

Another factor mentioned by the producers and press recurs in the viewer responses: namely, recognition of the main character and her insecurities about the way she looks. Despite the exaggerated nature of Sara's portrayal, many describe her as realistic and natural. This reading recalls the 'emotional realism' identified by Ien Ang (1982) in her audience study on the appeal of *Dallas* (1978–91): despite exaggerations, it 'feels' real. Viewers express a huge sympathy for Sara, supporting her with cheers such as, 'Come on, Sara. Stand up for yourself!' Echoing the claims of producers and critics, the viewers clearly sympathize with Sara's insecurity and 'underdog status', an element that (although it is present in every version of *Ugly Betty*) is perceived as 'typically Flemish'. This sympathy does not necessarily imply explicit identification, but instead a comparison to one's own life: 'As a man you watch Sara and you think "My wife isn't all that bad" or as a woman "Well I'm still a bit prettier than Sara", you see? And that helps your self-esteem' (Tony 57).

In line with comments about recognition of the main character, many respondents agree that the show is 'very Flemish', but they have a hard time explaining what exactly makes it Flemish, which confirms similar findings for other drama (Dhoest, 2009). When asked to elaborate, they comment on the language use, the 'typically Flemish' clothes and character traits, the interior design of Sara's house and the bar she goes to, the setting in the actual city of Antwerp and even the habit of eating a Chocotoff (a particular kind of candy). Although many interviewees state that this story could happen anywhere, they appreciate the little details that make it recognizable. Audiences were also acquainted with the local Flemish actors, such as the popular Kürt Rogiers, who is cast against type as the unpleasant Alexander de Lannoy. Clearly, recognition works on many levels, but all bring fiction 'closer to home'.

Conclusion: Sara as 'National' TV

Based on an analysis of the discourses surrounding *Sara,* it appears that it firmly put a new genre on the map of Flemish television. Both the producers and the viewers stress its novelty and its difference from the more familiar soap opera. This *telenovela* was so warmly embraced because it was 'something different' as well as pleasant, comforting viewing. Despite being an adaptation of an established, foreign genre, an already proven format, and offering a 'universal', melodramatic viewing experience, *Sara* also created a strong sense of cultural proximity by situating the story firmly in contemporary Flanders. In this way, it illustrates one of the central – seeming – contradictions of the globalized media market: despite the increased opportunities to consume media products from across the globe, at least as far as television is concerned, the 'national' is generally preferred. The rapid global expansion of the format trade in the era of digital convergence and privatization confirms the key observation that globalization does not lead to one uniform culture, instead going hand in hand with processes of localization, heterogenization and the formation of hybrid 'glocal' forms of the global (Kraidy 2005). Format adaptations are a good example of such glocalization, flexible frameworks allowing for nationally flavoured programmes. For, indeed, it is on the national level that these 'local' adaptations operate, which leads Moran to comment on the endurance and reappearance of the national in television:

> The TV format industry's maturation as a mainstay of an international system of cultural exchange seems to point not to a strengthening of the global and the local at the expense of the national, but to an enhancement of the national that may be to the detriment of those other two levels (2009: 157).

The very fact that local adaptations are generally preferred over imported programmes confirms the audience need for national viewing, because in a privatized television market it would be more economically profitable to buy and broadcast the finished show if it attracted similar audiences. *Ugly Betty*, with its numerous adaptations, illustrates exactly that: on the one hand, it is a key example of the global trade of a 'universal' format, while on the other hand, it is customizable and can therefore reflect local specificities (Miller 2010).

While broadcasters worldwide continue to buy high-profile, mostly US drama in genres which necessitate high budgets such as action and adventure (e.g. *Prison Break* [Fox, 2005–9], *CSI: Crime Scene Investigation* [CBS, 2000–present], and *Lost* [ABC, 2004–10]), in cheaper genres such as soaps, reality TV and game shows, domestic programmes or adaptations are preferred. As argued by many, these seemingly similar national versions do differ in essential and nationally specific aspects such as media rituals, settings, themes and conventions (Aslama and Pantti 2007) and banal references to the nation (Van den Bulck and Sinardet 2005). References to the national context may be implicit most of the time, but they do make part of the persistent omnipresence and self-evidence of nations in what Michael Billig (1995) calls 'banal nationalism', the continuous, largely unnoticed everyday references to, and confirmations of, the national. When budgets are less of an issue, for instance in the US market, even high-profile genres and programmes are adapted or 're-made', as is the custom with successful European films. Similarly, culturally specific genres like comedy can be remade to accommodate national tastes more closely, as the US adaptation of *The Office* (NBC, 2005–present) illustrates. Alexandra Beeden and Joost de Bruin (2010) argue that its US version was successful only because it more closely fitted the American social, cultural and institutional national context.

If we take a closer look at the elements that are changed to add national specificity, we could say that many small, seemingly superficial changes conspire to give programmes a fundamentally different feel. While many secondary narratives and characters were changed in the Flemish version of *Yo soy Betty, la fea*, the overall storyline was identical, as was the characterization of the main characters. At this level, the 'universal', melodramatic/comic storylines and archetypes are at play, which remained untouched as they ensured a broad appeal. The 'national' flavour seems to be situated mostly in the mundane details of everyday life, which may seem superficial but are fundamental in order to create cultural credibility. The very fact that Flemish actors were used, speaking Dutch with a familiar accent, is crucial to Flemish viewers. Although Flanders shares the same language with the Netherlands, television programmes do not travel well or often. While some crime and 'quality' drama is exchanged between Flanders and the Netherlands, in genres strongly rooted in daily life such as soap operas or *telenovelas* this is unheard of. Indeed, it seems to be particularly on the level of everyday life that cultural specificity is to be situated: ordinary people and accents, clothes and cars, landscapes and interiors, values and common sense. This echoes the statements by many authors on soap operas, which are generally considered to be representations of 'ordinary', everyday life in the nation (Turner 2005; O'Donnell 1999), complementing universal conventions with 'local' elements such as stars, settings and iconography (Moran 1998), accents and locations (Moran 2000), landscapes and lifestyles (Dunleavy 2005), (minority) languages and cultural assumptions (Franco 2001; O'Donnell 2001) and cultural values (Kreutzner and Seiter 1991).

In this view, the domestic *telenovela* is more closely related to the domestic soap than the discursive analysis above indicates. It may be perceived as 'new' and 'different', but it is equally strongly rooted in the everyday life of the nation. Cultural familiarity is a key ingredient to the success of this adaptation, as it is for the continued popularity of domestic soap operas that are never threatened by imported programmes. In this sense, Straubhaar's (2007) observations on the continued importance of cultural proximity in television viewing are crucial to understanding the success of *Sara:* viewers still tend to prefer cultural products that are close in cultural content and style to their own culture. More generally, the case of *Sara* confirms the importance of taken-for-granted, unreflexive, 'everyday' popular culture and television to the constitution of national identities and communities (Edensor 2002). As noted by Frances Bonner (2003), 'ordinary television' – often unnoticed, lightweight entertainment programmes such as game shows, talk shows and food programmes – are generally 'local' and show everyday life in the nation. Despite its partly escapist and humoristic tone, *Sara* is also to be situated within this category of 'ordinary' representations of Flanders, building on a global format but domesticating it through 'everyday' nationalism.

Works Cited

Ang, Ien, *Het geval Dallas: Populaire cultuur, plezier en ideologie* [The Dallas Case: Popular Culture, Pleasure and Ideology] (Amsterdam: SUA, 1982).

Altman, Rick, *Film/Genre* (London: BFI Publishing, 1999).

Aslama, Minna, and Pantti, Mervi, 'Flagging Finnishness: Reproducing National Identity in Reality Television', *Television & New Media*, vol. 8, no. 1 (2007), pp. 49–67.

Beeden, Alexandra, and de Bruin, Joost, '*The Office*: Articulations of National Identity in Television Format Adaptation', *Television & New Media*, vol. 11, no. 3 (2010), pp. 3–19.

Billig, Michael, *Banal Nationalism* (London: Sage, 1995).

Bonner, Frances, *Ordinary television* (London: Sage, 2003).

Creuwels, Jan, VMMA producer, Personal interview with Manon Mertens, Vilvoorde (1 March 2009).

Dewit, Reinhilde, Creative Director Fremantle, Personal interview with Manon Mertens, Opwijk (29 March 2009).

Dhoest, Alexander, 'The National Everyday in Contemporary European Television Fiction: The Flemish Case', *Critical Studies in Television*, vol. 2, no. 2 (2007), pp. 60–76.

——, 'Do We Really Use Soaps to Construct Our Identities? Everyday Nationalism in TV Fiction: the Audience's View', in Enric Castelló, Alexander Dhoest and Hugh O'Donnell (eds), *The Nation on Screen. Discourses of the National on Global Television* (Cambridge: Cambridge Scholars Publishing, 2009), pp. 79–96.

Dunleavy, Trisha, '*Coronation Street, Neighbours, Shortland Street*: Localness and Universality in the Primetime Soap', *Television & New Media*, vol. 6, no. 4 (2005), pp. 370–82.

Edensor, Tim, *National Identity, Popular Culture and Everyday Life* (Oxford: Berg, 2002).

Franco, Judith, 'Cultural Identity in the Community Soap: A Comparative Analysis of *Thuis* (*At Home*) and *Eastenders*', *European Journal of Cultural Studies*, vol. 4, no. 4 (2001), pp. 449–72.

Kraidy, Marwan, *Hybridity, or the Cultural Logic of Globalization* (Philadelphia: Temple University Press, 2005).

Kreutzner, Gabriele, and Seiter, Ellen, 'Not All "Soaps" Are Created Equal: Towards a Crosscultural Criticism of Television Serials', *Screen*, vol. 32, no. 2 (1991), pp. 154–72.

Neale, Steve, *Genre and Hollywood* (London: Routledge, 2000).

Miller, Jade L., '*Ugly Betty* Goes Global: Global Networks of Localized Content in the *telenovela* Industry', *Global Media and Communication*, vol. 6, no. 2 (2010), pp. 198–217.

Moran, Albert, *Copycat TV. Globalization, Program Formats and Cultural Identity* (Luton: University of Luton Press, 1998).

——, 'Popular Drama: Travelling Templates and National Fictions', in Jan Wieten, Graham Murdock and Peter Dahlgren (eds), *Television across Europe: Comparative Introduction.* London: Sage, 2000), pp. 84–93.

——, 'Reasserting the National? Programme Formats, International Television and Domestic Culture', in Graeme Turner and Jinna Tay (eds), *Television Studies After TV: Understanding Television in the Post-Broadcast Era* (London: Routledge, 2009), pp. 149–58.

Mittell, Jason, 'A Cultural Approach to Television Genre Theory', *Cinema Journal*, vol. 40, no. 3 (2001), pp. 3–24.

——, *Genre and Television: From Cop Show to Cartoons in American Culture* (New York: Routledge, 2004).

O'Donnell, Hugh, *Good Times, Bad Times: Soap Operas and Society in Western Europe* (London and New York: Leicester University Press, 1999).

——, 'Peripheral Fissions? Soap Operas and Identity in Scotland, Ireland and the Basque Country', *EnterText*, vol. 2, no. 1 (2001), pp. 173–97.

Ryall, Tom, 'Teaching through Genre', *Screen Education*, vol 17 (1975), pp. 27–33.

Straubhaar, Joseph D., *World Television: From Global to Local* (Thousand Oaks, CA: Sage, 2007).

Turner, Graeme, 'Cultural Identity, Soap Narrative, and Reality TV', *Television & New Media*, vol. 6, no. 4 (2005), pp. 415–22.

Van den Bulck, Hilde, and Sinardet, Dave, 'The Nation: Not Yet the Weakest Link? The Articulation of National Identity in a Globalized Popular Television Format', in Lennard Højberg and Henrik Søndergaard (eds), *European Film and Media Culture* (Copenhagen: Museum Tusculanum Press, 2005), pp. 137–58.

Van Laere, Hugo, screenwriter *Sara*, Personal interview with Manon Mertens (Gent, 6 April 2009).

Endnote

1   The interviews were all effectuated and transcribed by Manon Mertens in February and March 2009. All quotes are literal translations by the authors. For the sake of confidentiality, we refer to the interviewees using an 'alias' as well as their age.

Recreating Betty's
World in Spain

Stefania Carini

FremantleMedia[1] holds the European franchise to *Yo soy Betty, la fea* (*I Am Betty, the Ugly One* [RCN, 1999–2001]) the Colombian *telenovela* created by Fernando Gaitán, and entrusts the local adaptation to affiliated studios operating individually at a national level. Grundy UFA takes responsibility for the German adaptation, *Verliebt in Berlin* (*In Love in/with Berlin* [SAT.1, 2005–7]), while Grundy Italia co-operates with Grundy Producciones to develop the Spanish version, *Yo soy Bea* (*I am Bea* [Telecinco, 2006–9]).

Yo soy Betty, la fea was first broadcast on the Spanish terrestrial TV channel, Antena 3, in 2000–1; but some years later, a second commercial channel, Telecinco, decided to adapt the Colombian *telenovela*. Co-operation with Grundy Italia followed, due in part to an agreement between Paulo Vasile, chief executive officer at Telecinco, and his counterpart at Grundy Italia, Roberto Sessa. *Yo soy Bea* first aired on 10 July 2006 and became Spain's top-rated daytime programme, regularly attracting over 4 million viewers (35 per cent audience share).

The Spanish adaptation proves an interesting case study, as it allows us to trace a flow of content, creative practice and production procedures between several different countries. The Colombian *telenovela* was adapted in Spain thanks primarily to an Italian-based studio and the flow of know-how from one European country to another; and in both cases, the studios, in turn, adopted a model for producing soap opera originating from Australia and shaped by British social-realist traditions.

Drawing on an extensive interview I conducted with Roberto Sessa,[2] this chapter focuses on Grundy Italia, the Italian-based studio that produced *Yo soy Bea*, and how its production knowledge, predicated on Australian-based know-how, shaped the Spanish adaptation, before considering why the adaptation, despite being produced in Italy, did not find success in that country. According to Sessa, a good adaptation is the result of 'a good, winning original idea – that is, from a *concept* – and then from the re-construction of a world that viewers can perceive as close as possible [to their own]'. In an attempt to develop what Sessa says, the chapter asks: what were the challenges – economic, creative, cultural – involved in adapting the Colombian format for the Spanish market?

Betty Is a Universal Story[3]

Yo soy Betty, la fea became an instant hit when it debuted in Colombia in 1999. Over the next few years, the *telenovela* was successfully exported to several foreign territories. In addition, *Yo soy Betty, la fea* took on the shape of a global format with numerous local adaptations. Of why Gaitán's story of the ugly duckling travelled so well, Sessa says:

> The strength of *Betty* lies in its core idea: while the premise may be banal – in its allusions to the 'Ugly Duckling' and 'Cinderella' – it allows for easy access, since the public can enter the tale straightaway. Moreover, when the tale is delivered, through well-written characters plunged into a world able to stimulate the viewers' curiosity, the story becomes universal. This accounts for the success of *Betty* in both its dubbed and adapted versions (2009).

The Betty story is as universal as it is recognizable. It draws on a well-established formula, while at the same time repackaging it into a range of different TV forms – a primetime drama, soap opera or *telenovela*. Given its archetypal nature, *Yo soy Betty, la fea* contained elements of its future adaptation from the beginning. The well-known narrative thus offers the audience immediate accessibility, made easier by pre-existing knowledge of the overall plot.

What turns the story into an international format is that *Yo soy Betty, la fea* never hid its core themes or narrative structure. Gaitán's *telenovela* is a fable about physical (Ugly Duckling) and social (Cinderella) transformation. Betty *is* transformation *par excellence*: the makeover is at the narrative centre both literally and figuratively. The 'content scheme' of the work is also easy to identify, vividly displayed as it is across the heroine's body.

Moreover, *Yo soy Betty, la fea*'s narrative progression shares development patterns similar to those contained in fables as well as the 'hero's journey' most famously analysed by Joseph Campbell (1949), and Hollywood story analyst Chris Vogler (1992). The hero's journey develops through 12 stages: the hero leaves the ordinary world to enter an extraordinary (often unknown) one; they must next face a long journey which involves inner transformation; and only when that transformation is complete can the hero reach their goal. The original *telenovela* exploits such a sequential pattern expanded across a huge number of episodes.

Yo soy Betty, la fea is the story of a heroine's transformative journey. It conceals neither its theme nor the path that the heroine must take. It displays transparent content and structure, making the story accessible. From a production viewpoint, such formal features expedite the transformation into a format, with the ability to replicate it in different regions around the world. At the same time, Betty's journey is also possible thanks to a new global dimension in the television market, which has allowed Fremantle Media to acquire the format and disseminate it in different territories via local affiliates, triggering a fertile exchange of creative and productive practices.

Betty in Spain: Grundy Style

Successfully broadcast on Antena 3 in 2001–2, *Yo Soy Betty, la fea* made a Spanish version more tempting because, according to Sessa: 'brand reputation helps the product deployment, since it triggers visibility'. For this reason, in 2006, the privately run commercial network Telecinco and Grundy Italia put forward the idea of a Spanish version. 'The adaptation,' recalls Sessa, '[stemmed] from the intuition of Paolo Vasile's, CEO at Telecinco. During a meeting about other projects, I told him we had already secured the rights to adapt *Yo soy Betty, la fea*. Telecinco was looking for a Spanish-produced daily series, something with a comedy-theme. We stepped in at the right time.'

Grundy Italia found fertile ground in Spain. *Yo soy Betty, la fea* was already well known as a successful brand, both in terms of its original version as well as its German adaptation by Grundy UFA. Since Telecinco were searching for a daily daytime series, an adaptation of *Yo soy Betty, la fea* looked like a feasible solution, based on past success. Vasile wanted Sessa and his team to lead the project for several reasons: first, they had the franchise and, second, they possessed the knowledge of how to produce a daily daytime series. Grundy Italia welcomed Grundy Producciones under their aegis, which, in turn, allowed for the co-operation to happen. As Sessa recalls: 'At first, we created a mixed formula with Italian editors, a creative producer and production manager supporting the Spanish team. The Italian activity was progressively reduced, as a Spanish staff was assembled.' This gradual shift in personnel reveals how 'localization' is also about the distribution of creative know-how. It entailed a double migration: first, from the original *telenovela* to the Italian creative group, and then to the Spanish team. Circulation of formats involves a movement in terms of transnational collaboration and production routines. The joint work of Italy and Spain, for example, enabled the consolidation of Grundy's Spanish branch, due in part to the success of another Grundy-produced show, *Sin tetas no hay paraíso* (*Without Breasts There Is No Paradise* [Televisa, 2008]), a Mexican adaptation of the popular Colombian telenovela of the same name (Canal Caracol, 2006). In October 2008, Telecinco signed a two-year agreement with Grundy Producciones to produce new daytime and primetime shows. What the case of Grundy Italia-Grundy Producciones also highlights is another, much older, creative migration related to the flow of TV programmes between Europe and Australia, dating as far back as the 1970s.

Grundy has led the market in Australian soap operas since the 1980s, owing to its success with *Neighbours* (7 Network, 1985–6, Network Ten, 1986–present). The company managed to export its style across Europe, including Italy, rooted in the British realist tradition (particularly *Coronation Street* [ITV, 1960–present]), and imported to Australia in 1967.

As Trisha Dunleavy argues, Australian audiences favoured the 'ordinary' British style over the excessive US one when it came to producing local Australian soaps (2005: 6). These continuing serials developed a recognizable style, combining the day-to-day realism of British soaps with the Australian sun, as well as a distinct format: five days a week in primetime. In the mid-1990s, Grundy moved into the Italian market. The company was initially formed through the acquisition of Pearson TV with the co-operation of Aran – a society co-founded by Sessa at the end of the 1980s. In 1998, the Pearson group acquired Mastrofilm, another company belonging to Sessa, and it evolved into Grundy Italia with Sessa at the helm. Its main goal was to produce *Un posto al sole* (*A Place in the Sun* [RAI, 1996–present]), Italy's first continuing serial. Grundy Italia, in fact, learnt how to produce this kind of television from adapting the *Neighbours* format (Buonanno 2009), before it emerged as one of the most important production companies in Italy, which in turn allowed for the co-operation with Grundy Producciones – and the Spanish version of *Yo soy Betty, la fea*.

In our interview Sessa stated that Grundy Italia and Grundy UFA had no contact whatsoever with each other concerning the different adaptations of the Colombian original. However, both companies appeared to operate with the same goal in mind, to tacitly follow the 'Grundy Style': Betty's excesses are soothed out, and a sense of ordinariness is foregrounded. This rejection of excess and focus on realism is confirmed by Michael Esser, scriptwriter for the German adaptation, *Verliebt in Berlin*: 'The main adaptive changes involved the softening of the original cheerfulness and the introduction of a more realistic dash, so that the German viewers could intimately relate to the characters' (quoted in Lippert 2008: 29).

Even the narrative tone of *Yo soy Bea* was adapted in accordance to the 'Grundy style' with its realism and portrayal of ordinary, everyday life: the social description mimics comedy, but avoids the excessive farce of the original. Realism is a common narrative solution in the European daily soap operas adopting the Grundy style, but as Sessa explains, 'In our adaptation, we altered the overall tone, trading farce for realism. Also, the visual style is realistic.' *Yo soy Bea* emerges as a comedy, not a farce. The shift implies a change in linguistic register towards a 'realistic', more ordinary and less excessive mode. It is this 'realistic' tone that distinguishes the Spanish *Bea* from the Colombian and American *Betties*, and is key to the way in which the plot engaged the Spanish viewers.

Transmission replicated the Australian model, with *Yo soy Bea* broadcast five days a week, Monday to Friday, the only difference being the time of broadcast. Telecinco scheduled it in the afternoon: although the actual time varied from season to season, *Yo soy Bea* eventually found a regular time slot at 7 pm (with primetime in Spain starting at 8 pm).

All these changes turned *Betty* into *Bea* – that is, into a Grundy-style soap opera. Such a transformation was the first step towards the local adaptation of Gaitán's Colombian *telenovela*. A format adaptation linked to a country's own culture, a combination of formal and production factors related to the evolution of a TV format involving global synthesis and local needs. Local-ness appeals to a country's specific audiovisual tradition, and the adaptation of an international format fosters the creation of what may be defined as a 'televisual sense of place'. In the Spanish adaptation by Grundy Italia, the recreation of a 'televisual sense of place' was supplied by the 'Grundy style', fusing British and Australian traditions now popular in several European countries.

Betty Becomes *Bea*

Adapting to the local context, *Yo soy Betty, la fea* went through further revisions. Local-ness is produced in and through the *mise en scène*, as well as stylistic and narrative choices of the show, with its particular awareness of regional peculiarities and its specific Spanish town setting: Madrid and its local vicinity. Of which, Sessa says, 'We took the characters and plunged them into their reference world – the outskirts of Madrid. We brought the characters closer to the viewers' daily world.' Local-ness in this context refers to placing a universal story into a specific spatial location. Archetypal characters are given a local stage – one that is known and familiar to viewers.

It is not only a matter of changing the location for the heroine's adventures, but adapting to Spanish television's specific needs and stylistic preferences. Local-ness thus relates to network practices and specific scheduling requirements. The universal story had to find an exact collocation inside Telecinco and its contents had to fit the local mould. *Yo soy Betty, la fea* was re-thought according to three factors: the time slots of the Spanish network, the number of requested episodes and new demands prompted by its wide success. Sessa explains as follows:

> We adapted the format to the scheduling needs: the original episodes ran for 25 minutes, whereas Telecinco wanted them to be 35 minutes long. Therefore we created new features and storylines, including a mystery element absent in the original. The original series comprised of 300 episodes, whereas our adaptation had to clock in at around 400. In the end, we stopped short of episode 500.

Firstly, there were the specific time requirements: more minutes, more episodes. *Betty*'s time expands to fit *Bea*'s, with a much more inflated storyline. The core plot has to be stretched over more episodes, without diluting the story. Conversely, new plotlines were added, making the original storyline far more complex, including mixing in a new genre.

Around episode 500, however, 'the story was really exhausted: the two main characters were to marry, and that would be it'. Continuing, Sessa says:

> Although an ending was scheduled, Vasile asked us to keep going. We definitely turned the product into a never-ending story: that is, into a real soap opera. The story typology was similar, but all characters and situations were changed, and we devised a new location. The passage from *telenovela* to soap opera is an innovative, seldom performed, operation.

Once the original storyline played out, *Bea*'s world had to experience a dramatic twist in its temporal dimension. Both soap opera and *telenovela* are continuous serial forms involving a huge number of episodes and an almost endless narrative development (Buonanno 2008). The closed continuous serial, with a distinct ending of the story, is a feature of the *telenovela*. By contrast, a soap opera displays an open continuous form with no clear conclusion of the plot available or foreseeable.

Yo soy Bea represents a distinct and discernable attempt to shift its narrative form from *telenovela* to soap opera through a double transition, from closed to open. Similar to the original *telenovela Yo soy Bea* offered a conclusion to its main plot: Bea's transformation and her finding love. However, the writers decided not to end the narrative world, but rather unravel the *telenovela* and create numerous new soap opera possibilities. Be Berlanga Echegaray (Patricia Montero) facilitates Bea's makeover at the end of the first season and becomes the new protagonist of the next. The twist in this tale is that, unlike Bea, she is already a beauty, if a rather spoilt one. Be's challenge over the course of season two is to prove to everyone, above all her mother, that she is not just a pretty face and that she should be taken seriously. From the original world created in *Yo Soy Bea*, the *diegesis* survived: the narrative space was contiguous with the previous one, while new characters were introduced.

It is, of course, a risky move; and it reminds us of other attempts to extend the *Betty* narrative world through spin-offs, such as in Colombia *EcoModa* (RCN, 2001–2) and in Germany *Verliebt in Berlin II* (S.A.T.1, 2006–7). The Spanish route, however, proved more complex, as it entailed a change in the original format to further the narrative world indefinitely. The commercial results of the new format were disappointing. Because of low ratings (average 17.2 per cent share),[4] Telecinco decided to cancel the show on 16 August 2009, after 773 episodes. Perhaps *Yo soy Bea* suffered from the substitution of the heroine, who did not have an equally universal appeal. Bea's transformation in the original version, for example, equates physical change with feminine success, a story that has long been sold to women across the world as a fairytale of self-fulfilment and personal happiness. Bea's final goal, therefore, is more concrete, more easily identified with, as it embodies some very common aspirations. The new heroine of the Spanish version, Be, on the other hand, has a less tangible desire and, not being tied to a physical transformation, her journey is not bound up with the makeover myths for our times: 'Bea had to find her external beauty, the process is reversed for Be.'[5] Be is already a beauty with many advantages in life and her transformation is internal, a journey towards independence and less believable for the audience, which may explain why the identification process proved more difficult.

Nevertheless, local-ness does require a real body. Of this Sessa insisted on a particular choice of lead actress: she had to be 'believable' in her role: 'Our characters are realistic. Our Betty is slim, almost skinny, and quite believable; in the German adaptation, for example, she was played by a gorgeous girl spoilt by makeup.' Actress Ruth Núñez, who played *Bea* in the Spanish version, is not a striking beauty, but rather has a common Mediterranean look. Núñez does not display the usual physical exuberance of Spanish women: her body is slim and lean. She makes visible the common Spanish girl, made uglier by badly applied makeup and a terrible dress sense. Her final transformation is not as jaw-dropping as her German counterpart, but is far more realistic. In this respect, Núñez embodies a sense of transformation that is more natural in keeping with the Grundy style.

Betty (not) in Italy

Betty is a modern fairytale: a remake of the Ugly Duckling, an adaptation of Cinderella. It roams the world as ancient fables have always done while embedding themselves in specific national contexts in accordance with a complex set of economic, institutional, cultural and aesthetic factors unique to that territory and its televisual and broadcasting traditions.

However, the globalization of television markets does not imply an unproblematic flow of texts from one country to another. Recounting the events leading to the Spanish adaption of *Yo soy Betty, la fea*, Sessa stresses the importance of the 'right time'. What he means is that the favourable convergence of productive and market logics cannot be underestimated. The circulation of formats depends on local and international conjunctures, often deeply intertwined.

This is exactly what has happened in Italy, where no local version was ever produced despite Grundy Italia's involvement with the Spanish adaptation. 'Even if the Spanish adaptation had been a stratospheric success in Spain – a country similar to Italy – and was produced by a "cousin" network, nothing similar could be done [in Italy],' concludes Sessa.

What he is alluding to is a series of trade relationships, which seek to block the flow of TV content. Telecinco is a private network with 50.1 per cent controlled by Mediaset, the media group (hence the 'cousin' status) owned by Silvio Berlusconi, and currently operating three on-air Italian networks. However, at the time of the interview, Mediaset decided against an Italian adaptation of *Yo soy Betty, la fea* because of a concurrent international agreement it had signed with Endemol.[6] Because of this exclusive deal, Grundy Italia could not develop daytime soap for Mediaset.[7] Something similar happened in 2006, when Antena 3 broadcast the Mexican version, *La fea más bella* (*The Most Beautiful Ugly Girl* [Televisa, 2006–7]), together with *Yo soy, Bea*, without much success. Some time later, Cuarto acquired the rights for the US version, but Telecinco blocked its broadcast until 2008, since it owned the rights for the Colombian original and thus asserted complete monopoly over its transmission (Lippert 2008).

It was summer 2007 and Alessandro Salem, content director of RTI (Mediaset's editorial branch), offered Sessa the chance to develop a primetime-oriented version of *Yo soy Betty, la fea* (which anticipated the ABC version). However, he declined, believing that the potential for the format was more suited to the daytime schedule. Moreover, Sessa had already been in talks with state-owned television RAI (for which Grundy Italia had already developed *Un posto al sole* and RaiFiction's director, Agostino Saccà.[8] Even though project manager Paolo Terracciano had worked for six months on the Italian version of *Yo soy Betty, la fea*, even reaching the audition stage, the project was eventually cancelled.

Although Spain had been the main exporter of formats to Italy (for example, *I Cesaroni* [*The Cesaronis* (Mediaset, 2006–present)] inspired *Los Serranos* [*The Serranos* (Telecinco, 2003–8)], and *Médico de familia* [*A Doctor in the Family* (Telecinco, 1995–9)] prompted *Un medico in famiglia* [Rai Uno, 1998–present]), the pairing of the two nations, further favoured by the presence of Grundy Italia, failed.

In 2011, RCN sold the *Yo soy Betty, la fea* rights to Televisa. The company, in turn, granted the Italian rights to EuroProduzione, a production company founded in 2000 and the Italian branch of the Spanish Grupo Europroducciones. Stefano Torrisi, vice-president and chief executive officer of EuroTV, resurrected the idea of an Italian Betty when he brought the project for a primetime adaptation to Mediaset. The media group were doubtful about its success and rejected the project. Torrisi has not given up hope, but as of now the future of the Italian *Betty* remains uncertain.

So in Italy, the seemingly unstoppable *Yo soy Betty la fea* franchise has come to a halt. Italian viewers had a chance to watch Gaitán's original (Happy Channel and Lady Channel from Sky; as well as regional channels such as Teleroma 56, Telenorba, TV Centro Marche, Videocalabria, Antenna Sicilia), the US version (on Italia 1, a channel owned by Mediaset, and on FoxLife, channel of pay-TV platform Sky), and even the Chinese one (Bonsai.tv, a web TV owned by Telecom Italia). Unfortunately, Italians were deprived of the chance to taste a local adaptation. The heroine's global journey makes a temporary stop in Italy. It has not affected the story, as it did manage to conquer Italian screens, but it has temporarily halted the international franchise. As the Italian case demonstrates, the circulation of TV formats can be compromised by international trade agreements, or it can meet with failure when it does not find the 'right time' at a local level because of adverse economical, productive or institutional circumstances.

Works Cited

Buonanno, Milly, *Le formule del racconto televisivo* (Milan: Rcs, 2002).

———, 'From Literary to Format Adaptation: Multiple Interactions Between the Foreign and Domestic in Italian TV Drama', *Critical Studies in Television*, vol. 4, no. 1 (Spring 2009), pp. 65–83.

Campbell, Joseph, *The Hero with a Thousand Faces* (Princeton: Princeton University Press, 1949).

Dunleavy, Trisha, '*Coronation Street, Neighbours, Shortland Street*: Localness and Universality in the Primetime Soap', *Television & New Media*, vol. 6, no. 4 (November 2005), pp. 370–82.

Grasso, Aldo, and Scaglioni, Massimo, *Che cos'è la televisione* (Milan: Garzanti, 2003).

Lippert, Bianca, 'The "Bettyer" Way to Success', *Critical Studies in Television*, vol. 3, no. 2 (Autumn 2008), pp. 19–39.

Nelson, Robin, 'TV Fiction Exchange: Local/Regional/National/Global', *Critical Studies in Television*, vol. 2, no. 2 (Autumn 2007), pp. 4–17.

Taggi, Paolo, *Morfologia dei format televisivi* (Rome: Rai Eri, 2007).

Vogler, Chris, *The Writer's Journey: Mythic Structure for Writers* (Studio City, CA: Michael Wiese Productions, 1992).

Endnotes

1   FremantleMedia is a large global media conglomerate owned by the RTL Group, one of Europe's largest television and radio broadcast companies, with interests in 42 television and 32 radio stations scattered in 10 European countries. RTL is the 90 per cent property of Bertelsmann AG. Created in 2001, FremantleMedia comprises a number of companies: some of these have been operating for many

years under Pearson Television, which, in 1995, acquired the Australian society Grundy together with its local branches. Of course, all these studios became part of the Fremantle portfolio in 2001 when Pearson began to operate under the FremantleMedia umbrella. In May 2010, Grundy Italia changed its name to Fremantle and combined with the Italian studio Wilder, whose head, Lorenzo Mieli, is now chief executive.

2   The author recorded the interview with Roberto Sessa on 16 July 2009. All unspecified direct quotations appearing in this chapter originate from this interview. Roberto Sessa left Grundy Italia in December 2009. He was the first promoter of the co-operation between Spain and Italy that ultimately brought about the Spanish version of *Betty*.

3   In the 1990s, globalization in the television sector called for TV shows that used a well-defined format: it was a sort of 'sacred grail' for both producers and broadcasters.

4   See 'Se acerca el final', online at: www.formulatv.com.

5   See http://www.telecinco.es/yosoybea/biography/biography4240.shtml.

6   In 1999, Endemol and Mediaset founded Mediavivere, a production company born to produce *Vivere* (1999–2008), Mediaset's first soap opera. Mediavivere also produced the other successful soap opera of Canale 5, *CentoVetrine* (2001–present).

7   See 'Roberto Sessa della Grundy a TvBlog: Un errore non aver realizzato Yo soy Bea in Italia', online at: www.Tvblog.it.

8   Idem.

Towards a Cultural Economy of *Chou Nu (Nv) Wu Di*: The *Yo soy Betty, la fea* Franchise in the People's Republic of China*

Xiaolu Ma and Albert Moran

Introduction

The first decade of the twenty-first century has seen the maturation of a worldwide television system, which, while transnational, also possesses a central dynamic that localizes and/or nationalizes the end product. The People's Republic of China (PRC) is a key player in this new system, with a domestic market comprising the world's largest audience. Technology transfer is a crucial mechanism in this process of growth whereby the People's Republic seeks to value-add crucial knowledge, practice and know-how to its existing resources, thus giving it a prime position so far as dominant international advantage is concerned. In this respect, technology comes in various forms, including those found in machinery and physical goods, as well as ideas and know-how; TV programme formats are a good example of these second-order technologies. They contain not only specific knowledges about particular television programmes, but also offer more general lessons and insights into the framework and structures

---

* Because of the closed nature of the Chinese broadcasting system we were unable to source various production details and dates in this chapter.

from which they are derived. As this edited collection demonstrates, the Colombian *telenovela*, *Yo soy Betty, la fea* (*I Am Betty, the Ugly One* [RCN 1999–2001]) better known in the West as *Ugly Betty* (ABC, 2006–10), has repeated a pattern of cultural and commercial transfer in many different broadcast territories. It has also reproduced a pattern of novelty by serving to introduce the production, broadcasting and textual regimes of the genre of the Latin American *telenovela* to a host of territories across the globe that were hitherto ignorant of, and unskilled in, this content genre.

Chinese television was a relatively late starter among national television systems, and this lag persisted until recently. It mostly missed the cycle of licensed mega-format import and remake that occurred elsewhere in the early 2000s (Moran 2009). Times change, however. *Chou Nu (Nv) Wu Di* (*The Ugly Girl Is Matchless* [Hunan TV, 2008]) constitutes a significant moment of rapprochement between an already globalizing (Western) television system and a globally emergent Chinese structure of broadcasting. Our chapter addresses the *Yo soy Betty, la fea* format in the PRC and its adaptation into *Chou Nu (Nv) Wu Di*, a remake of Televisa's *La fea más bella* (*The Most Beautiful Ugly Girl* [Televisa, 2006–7]), based on, and licensed from, the Colombian original. This television programme format franchising is part of a process wherein Chinese television becomes a highly significant player in the world television system, itself part of an even larger story in which the PRC attains the dominant cultural and commercial position in an evolving world system.

Our argument is that the adaptation and remaking of a television programme format in China is most usefully approached from a cultural economy perspective. This emphasizes the fact that the programme concept, with its dramatic premises, multiple storylines, regimes of character, and so on, is only a small part – the tip of the iceberg – as far as commodity exchange is concerned. Institutionally, Chinese television synchronized a series of cultural and commercial arrangements related to the programme format transfer in order to achieve a fit with the global television system, even while that system, in the form of *Yo soy Betty, la fea*, settles into a rapprochement with television in the PRC. Cultural imperialism is not in play here; rather, a series of necessary recalibrations of both a business and social nature have taken place, whereby the format could be successfully 'sinofied'. Deciding to license a programme format of the Latin American *telenovela* was a deliberate commercial decision. This fact is underlined in our analysis, which concentrates on the chain of industrial and cultural gate-keeping decision-making involved in the implementation of the series. Meanwhile, in the second part of our argument, we suggest that the textual changes in the remake were designed to customize the programme for its Chinese audience.

The Mexican Connection

Licensing of TV formats already successful in other overseas territories is an obvious way for a new broadcaster to gain rapid ground in a competitive television marketplace. In 2007, the new production company Xiang Chao Guo Ji decided to attend the Shanghai TV Festival with a view to acquiring franchise properties for just this kind of boost. In the past, Chinese broadcasting and production companies have simply copied television programmes from other places without bothering to acquire licensing rights over these shows. However, in joining the World Trade Organization, China signalled its desire to play by the rules of intellectual property conventions. Xiang Chao Guo Ji was itself ready to join the international worldwide television industry.

The Shanghai Television Festival began in 1986 as a practical means of continuing to open up Chinese television to the world. HNSTV has developed a series of well-known programmes, including *Joyful Base Camp*, *Rose Engagement*, *Evening News*, *New Youth*, *Music Forever* and *Today Talk*. Indeed, the years since 2003 have witnessed a golden period in its programming fortunes and popularity as a network. Nor has it been a stranger to the practice of format licensing of programmes from elsewhere. Its Chinese adaptation of *Pop Idol* in the form of *Super Girl, Super Boy* has been hugely successful, further helping to build the youth/entertainment branding of the network (HunanTV.com, 2009).

As a satellite broadcaster, the company needed a television programme supplier to guarantee sufficient content for its delivery service. Accordingly, in 2007 HNSTV took advantage of its personnel and corporate wealth to establish an independent media production company, Xiang Chao Guo Ji, in co-operation with Beijing Tong Dao Media Production. Hunan TV is the controlling shareholder in this venture, while Xiang Chao Guo Ji's task is to supply programming to the network.

In 2007, executives of the new Chinese production company met sales representatives from Mexican multimedia conglomerate Televisa, the largest media company in the Spanish-speaking world, with an extensive global distribution operation. The hottest-format property being hawked by the latter at that time was *Yo soy Betty, la fea*, which Televisa had acquired from the original devisor and owner, the Colombian private television network, RCN. RCN's core business was and is television broadcasting, so after its 1999 success with the *telenovela*, it sold on the international format licence to the Televisa conglomerate. As TV format researchers have pointed out elsewhere (Moran 1998: 13–26; Moran and Malbon 2006: 19–27), a format licensing fee may not be financially lucrative in itself, but it gains in value from a package of complementary production and marketing services made available by the licensor to the licensee. In other words, at the Shanghai TV Festival, Televisa was seeking a Chinese partner to help franchise the Mexican/Colombian version of the format in that market.

Originally there was some resistance to the idea of a Chinese spin-off of *Yo soy Betty, la fea* among Chinese television production executives. When Hao Xiaojiang, the executive producer and vice-president of the Xiang Chao Guo Ji production company, first spoke with Televisa, he had a sense that a business and cultural innovation in the form of a television format remake might not be suitable for a Chinese audience.[1] However, the franchise of *Yo soy Betty, la fea* had achieved impressive international commercial returns over the previous decade, so Hao Xiaojiang overcame his early reluctance to license a format franchise. An oral agreement was struck and a formal contract signed in Beijing between Xiang Chao Guo Ji and Televisa.[2]

Television format remaking involves knowledge transfer from one place to another. Albert Moran (2009a: 9–15) suggests that, depending on prior imbalances of production knowledge, technology access, generic background and other bodies of know-how that may or may not be common to licensor and licensee, far more than textual programme knowledge, must be made available in a format exchange. This was certainly the case with the *Yo soy Betty, la fea* franchise transfer to China. Xiang Chao Guo Ji sent staff to Central America in order to observe and study the routines of production in operation at Televisa's studios in Mexico City. The Chinese learned not only about the organization and patterns at work in the making of a television series, but much else as well. This included financial decisions to do with such matters as product placement, artist packaging services, programme promotion and derivative product arrangements. This amounted to assimilating a new kind of television, with Xiang Chao Guo Ji emulating the production and marketing model it had learned from the Mexicans.

Production, Marketing and Publicity

After the intensive crash course at Televisa, it was time for Xiang Chao Guo Ji to go to work. Events moved quickly. Xiang Chao Guo Ji is located in Beijing, and it was decided to produce at least the first season of *Chou Nu (Nv) Wu Di* there. In July 2007, a hotel near the city's northern fourth ring became the production base. The company rented five levels of the hotel as a site for script development and as a venue for auditioning actors. 'Discovering' possible celebrities among these relative unknowns avoided the costs associated with the use of already famous screen stars, opened up the possibility of the company becoming their agent, and helped create valuable publicity for *Chou Nu (Nv) Wu Di*.

Earlier script packages associated with productions elsewhere, including Mexico, were made available as part of the format franchising deal between Televisa and Xiang Chao Guo Ji. However, scripts for individual episodes, as well as overall storylines, had to undergo extensive change to take account of the new national setting for the *Yo soy Betty la fea* story. One of these cultural changes involved replacing the gay male assistant working at the fashion magazine in the US *Ugly Betty* version of the *telenovela* with a heterosexual male in love with one of the other female characters. This change occurred in the first season. The new character was Chen Jiaming (Wang Kai), an art director, who was soft and feminine, thereby balancing his tomboy girlfriend Liang Wushuang (Hou Wen). The change seems to have occurred for dramatic rather than political reasons.

Generally, what interested the production company most was not the black ink used on scripts of the series, but rather the black ink the series might leave on the account books. Product placement was just as important for executives of the Xiang Chao Guo Ji group as the Ugly Duckling story was for the programme's audience. Product placement was a key element of the Mexican format, explaining why the Chinese licensed *La fea más bella* rather than the Colombian original (Sinclair 2009: 31). Suggested here is that branded content drives the narrative and provides a lucrative revenue stream for the producing company. Learning a lesson from the Mexican production of the series, sales executives at Xiang Chao Guo Ji began a search for companies that might take out sponsorships in return for the placement of their products in one or other of the story's many settings. Initially, several domestic enterprises were hesitant to buy in to this kind of service. However, ShareMinds under WPP Group 3, one of the biggest media consultant companies in the world, offered encouraging recommendations to clients and sponsors soon came on board. In the first season, these included such global corporate players as Bausch & Lomb, Patek Philippe & Co (PP) and Group Bimbo. Underlining the general internationalization of the Chinese economy as a whole, these had such national origins as the United States, Switzerland and Mexico, while their goods for product placement included eye health items such as contact lenses and lens care goods, luxury watches and bakery foodstuffs (Lu 2008).

An extensive publicity campaign was conducted, both in digital environments and in the more public domain. Hunan TV engaged in an aggressive effort to heighten public awareness of the upcoming production and broadcast of *Chou Nu (Nv) Wu Di*. The channel featured preview trailers dropped into the regular flow of scheduled programmes, and viewers became used to seeing members of the production team turn up as regular guests on many of the network's talk shows. The channel also launched several interactive situations on its official website to help attract young viewers. Meanwhile, joint-venture multinational Union Liver displayed stage photos and posters of *Chou Nu (Nv) Wu Di* in its big-brand monopoly stores during the show's broadcast seasons. The issue remained: what kind of cultural resonances would the programme have with Chinese audiences? How might viewers assimilate fictional programming into their cultural universe? Let us turn to some considerations of the images and sounds that formed part of *Chou Nu (Nv) Wu Di*.

Fiction Imports: Canned and Format

The franchising of the *La fea más bella* format by producer Xiaodong Chen, director Feng Zhang, and scriptwriters Yang Han and Zhan Shi (Season One) on behalf of HSNTV was a major commercial and cultural gamble. It presupposed that a drama serial first produced on the other side of the world could be licensed and successfully remade for an audience in the PRC. The risk was twofold: first, that a licensed remake would be successful, and second, that the fictional *telenovela* form could be effectively transplanted to China. Television was a political instrument in China from its innovation in 1958 until around 1980. It has only been over the past 30 years that this form of broadcasting has begun to expand and define itself along lines familiar in the West. Not surprisingly, the television service has been ready to involve itself in all forms of technology transfer, given both the very large territory to be covered and the massive size of the audience to be reached. This kind of exchange with the outside world may take material or ideational form, or both. The adaptation and remake of popular television programmes derived from more established centres of television production, including the United States and the United Kingdom, fall under this label. Many television entertainment programme formats have turned up in domestic forms on Chinese television over the past decade. Repeating a history of TV format circulation in the West, many of the Chinese adaptations were pirated and, more recently, others have been remade under licence agreement. Michael Keane, Anthony Y.H. Fung and Moran report on one such instance, *Into Shangrila*, which bears a close resemblance to the reality show, *Survivor* (2007: 141–59).

Other programmes to spawn Chinese lookalikes have turned up in several different generic modes, some unauthorized and others unlicensed. Fiction series have included: *Sex and the City/Hao Xiang Hao Xiang Tan Lian Ai* (*I'm Looking Forward to Being Loved* [Anhui Television, 2004]), *Friends/Huan Le Qing Chun* (*Happy Youth* [Bei Da Hua Yi, 2002]), *Desperate Housewives/Mei Li Zhu Fu* (*Beautiful Housewives* [Tian Di Zong Heng, 2004]), and *24/Wei Qing 24 Xiao Shi* (*Danger 24 Hours* [Hua Yi Brothers, 2004]). Similarly, in the live entertainment mode, there has been *Dancing with the Stars/Wu Lin Da Hui* (*Dancing with Stars* [Shanghai Media Group, 2006–present]), *Strictly Come Dancing/Wu*

Dong Gi Ji (*Dancing Miracle* [Hunan TV, 2007–present]), *American Idol/Chao Ji Nv Sheng* (*Super Girl* [Hunan TV, 2004–present]), *Who Wants to Be a Millionaire?/Kai Xin Ci Dian* (*Happy Dictionary* [China Central TV (CCTV), 2000–present]), and *America's Got Talent/Meng Xiang Zhong Guo* (*China Dream* [CCTV, 2004–present]) (Keane, Fung and Moran 2007: 127–59).

Thus there was already a history of remaking successful programme formats from elsewhere when the opportunity arose to develop a Chinese lookalike of a Latin American *telenovela*. But what of the narrative rhythms and expectations associated with this kind of long-form fictional form? There was no direct precedent in Chinese television for the generic departure in production, transmission or viewing represented by *Chou Nu (Nv) Wu Di*, although, paradoxically, broadcasters and audiences were familiar with the finite long-form fiction involved with the genre of the *telenovela* (Patna 2004: 3456–8). The initial impulse leading to this adoption had its roots in the 1980s, with the reorientation of Chinese television towards private commercial broadcasting. Like their professional counterparts elsewhere, such as Western Europe, the rapid expansion of broadcast hours caused Chinese television executives to import overseas programming to help fill the television schedule (*see* Silj 1988: 1–9; Tunstall 2008: 1–15). The Latin American *telenovela* was attractive not only because of the large volume of potential broadcast slots that it would fill, but also because its origin was not the United States. Early in 1984, Beijing TV imported and played its first *telenovela* in the form of the Brazilian series *Escrava Isaura* (*The Slave Isaura* [Rede Globo, 1976-7]). Dubbed into Mandarin, the 60-minute episodes proved very popular with audiences. Around the same time, another Latin American *telenovela*, *Bianca Vidal* (Televisa, 1982–3) – this time from Mexico – broadcast on Beijing TV with 108 episodes. It also succeeded in gathering significant numbers of enthusiastic viewers.

The largest Chinese broadcaster, CCTV, continues to import *telenovelas* from different television markets as a means of helping to fill its schedule. In recent years, Chinese audiences have become used to a more regional version of the form, largely thanks to the advent of *telenovelas* produced in neighbouring parts of East Asia. In 2007, for example, CCTV imported a 526-episode Taiwanese series, *Yi Nan Wang* (*The Unforgettable Memory* [Formosa TV, 2004–6]). South Korean *telenovelas* are just as popular with broadcasters and audiences, although they are often shorter in running time. Thus *In-eo A-ga-ssi* (*Miss Mermaid*, 2002, consisting of 164 episodes), *Men in the Bathhouse's Boss Family* (87 episodes) and *See It Again* (168 episodes) turn up regularly on different channels in Mainland China.

Despite this quarter-century of importing and broadcasting *telenovelas*, the common view among television experts and scholars in the PRC has been that a locally produced, long-form series would struggle to find an audience. For instance, the vice-president of the China Television Artists' Association, Ming Li, believed that the plan of producing and broadcasting at approximately the same time would be a difficult practice to introduce because the mainland audience had different viewing habits compared with other territories (Lin 2007). This audience, he claimed, expected to watch a complete television story in a limited period of time rather than waiting for further story episodes in later seasons. This same view also seems to pertain in South Korea. Television stations usually broadcast five different series each weekday on the basis of one episode a day. Given this slower pace of broadcast, production companies have sufficient time to produce episodes that respond to audience feedback and ratings.

Taiwan, on the other hand, helped determine the *telenovela* broadcast system for Mainland China. There, the broadcast pattern is to transmit at least two episodes each day; however, production companies still manage to produce at a comparable rate. Usually, about 20 episodes of a new *telenovela* are completed before this routine swings into operation. Producers, then, have the flexibility of a potential daily response to ratings, possibly adjusting future storylines as it is deemed necessary (Lin 2007).[3] This offshore model helped to set the broadcast and production routines of *Chou Nu (Nv) Wu Di*, the first *telenovela* produced in Mainland China and a successful pioneer of new television methods for programme output and circulation.

The Chinese Remake as Text

Chou Nu (Nv) Wu Di has been a sprawling textual affair, running to almost 200 hours of fiction. It depicts the love of an ugly duckling girl for her male boss. Three significant areas of difference can be outlined as a means of indicating a larger pattern of continuity and bounded variation at work in the Chinese version.

Title and Protagonist

Although the original *Yo soy Betty, la fea* prototype was produced for Colombian television in 1999 and subsequently licensed on as a programme format, the Chinese remake was two stages removed from it. After its outstanding string of successes in other markets, both as a finished show and as a format adaptation over the next seven years, Mexico's Televisa bought the original Colombian format and proceeded to adapt its own variation, *La fea más bella*. It began on Mexican television in early 2006 and ended 13 months later in 2007. Thus, when it came to licensing the format to Xiang Chao Guo Ji, Televisa had two prototypes available: the Colombian *Yo soy Betty, la fea* and the Mexican *La fea más bella*. As Moran suggests elsewhere (1998: 13–71), the production, marketing and financial know-how offered in a format package is just as important as content elements. Consequently, *La fea más bella* proved the more attractive franchise option so far as the Chinese were concerned because the industry knowledge accumulated in its franchising process was more recent and appropriate to the large Chinese market. The Mexican adaptation had also had two other successful airings in the United States (Univision) and in the Philippines (ABC5 network), thereby further strengthening its appeal to its East Asian licensor.

Additionally, if the format title varied, so too would the name of the female protagonist. The newer, more paradoxical title invited national variations on names for the heroine. In the Mexican version, the figure was known as Betty. She became Bea (Beatriz) in the Spanish Telecinco 2006 remake and identified as Wudi in the Chinese version. Finally, in late 2009, Xiaojiang Hao from the production company Xiang Chao Guo Ji announced that for the fourth and final season of the *telenovela* format remake (see Appendix), its title would change to *Chou Nu(v) Da Fan Shen* (*The Transformation of Ugly Girl*). This move was necessary to comply with a new ruling by the Chinese State Administration of Radio, Film and Television (SARFT) designed to curb the practice of television and film sequels. Season Five was cancelled, with the Wudi (Betty) story ending on a high note – albeit with an open ending, where the heroine triumphs in business and finds a host of suitors (Sina.com 2009).

Storytelling: Production, Audience Input and Musical Variation

There were at least three significant variations or attempted ones in the narrative arc of the Chinese *telenovela* format adaptation. The first was the transplanting of the idea of the television season. Previously China had no specific notion of this broadcasting convention and its attendant production practices. Instead of producing a season's batch of shows, the standard practice had been for production companies to make programmes on a one-off basis and sell these to television stations in different places. CUB was the first TV series to import the season notion in PRC. Under this novel arrangement, most of the filming of a season of *Chou Nu (Nv) Wu Di* would already have taken place when broadcasting of early episodes started. In other words, the programme was both a test and an experiment in commercial and cultural routines and schedules.

Initially the aim was to produce 500 episodes of the Chinese *telenovela*, with each episode running 30 minutes. Once production and broadcasting began, however, crucial changes were made. Season Two saw the first of these modifications. One of the audience pleasures associated with seemingly open-ended story forms such as the soap opera or the *telenovela* is the apparent opportunity for viewers to have an influence over direction of future story lines. It is sometimes assumed that viewer feedback can provide ideas for producers and writers about such elements as future developments, character/actor importance and types of story. The availability of new production technologies only seems to increase the possible speed and efficiency of such feedback. Season Two of *Chou Nu (Nv) Wu Di*, and the producer decided to increase this interactivity. Hunan TV, in association with Sina.com – the largest Chinese-language infotainment web portal – increased online feedback between the production company and the audience. However, while this interactivity was useful in providing viewer opinion to the production company, the latter paid no heed to polling so far as character retention in the next season was concerned. Interactivity is not a two-way street.

Season Three introduced another novelty in storytelling in the form of a musicalization of *Chou Nu (Nv) Wu Di*. In China, film musicals date back to the 1930s, although musical fiction on television – incorporating song and dance – is a more recent phenomenon. One such programme originated from Taiwan. Adapting conventions of Chinese traditional opera into the dialogue as song, *The Legend of White Snake* (1994) proved very popular and influential with Mainland Chinese audiences.[4] Despite precedents of this sort, however, *Chou Nu (Nv) Wu Di*'s production company claimed that the third season was the first 'real TV musical'. To accommodate the shift in form and style, several changes had to be made in the storytelling structures of the *telenovela* remake. Jiong Lei (Deng Anqi), a new central character, was introduced to lead the dancing and singing. Additionally, a new main setting – a bar – became the location for the musical numbers. Unfortunately, the two main characters, Lin Wu Di (Li Xin Ru) and her boss, De Nan Fei (Liu Xiao Hu), were marginalized in the process of this musicalization.

Overall, this generic hybridization was not especially successful. Several shortcomings soon became apparent. In particular, the song and dance numbers were successful in expressing exuberance of spirit, but less satisfactory in conveying character emotion and/or internal psychological motivation. Moreover, the musical scenes tended to look stylistically similar and even repetitious – an effect probably due to the speed of production turnaround. As the end of the season approached, producers decided to end the experiment. Further prompted, no doubt, by audience feedback, which suggested that viewers did not appreciate the musical interludes delaying the story. Not surprisingly, the production decision was taken to abandon the musical elements in Season Four.

Cultural Variations

Further differences in *Chou Nu (Nv) Wu Di* can be highlighted by comparing three representative elements of the US, Mexican and Chinese adaptations. These relate to broad storytelling patterns: the love triangle involving the protagonist and her boss, and the depiction of the heroine and her father. Matters of storytelling have already been touched on in relation to the musicalization in Season Three of *Chou Nu (Nv) Wu Di*. It goes without saying that much that happens in the *telenovela* form generally has to be slow, deliberately retarding particular plot developments and elongating various fictional situations and relationships (Patna 2004: 3456–8). Yet various other plot events receive scant dramatic attention, and the story sometimes hurtles forward. Overall, the Chinese version falls somewhere between the Mexican and US adaptations, with new plot situations used frequently to keep the audience engaged. Significantly, Wudi's birthday celebration only occupied one episode whereas in the Mexican version, the party extended across four.

The main love story of the different national versions has generated several approaches. In the Colombian version, there is no narrative preoccupation with the virginal status of the heroine. Instead, Beatriz 'Betty' Pinzón Solano (Ana María Orozco) has sex with her boss, Armando Mendoza (Jorge Enrique Abello), and even moves in with him despite the fact that he already has a girlfriend. She becomes the third person in this love triangle and must wait for him to end the earlier affair. In the US version Betty Suarez (America Ferrera) enjoys a platonic relationship with her publishing boss, Daniel Meade (Eric Mabius), allowing several different story directions to remain open. In the Chinese remake, Lin Wu Di has a similar platonic relationship with the boss, Fei De Nan, but gives most of her emotional attention to work and solving work crises. Romantic feelings only begin to surface once her boss ends his relationship with Li An Qian (Li Xin Yi). This development is in line with traditional principles of Confucius that offer an ethical vision of orderly social relations with virtue and good manners playing a central role. It is unacceptable for a third person to break up a couple's relationship so that, finally, a gentle kiss between the two proved the most intense love scene in *Chou Nu (Nv) Wu Di*.

The third related variation has to do with traditional values and the heroine's family, as seen in the *telenovela* adaptations. The heroine's mother is already dead in the Chinese version's central story, so home life becomes an opportunity to work through issues relating to authority, gender and generational relations between father and daughter. In the Mexican version, the heroine's father is very conservative and highly protective – even over-protective – of his daughter. In the US version, by contrast, the heroine's family values are seen as emblematic of Latino Americans, and father, Ignacio Suarez (Tony Plana), becomes the narrative focus of several story lines involving murder, illegal migration and health care. In *Chou Nu (Nv) Wu Di*, in keeping with China's 'one child' policy, Wu Di is an only child. Traditional family values are emphasized even if they are – on occasion – mildly satirized. Hence, father Lin Wu Qing (Wang Ming) and daughter Lin Wu Di are both gentle and restrained in their approach to the world while the over-protectiveness of the former is, for instance, highlighted in the tender comedy when he visits Wu Di at work.

Summary

This chapter has been concerned with the importation and adaptation of cultural technology in China. As China seeks a dominant place in global affairs, so it has imported and adapted all kinds of know-how in both material and ideational form. This is the most useful context in which the *Chou Nu (Nv) Wu Di* programme format franchising can be understood. The *Yo soy Betty, la fea* telenovela adaptation represents a significant moment in this kind of knowledge traffic, and an important number of breakthroughs can be enumerated. First, as Hong (2004), Keane (2007) and Michael Curtin (2007) have shown respectively, Chinese television producers have long engaged in the practice of unauthorized copying of programme format knowledge from elsewhere. China's admittance to the WTO signals a new era in business and cultural relations. The licensing agreement leading to the birth of *Chou Nu (Nv) Wu Di* represents the first time that a Chinese production company has obtained legal authorization to franchise a fiction programme. Second, the occasion of the Chinese remake of *Yo soy Betty, la fea* via the Mexican adaptation, *La fea más bella,* represents the first time that a Chinese TV series has fully incorporated a comprehensive slate of commercials inserted into a broadcast show. Third, this placement constitutes the main profit source for the series rather than the copyright of the production broadcast sale. Additionally, *Chou Nu (Nv) Wu Di* facilitates the introduction of the concept of the television season eclipsing the past regime of production and broadcasting indeterminancy. The musicalization of part of the *telenovela* also constituted an unexpected and innovative generic variation in the remake.

Looking ahead, we should remember that incoming traffic in knowledge and ideas often gives rise to outgoing traffic. Cultural reception can trigger cultural transmission across borders. The socially engineered, commercial and cultural phenomenon in the PRC that is *Chou Nu (Nv) Wu Di* will disappear off production studio floors, television screens and even, in time, from popular memory. It will leave behind a legacy of creative and commercial knowledge about the current global television system that may eventually see the PRC become a dominant world centre for the creation and international export of its own mega-formats – even, perhaps, in the form of original Chinese *telenovelas* (*see* Jacques 2009: 403–6). *Chou Nu (Nv) Wu Di* is one step in this long journey. It is clearly part of an extended process of transition where knowledges developed elsewhere are integrated with Chinese practices in an ongoing reconfiguration of the television institution in the PRC. The adaptation does not mask or disguise this process of change but is instead wholly integral to such a movement. *Chou Nu (Nv) Wu Di* is better likened to an iceberg than to a Trojan Horse so far as its impact on Chinese television is concerned because what appears on screen is only a part of a larger package of effects that it entails.

Works Cited

Bao, Z.W., and Shi, Z.Q., '*Ugly Wudi*: The Reserve of Talents Is Insufficient in the Domestic Musical Films and TV Productions Market', *Film and TV Report*, 2009, online at: http://ent.yx48.eom/t/s/2009-09-17/00317.html (accessed 16 November 2009).

CSM.com.cn, 'About CSM Media Research', 2009, online at: http://www.csm.com.cn/en/about/index.html (accessed 16 November 2009).

Curtin, M., *Playing to the World's Biggest Audience: The Globalization of Chinese Film and TV* (Berkeley, CA: University of California Press, 2007).

Easynet Entertainment, 'Hot Topic of Ugly Wudi 3: Too Much Singing and Dancing & Infringing the Music Copyrights', 2009, online at: http://ent.163.com/09/0831/14/5I26J8OU00031GVS.html (accessed 16 November 2009).

Hong, J., 'China', in H. Newcomb (ed.), *The Museum of Broadcasting Communications Encyclopedia of Television*, 2nd rev. edn (New York: Taylor and Francis, 2004).

HunanTV.com, 'The Introduction of Hunan TV', 2009, online at: http://news.hunantv.com/English/NewsReport/200712/t2Q07122825013.html (accessed 16 November 2009).

Jacques, M., *When China Rules the World: The Rise of the Middle Kingdom and the End of the Western World* (London and New York: Allen Lane and Penguin Books, 2009).

Keane, M., *Created in China: The Great New Leap Forward* (London: Routledge, 2007).

——, Fung, A., and Moran, A. (eds), *New Television: Globalization, Television and the East Asian Imagination* (Hong Kong: Hong Kong University Press, 2007).

Lin, N., 'Soap Opera Brings Debate: It Is Hard to Broadcast While Production Still Takes Place in Mainland TV Industry', *Shenyang Evening News*, 2007, online at: http://ent.sina.com.cn/v/h/2007-09-19/09291721823.shtml (accessed 10 December 2009).

Lu, Q., 'Ugly Wudi: Introducing Commercial Advertisement and Season Broadcasting into the Production of TV Episodes', 2008, online at: http://www.51cmc.com/article/200811/20081106094847260647.shtml (accessed 6 November 2008).

Moran, A., *Copycat TV: Globalization, Program Formats and National Culture* (Bristol: Intellect, 1998).

——, *New Flows in Global TV* (Bristol: Intellect, 2009a).

——, *TV Formats Worldwide: Localizingg Global Programs* (Bristol: Intellect, 2009b).

——, and Keane, M. (eds), *Television Across Asia: Globalization, Industry and Formats* (London: Curzon/Routledge, 2004).

Moran, A., and Malbon, J., *Understanding the Global TV Format* (Bristol: Intellect, 2006).

Patna, A., 'Telenovela', in H. Newcomb (ed.), *The Museum of Broadcasting Communications Encyclopedia of Television*, 2nd rev. edn (New York: Taylor and Francis, 2004).

Silj, A. (ed.), *East of Dallas: The European Challenge to American Television* (London: BFI Publishing, 1988).

Sina.com, 'Ugly Wudi 4 Faces the New Restriction and Changes Title to the Transformation of Ugly Girl', 2009, online at: http://ent.sina.com.cn/v/m/2009–10–12/10362726286.shtml (accessed 10 November 2008).

Sinclair, J., 'The De-Centring of Cultural Flows', *Critical Studies in Television*, vol. 4, no. 1 (Spring 2009), pp. 26–38.

Tunstall, J., *The Media Were American: The US Mass Media in Decline* (New York: Oxford University Press, 2008).

Wang, Q.C., and Meng, H. Li, 'Why the *Ugly Wudi* Is Popular', *Media*, vol. 2 (2009a), pp. 72–3.

——, 'Why the *Ugly Wudi* Is the View: The Phenomenon of Ugly Wudi', *Advertising Panorama (Media Method)*, vol. 1 (2009b), p. 72.

Yan, X., Li, X., and Zou, T., '*Ugly Wudi*: The New Exploration of Product Placement in Marketing Communication', *Press Circles*, vol. 4 (2009), pp. 72–3.

Yang, M., '*Ugly Wudi*: The Audience Rating and Anti-Culture. Looking Through *Ugly Wudi* to See the Audience Rating and Anti-Cultural Tendency', *Advertising Panorama*, vol. 3 (2009), pp. 72–3.

Zhang, Y., '*Ugly Wudi* Season 3 on Air: Its Musical Elements Bring a Dramatic Debate', 2009, online at: http://yule.sohu.com/20090831/n266338735.shtml.

Appendix: *Chou Nu (Nv) Wu Di/ Chou Nu Da Fan Shen* Season Breakdown

Season 1: 40 episodes x 40 minutes. Broadcast September 2008.
Season 2: 64 episodes x 40 minutes. Broadcast January 2009.
Season 3: 48 episodes x 40 minutes. Broadcast August–September 2009.
Season 4: 30 episodes x 40 minutes. Broadcast early 2010.

Endnotes

1   Another important element in the overall Chinese commercial television landscape linking broadcasting, production, audiences and advertisers is an audience rating

service. Rating figures for *Chou Nu (Nv) Wu Di* are provided by CSN Media Research. This body is a joint venture between CTR Market Research, the leading market research company in China, and the TNS Group. CSM Media Research operates the world's largest television and radio audience measurement panel. Its operation covers China's 1.2 billion and Hong Kong SAR's 6.3 million television and radio audiences, involving 217 individual markets comprising the national entity, 24 provinces and 192 cities (including Hong Kong SAR), with some 55,600 homes and 183,700 panellists participating in the measurement of over 1,270 main channels and 396 radio frequencies, every day of the year (CSM.com.cn, 2009).

2   The information to do with Xiaojiang Hao's hesitation was given to the authors in strictest confidence so that the source cannot be revealed.

3   A reader has suggested that the producers' encouragement of viewers to believe in complete interactivity with the programme such that the audience can influence future directions of the story '... seems to be an important question relating to Democracy and Communism'. We are happy to pass on this suggestion although we believe that this is to misunderstand a market strategy that is common across culture industries, inside and outside of the PRC.

4   The Chinese version of the genre was markedly different from that of Hollywood with little dancing. Notable Chinese feature musicals have included *Street Angel* (Yuan Muzhi, 1937) *Ashima* (Qiong Liu, 1964) and *Liu San Jie* (Su Li, 1978).

How *Ugly* Can *Betty* Be in India?

Divya McMillin

I like the concept of a not-beautiful-girl because generally you have mega models in every serial. She comes from a middle-class family and … copes (with) everything and *nothing* can really *get* her *away* from her path. (Anujoth, 14-year-old female, Bangalore 2004)

I would make her look beautiful because that would give her more … um … self-confidence. That's *one* drawback. That she has a bad physical appearance [sic]. And if she becomes beautiful, then that drawback will not affect her. (Ashwin, 14-year-old male, Bangalore 2005)

My favourite would be *Khahani Ghar Ghar Ki* (*The Story of Every House*, Adnan Wai, 2004) on Star Plus because the heroine Parvati represents the ideal Indian woman. She does a *lot* for her family, keeps the family united. She sacrifices her happiness but ultimately she does not get what she deserves … She is modern but she still is traditional in her beliefs and values. (Uzma, 16-year-old female, Bangalore 2007)

The plain-faced heroine worked for a while. Fourteen-year-old Anujoth is talking about Jasmeet 'Jassi' Walia (Mona Singh), the Indian *Ugly Betty* in Sony Entertainment Television's (SET)[1] adaptation, *Jassi Jaisi Koi Nahin* (*There's Nobody Quite Like Jassi*, henceforth *JJKN*) which aired from 2003 to 2006. The bespectacled, thick-fringed, teeth-braced heroine resonated with Anujoth's own no-nonsense self-assessment – she saw herself as plain yet smart, popular at school because of her brains, not her looks. Interviewed during ethnographic fieldwork in Bangalore in 2004 as part of an international collaborative pilot project exploring the influence of favourite television characters on teen identity,[2] Anujoth believed Jassi was a refreshing break from the cookie-cutter, heavily made-up, curvaceous Bollywood heroines. By the time we moved onto another phase of fieldwork in 2005,[3] viewers seemed restless for a different type of Jassi. Audiences were weary of an unattractive heroine fighting against evil but gorgeous antagonists. Fourteen-year-old Ashwin's comments reflect this ethos; if only she were beautiful, he wished, the show would be perfect. By 2007, when *JJKN* was off the air, young viewers had come to accept the virtuous heroine as the standard – she had to straddle private and public spheres with elegance and confidence. Yet there was also a backlash, as we see in 16-year-old Uzma's statement. Her description of a protagonist who conformed to patriarchal constructions of the ideal woman indicates that audience responses to *JJKN*-type dramas are complexly drawn. They are a response to competing frameworks of meaning – the viewer's own background informed by integrated class, caste, religious, language and gender experiences; the increasingly transnational media environment where only certain programme formats and themes lend themselves to production; and voracious corporate sponsors that pounce on such robust formats to gain access to consuming viewers.

What is remarkable is that all these phases of fieldwork in Bangalore, the first two (in 2004 and 2005 respectively) focusing on the role of television in shaping teen identities, and the third in 2007 addressing the 'modern' woman emerging on Indian television, were not about *JJKN* at all. Yet in those phases, during in-depth conversations with the teens numbering over 200 in all, and ranging from 14 years to 18 years old, Jassi could very well have been sitting with us, peering myopically through her glasses, listening in. As we talked to respondents about their television habits, interests, family and school activities, and dreams and anxieties, *JJKN* served as intertextual wallpaper, with examples from the show used to illustrate the respondent's own opinions and experiences. Respondents wanted to be politically correct, initially arguing that looks were not important to get ahead, what mattered was only what was in one's head and heart. Gradually, when they relaxed a little and started joking around with the researcher, they confided that they wished Jassi could look as glamorous as her enemies then she could *really* teach them a thing or two. These teens were not the target audience for the show, yet they were among its most ardent fans and critics.

This chapter is a journey of sorts, going back into materials gathered from research conducted between 2004 and 2007 in Bangalore. Such materials include archived media library reports, transcripts of interviews with network executives, viewers' journals, scrapbooks and photographs, and extensive field notes from participant observation at networks and in viewer homes. The chapter begins with SET's unique marketing strategy and will briefly discuss the *telenovela* as a product of a globalized media environment. I will then dip a little into the storyline, to get a sense of the complications of private and public that the show engenders, at the same time looking at the viewer's engagements with the plot. Such engagements are drawn from interviews and fan forums online. The chapter ends with a critical discussion of Jassi as a sign of a carefully and artfully manipulated Indian womanhood that sits well with conservative longings for a woman who knows her place, as well as progressive fantasies of a woman who can navigate the public sphere without losing respect. *JJKN* is a dynamic economic and cultural product, capitalizing on an increasingly synergistic media environment and on the expanding credibility of the Indian woman in the public sphere.

Webs of Desire

In the complex web that is the Indian private television environment, SET is second only to Rupert Murdoch's Star Plus, and in the early 2000s, mergers and acquisitions marked television network activity in India (McMillin 2001). To stay afloat, networks indulged in the frenzied purchasing of programme format licenses that had proven successful in foreign markets. Many more adapted or plagiarized successful formats such as big prize game shows, surveillance reality shows, and MTV-style countdown music shows. By the end of 2003, it was clear that Star Plus had almost five times as many viewers as SET, primarily because of *Kaun Banega Crorepati?* (*Who will become a Crorepati?* [Starplus, 2000–6]), the

ABCL-cloned production of Celador's *Who Wants to Be a Millionaire?*, originating in 1998 on ITV and acquired and licensed by Sony Pictures Television in 2008.

The other private Hindi-language networks, Zee TV, Sahara TV, and SAB TV followed behind the top two. Star Plus continued its stronghold on audiences between 7.30 pm and 11.30 pm at the time of writing, primarily due to its robust programme inheritance strategy. With high-quality (in terms of production) in-house programming that includes family-oriented dramas, game shows and news, the network has been able to sustain audience flow from one programme to the next. In his over two decades of research studying inheritance effects in US programming, James G. Webster (2006) asserts that these are *the* most robust indicators of audience behaviours. Quite simply, such effects refer to the tendency of viewers to continue watching one programme after the previous one. This results in disproportionately large numbers of duplicated audiences, confounding the tracking of ratings for a particular show. Even with the availability of digital video recorders and video-on-demand in North American markets, Webster believes inheritance effects are hardly on the decline. In the Indian market, these technologies are available to less than 1 per cent of viewers; inheritance, audience duplication, and programme constancy are where network executives craft their strategies, as we shall see in the case of SET and *JJKN*.

Unable to break Star Plus' command over primetime audiences with *KBC* and facing stiff competition from Zee TV's popular K-dramas (*Kyunki Saas Bhi Kabhi Bahu Thi* [*Because a Mother-in-Law Was Once a Daughter-in-Law Too*, 1999–present] and *Kahaani Ghar Ghar Ki* [*The Story of Each Home*, 2000], for example) featuring the kitchen politics of upper-middle-class Gujarati families,[4] SET developed a strategy that could best be described as normative morphism,[5] where it followed those norms that proved to be best practices (see Keane 2004). Best practices in the cut-throat competition to be *the* 'family brand' channel of choice translated into women-centred narratives that simultaneously cast heroines as independent and needy. Examples illustrating this trend are the virtuous wives in *Mangalya* and *Kadambari* on the Kannada-language Udaya TV, fighting mothers and daughters in *Jhansi* and *Chakravakam*[6] on the Telugu-language Gemini TV, suffering daughters-in-law in *Kyunki Saas Bhi Kabhi Bahu Thi* (2000–8) on the Hindi-language Zee TV and

Kuch Apne Kuch Paraye (2006) on the Hindi-language Sahara One, and struggling urban women in *Main Aisi Kyun Hoon?* on Sahara One and *Saat Phere – Saloni Ka Safar* on Zee TV.

In this mimetic environment, SET launched its 'Understanding the Woman' audience research. The purpose was to obtain an intimate sense of target audiences' desires, needs and activities. The results were clear: urban Indian women were actually tiring of perpetually pained protagonists. They wanted serials that portrayed intelligent decision-makers. In a report in the India Times Publications' *Strategic Marketing Journal*,[7] SET executives Albert Almeida (senior vice-president of marketing), Sunil Lulla (executive vice-president of marketing) and Nina Jaipuria (assistant vice-president of marketing) summarized that female leads had to be modern housewives who also worked outside the home. They had to have multiple solutions at hand; no longer were audiences interested in women who quietly endured, or who were helpless economically and physically. The authors noted that the concept of the Colombian hit *Yo soy Betty, la fea* (*I Am Betty, the Ugly One* [RCN, 1999–2001]) was a perfect fit. They proposed that the adaptation in India, as *JJKN*, would be unlike that in any other market where it was either dubbed or subtitled. It would be recreated to suit the target female viewer who was quite possibly a homemaker but more likely employed, within the top three socio-economic groups, between 25 and 34 years of age, well educated, most likely married, and with two children. Such adaptation makes sense in the face of significant evidence that audiences prefer domestic, vernacular-language programmes over foreign ones, particularly with the improvements worldwide in production and reception quality beginning in the 1990s (Straubhaar 1991; Waterman and Rogers 1994). Subtitled foreign dramas are far less popular than those that are locally produced (Wang 1998; Dupagne and Waterman 1999).

The recreation of the Colombian *telenovela* can be considered an open adaptation. Albert Moran explains that a television format is a 'set of invariable elements in a programme out of which the variable elements of an individual episode are produced' (2004: 5). As an open adaptation, only part of the original format was incorporated in *JJKN* (such as the *telenovela* structure itself, as well as the protagonist's dark, fringed hair, thick-rimmed glasses, braces, conservative clothing and bubbling personality) and much was developed to transform it for local tastes, drawing heavily from Bollywood. Yet the plotlines departed significantly from the original. SET executives noted that the word 'ugly' would not sit well with middle-class audiences, neither would the name Betty. The title character was thus renamed Jassi and her honest and hard-working personality was played up, to distract audiences from her unattractiveness. The story was set in a fashion house (Gulmohar House) and plots were manipulated to suit Indian preferences for intensely emotional and complex narratives (Ganti 2002) that also connected intertextually with Hindu myths of female purity. The adaptation of *JJKN* reflects the best practices of a transnational television circuit as well as a robust Indian film industry from which television voraciously feeds. It illustrates durability, an essential component in highly competitive markets where viewers can be capricious and where brand loyalty, whether to programme or network, is elusive at best (Mukherjee and Roy 2006).

Deriving from the Indian film industry's practice of marketing movie songs and posters months in advance of the movie's debut and building 'buzz' through teasers and trailers on billboards and television advertisements, SET developed a striking and innovative marketing ploy that was unprecedented in the history of Indian television. Shifting from the standard larger-than-life glossy billboards advertising Bollywood films and Star and Zee serials, SET marketing executives decided that Jassi's face should remain a mystery before the launch of the show and even in its first weeks, until a critical viewership was achieved. Through placards at airports, train stations and malls, flyers distributed at traffic stops, SMS, flash mobs in public places yelling 'We Want Jassi', and advertisements in newspapers, magazines, radio and television asking the question, 'Who is Jassi?', the network was effectively able to stimulate widespread curiosity about the show. During the weeks leading up to the pilot, advertisements carried descriptions of Jassi's wonderful personality. These gave way to more advertisements depicting other characters on the show talking about Jassi. Finally, the Shaher Shaher Mein Charcha campaign was launched which featured a variety of people talking about Jassi. Exploring synergistic possibilities, SET promoted a Jassi 'Pals Club', Jassi merchandise, and even downloadable ring tones from the show. Right before it debuted, cast members with the exception of Jassi were introduced at the media launch. *Times of India* supplements in Mumbai, Delhi and Kolkata carried a picture of the cast, again with Jassi missing, and with the legend: 'Jassi manages to give the cameras a slip yet again.' Finally, a day before the pilot episode, a sneak preview was aired during primetime, followed by a half-hour 'mockumentary' on how the show was produced. During the first few weeks that the show aired, Jassi herself was treated like a star off the set, and was interviewed (in character) on the Aaj Tak television channel and Red FM radio.

The description of SET as a competitor in the Indian television market and its innovative marketing strategies with *JJKN* gives us an intimation of a plot that was constructed to cater to several demands: corporate sponsors, the network itself, the actress Mona Singh who played Jassi, and finally, the audience. From Jasmeet Walia to Jessica Bedi to Neha Shastri, Singh reported in various venues that she was as entranced by the twists and turns of *JJKN* as were her fans in India and abroad. In various magazine, newspaper and online reports, she commented on her scepticism regarding the bizarre experiences her character underwent – international travel, murder attempts, love triangles – despite being middle-class. Singh worried about being typecast as a dull and naive girl, a point we shall take up later.

Jassi is *Real*

JJKN follows the general pattern of *Yo soy Betty, la fea* by demonstrating fundamental strategies of the entertainment-education formats used by national governments of developing economies in Asia, Latin America and Africa in the 1960s through the 1980s (Papa et al. 2000). Other examples of such formats are *Crossroads* in Khazakhstan (Mandel 2002), *Hum Log* (1984–5) in India, *In a Lighter Time* in Nigeria, *Twende na Wakati* in Tanzania, and *Neria* and *More Time* in Zimbabwe (Brown and Singhal 1990), where varied characters are used to provide positive and negative models for audiences to learn from. While the focus of these *telenovelas* is social development, they represent abundant opportunities for product placement and programme sponsorship. In *JJKN,* Jassi, who we recall is an employee at Gulmohar House, is in love with her boss Armaan Suri (Apurva Agnihotri), and is taunted by her more attractive colleagues, mostly female. Her nemesis is the gorgeous Mallika Seth (Rakhshanda Khan) Arman's fiancée. Gradually Jassi wins the hearts of almost all. By February 2004, SET recorded that *JJKN* was its top-rated show, and that its share in the 9.30 pm slot grew from 8.2 per cent to 32.4 per cent within the first three months of the show. On the other hand, Star Plus's share for that timeslot dropped from 81.8 per cent to 62.6 per cent in the same time period. SET advertising rates were raised 50 per cent and the network still witnessed an exponential increase in sponsors (from 1 to 12). A single email advertising the Jassi 'Pals' Club sent to 46,000 viewers resulted in 4,000 members and over 100,000 viewers responding to an SMS question about Jassi's next step when faced with a moral dilemma. Over 80,000 viewers downloaded the *Jassi* ring tone in the first two weeks of the campaign.

By 2004, when the pilot study exploring television and teen identities began (see Endnotes), *JJKN* was leading the ratings game, still not overtaking Star Plus's *KBC*, but comfortably ahead of dramas on Zee TV and the other Hindi-language channels. Fieldwork included the components of ethnography – participant observation, in-depth conversations, and for the researchers who either lived or grew up in the very locales as the respondents, long-term immersion in the field.[8] The pilot study spanning six months (February through July) required participants to collect newspaper and magazine clippings of their favourite television and movie actors and maintain a journal of their daily activities. Much of these activities revolved around school and family since they were facing the highly competitive 10th-grade state and nationwide examinations. Their television watching was highly selective, making their involvement with *JJKN* purposeful, not random. Quite predictably, language familiarity determined whether the show was watched at all. Rural participants who were native Kannada speakers kept to the Kannada-language channels, while urban, middle-, and upper-middle-class Hindi speakers watched the show regularly. We focus here on the responses of two viewers, 14-year-old Anujoth and 14-year-old Zohrab, because they articulated the dominant views on the serial expressed by other middle-income teens in the study.

Anujoth, an extremely introspective and high-achieving teen, immediately connected with Jassi. While this participant's experiences and media behaviours are discussed more extensively elsewhere (see McMillin 2009), I will spend a little time here on her views about Jassi. She said:

Jassi has really impressed me. Initially her character was a little boring and she was quite gullible. But the way she emerged successful in spite of being not very good looking was inspiring. It helped me understand that it's not only looks that matter; personality indeed is what matters. Now she has the same personality but she made a few changes. She is now more self-centred which is very good according to me. In today's world, it's good to be a little selfish!

Anujoth was often irritated with the Zee TV and Star Plus family-oriented dramas that her mother watched, because of their numerous characters and intertwining relationships. *JJKN* offered a certain simplicity and realism in its use of a plain-faced character. It appealed to Anujoth's scientific bent; and she talked repeatedly about Jassi being just like her: neat in appearance, minimally fashionable, but more interested in doing her job well and in maintaining long-lasting relationships. Jassi really was her favourite television character because:

> She has come across a lot of problems in her life and … I think that in today's world there may be a lot of distractions but if you *want to*, you win. If you want to stick to the path, to the goal you are trying to get to, you will *definitely*.

Zohrab, on the other hand, hardly *talked* about Jassi. He said he primarily watched English-language serials on the Star network. Yet his media diary revealed that *JJKN* was the serial he watched the most. His notes were a combination of programme description and personal thoughts. As *JJKN*'s plot unravelled, Jassi's boss Armaan is exposed as manipulative and conniving, conjuring ways to get Jassi to falsify Gulmohar House's accounts to cover up losses. Zohrab noted in his journal on 13 April 2004:

> I don't like Jassi's boss Armaan in this episode. He is okay in looks but he keeps spying on everybody, he does not trust anybody. Because of Jassi, the Gulmohar Fashion Show was a success so there was a party for which Armaan invited Jassi but Nandu, Jassi's childhood friend, had other plans for the evening as he had asked Jassi first. She went with him for her 'surprise'. Armaan

likes Jassi and got jealous. He started following them and spied on them.

During subsequent episodes, Zohrab seemed to connect with the realism of the characters. He described the 16 April episode where Armaan, who is very rich, is out-of-sorts eating with his hand, a common practice in India. Zohrab wrote, 'I liked the part where … he ate with his hands. I liked it because he was rich and had never eaten without a spoon so he did not know how to use his hand and made a big mess!' In another episode a week later, Armaan and Jassi are at a roadside stall where they are about to eat *pani puris* which consist of deep-fried, puffed pastries filled with a tangy tamarind and onion sauce. Zohrab enjoyed watching Armaan's consternation:

> He hesitated to eat *pani puri* from a roadside stall. He was rich and was afraid! It's funny … the man messes up and Jassi tells him, "you have to put the whole thing in your mouth." I love eating *pani puris* – sometimes they are too big for your mouth and splash all over, but they always taste great.

It is apparent here that Zohrab is deriving pleasure from the discomfort of the rich and conniving Armaan. The show effectively allowed at least a momentary subversion of an integrated class, gender and appearance hierarchy. Such subversion was quite likely cathartic to Zohrab, who candidly talked about his frustration at being from a low-income household, yet with an upper-middle-class upbringing. During lengthy interview sessions, Zohrab talked passionately about the liberation he felt on stage. There he could say what he wanted, could talk about taboo subjects, and it would all be just fine. *JJKN* provided him a lab of sorts.

Jassi is Real … But Has to Be *Beautiful*

During fieldwork in 2005 designed to expand on the insights learned in the 2004 phase (McMillin, 2009), we interacted closely with 30 teens. Participant observation and interviews again spanned several months with respondents collecting materials on their favourite media celebrities while maintaining a media and personal diary. By this time, the *JJKN* plot had become significantly more complex. Jassi had accepted a proposal of marriage from Purab Mehra (Samir Soni), despairing that Armaan would ever be interested in her romantically. Jassi fled to Mauritius when she discovered Armaan had been manipulating her all along and when Purab withdrew his proposal on his friend's ill-meaning advice. Jassi's sudden departure was quite likely in response to strong viewer feedback regarding her looks. Online forums such as Indiaforum.com and Mouthshut.com contained literally hundreds of messages describing intense involvement with the show. Legions of fans discussed the show as an extension of their families; they were addicted and would not miss even a single episode. They were very critical of Jassi's looks, believing that she could avenge her enemies by just changing her appearance, and at the very least, dressing more fashionably. Fieldwork showed that while urban teens in Bangalore professed a rich variety of programme preferences, Jassi was still a primary choice. This time, *JJKN* served as a standard of reference – other primetime serials were considered just as ridiculous and convoluted as the *telenovela*, or a refreshing change from it. *JJKN,* developed to be unique, was increasingly becoming indistinguishable from its competitors.

Again, I will focus on two teens, Ashwin (middle-income) and Kirthana (upper-income), both aged 14, who best reflected the views of the other participants regarding *JJKN*. Ashwin spoke at length about how he felt Jassi was like his sister. She always wanted to help others even if she was wronged. He was conflicted about her appearance; while he insisted that, 'It doesn't matter if you are ugly or beautiful, Jassi catches [*sic*] people's hearts.' He would also end his descriptions of her each time with, 'She *has* to become beautiful, she has to *be* beautiful, *then* she will have a greater impact.'

With the strong feedback that Jassi should receive a makeover from viewers such as Ashwin,[9] SET saw more advertising potential. The actress herself, Mona Singh, was flexing her muscles, aware that other female leads such as Nausheen Ali Sardar of SET's own *Kkusum ... Ek Aam Ladki Ki Kahani* (produced by Balaji Telefilms, 2001–5) had walked off the highly profitable set fearing she would be typecast as a drab, older woman. Jassi's makeover seemed inevitable as Singh was increasingly fielding questions from the press about her prospects in the industry when she portrayed such an unexciting character. Months before her transformation, cosmetic companies and department stores were solicited for sponsorship. Executive vice-president of programming, Tarun Katial, in the 30 January 2005 Business section of *The Times of India*, said that the new plot twists would allow for significant brand placement opportunities. And so it went – Jassi received a total makeover while in Mauritius and returned to India as Jessica Bedi, a model. Back at Gulmohar, Mallika attempted to frame 'Jessica' for the murder of Jassi. Jessica revealed that she was Jassi herself and reunited with Armaan who was now ready to marry her. Viewers were livid at the turn of events, however, particularly Jassi's desertion to be at her friend Purab's side while he was dying of cancer and Armaan's eventual marriage to another woman, Mallika.

The popular press had followed preparations for Jassi's wedding for weeks. Fans were relating to her as a real person. Rediff.com's India Abroad website reported on 3 August 2005 that in just a couple of days, the elaborate wedding would be featured, with Jassi wearing a wedding sari designed by Neeta Lulla, India's famed Bollywood designer (with credits such as the period dramas *Jodha Akbar* [Bharat, 2008] and *Devdas* [Mega Bollywood, 2002]). Lulla's crafting of the 5-kilogramme red and gold sari with exquisite brocade, crystals and precious stones provided the stamp of Bollywood legitimacy. Jassi had moved not just from ordinary to superstar status within the serial, but had elbowed her way out of the small screen platform to the glittering Bollywood wedding hall, an ingenious step to signal her viability and availability for the movie circuit. When Armaan wed Mallika instead of Jassi, thousands of viewers emailed, called and texted their disbelief at the ultimate betrayal.

During this mayhem, 14-year-old Kirthana discussed her views about the show and its many spin-offs. Describing herself as a faithful viewer of all primetime dramas, Kirthana was impatient with the soaps on Zee TV because of the difficulty of following the highly convoluted plots. On the other hand, *JJKN* seemed 'natural' and 'real'. Jassi, to Kirthana, 'is a very good actress … and then the serial seems very natural as if it is happening to a real (person), it is happening *really* and it doesn't seem like a serial'. Like Ashwin, Kirthana occupied ambiguous territory. She could relate to the drab heroine, yet that sort of ideal 'realism' was unreal; in her 'real' world, looks *were* necessary to get ahead. Despite Kirthana's claims that *JJKN* was refreshingly different, she welcomed Jassi's metamorphosis into the glamorous model Jessica Bedi. Asked to comment on this 'evolution', Kirthana said she did not like Jassi earlier when she was not good-looking, despite strongly identifying with the heroine.

By the end of 2005, *JJKN* was in its third year, airing right after another hit, the cloned *Indian Idol* (SET, 2004–present), inheriting audiences and sustaining flow from that programme. *JJKN* became the poster child for product placements. It had already woven in promotion for a Bollywood film, *Hum Tum* (*You and Me* [Kunal Kohli, 2004]), itself loosely based on Columbia Pictures' *When Harry Met Sally* (Rob Reiner, 1989). Lead actor Saif Ali Khan, who portrayed cartoonist Karan Kapoor in the film, stirred up conflict in *JJKN* by arguing with Jassi and the other fashion staff about the male point of view presented in his comic strip. In 2005, there was no dearth of contenders for product placement. Prominent examples are Maruti Zen and Mercedes automobiles, L'Oreal cosmetics, Asmi jewellery and Samsung phones. Even locales proved fertile ground for advertising: sinister events were designed to unfold in foreign locales, providing effective sponsorship for Singapore Tourism, to name but one example. The automobiles found abundant coverage in Jassi's ventures in Nainital.

Transformations and Interconnections

For the thousands and possibly millions of Jassi fans in urban India and abroad, *JJKN* provided an intriguing world in which to participate at multiple levels. From the brief audience comments recounted here, it is apparent that Jassi provided teens with a very real sense of what was possible. Her awkward adolescent persona struggling to make it in a competitive adult world resonated with their own experiences. Jassi told them to stay true to themselves, to stay focused on what was good in people. Yet for audiences bred on super slick Bollywood heroines and K-dramas on the other Hindi-language competitors such as Star Plus and Zee TV, Jassi was unreal in her realness. Her transformation was fuelled by product placement opportunities, no doubt, but also serves as an important sign of what is necessary to be successful in urban India. The transformation can be a journey from adolescence to adulthood, from backwardness to modernity, from ugliness to beauty. The ideologies that are embedded in the process and that legitimize the journey from one to the other are apparent, as is intricately explained in a wealth of postcolonial scholarship (see, for example, Seuerquebahn 2007; Ashcroft 2001). The 'consumable hero(ine)', to borrow from Sudhanva Deshpande (2005: 202) is in essence a creation of the liberalized market. Such a hero has a high disposable income, a jet-setting lifestyle, shops and vacations overseas. While Deshpande is talking about the Bollywood male hero who is catering to not just domestic audiences but also expatriates who fund movie production, his comments are relevant for Jassi. Her transformation and extensive travels were absolutely necessary to keep the interest of the diasporic community; her increased materialism was necessary to keep corporate sponsors coming back. As discussed elsewhere (McMillin 2009), the heroine in Hindi dramas consumed by young urban audiences whose labour is desperately sought after in an increasingly transnational workplace offers crucial lessons on what is desirable and what signifies entry into an adequate standard of living. The heroine with brains, beauty and capital becomes a sign of progress and agency. Such a sign also legitimizes a range of behaviours such as sexism, classism and consumerism, to name but a few, as *the* only way to get ahead.

The beautification of Jassi itself carries realism and connects with fieldwork observations over several research projects. For example, fieldwork in 2003 among sweatshop labourers showed that beauty parlours were rapidly increasing in number around the semi-urban ancillary factories and slums. Young assembly-line workers were regular clients (McMillin 2003). A visit to the outcaste Balmiki (sweeper) community in New Delhi in 2006 showed that in the heart of the slums, social workers were training young women to work at beauty parlours; conversations with these women revealed that this was how they could make an easy income without formal education. Fieldwork at call centres provided another layer of observations that supported the importance of television and primetime dramas in grooming young men and women for the corporate workplace (McMillin 2006).

One possible conclusion is that *JJKN* serves, with other similar dramas not just in Hindi but also in vernacular adaptations, to channel rich diversity and teen rawness into a standardized version of the global urban individual – slim, beautiful and well groomed. As a structured product carefully engineered for the marketing of a wide range of products – from cosmetics to automobiles – it simultaneously propagates ideologies of gender, nation, caste and class.

However, this misses the larger context in which the teens were embedded, where family environment, religion and class experiences, to name just a few influences, may texture how they perceive the protagonist's and their own agency. Reponses to a single text are useful, but also could be reductionist if they are not adequately contextualized. It is important to reiterate that many of the teens articulated displeasure at the representation of women on primetime dramas. These young women were not limited to just television for their understanding of womanhood and femininity. Their exposure to critical theory (an addition to the introductory curriculum in primarily private colleges that are autonomous from the state university system) provided them with a certain vantage point, a privileged eye, as it were. They were able to see Jassi as a sign of independence and also, in later episodes, a sign of an integrated television-film environment where her transformation was necessary to further her own career, not just the plot. For some others, such analysis caused them to pause and reaffirm conservative notions of woman as selfless caregiver. The latter position reminds us that viewers are situated individuals, attached to enduring structures. They may critique that which confines them and seek to shift out of it, yet how much mobility can such critique really provide? And is such mobility really desired? While many of the teens were able to inject a counter discourse, such discourse cannot be held up as a sign of mobility and agency because the material benefits of the system still largely accrue to those in control of the representations. The discussions of the production environment of *JJKN* and its accommodation by viewers at various stages of plot development leave us with a few avenues for further exploration. First, the character of programme adaptations needs continued scrutiny – what is lost or gained in the translation? How is gender localized for consumption? Second, what kinds of transformations are necessary for young viewers to participate in a globalizing world, as workers and consumers? Finally, how may we theorize the opportunism in such transformations by all constituents involved? What may we say about the subject whose identity feeds from a system that pleasurably puts her in place?

Works Cited

Ashcroft, B., *Post-Colonial Transformation* (London and New York: Routledge, 2001).

Brown, W.J., and Singhal, A., 'Ethical Dilemmas of Prosocial Television', *Communication Quarterly*, vol. 38 (1990), pp. 206–19.

Dickey, S., *Cinema and the Urban Poor in South India* (Cambridge: Cambridge University Press, 1993).

Eder, W., and Corsaro, D., 'Ethnographic Studies of Children and Youth: Theoretical and Ethical Issues', *Journal of Contemporary Ethnography*, vol. 28 (1999), pp. 520–31.

Fernandes, L., 'Nationalizing "the Global": Media Images, Cultural Politics and the Middle Class in India', *Media, Culture & Society*, vol. 22 (2000), pp. 611–28.

Gangoli, G., 'Sexuality, Sensuality and Belonging: Representations of the "Anglo-Indian" and the "Western" Woman in Hindi Cinema', in R. Kaur and A.J. Sinha (eds), *Bollyworld: Popular Indian Cinema Through a Transnational Lens* (New Delhi: Sage, 2005), pp. 143–62.

Jeffrey, C., Jeffery P., and Jeffery, R., *Degrees Without Freedom? Education, Masculinities and Unemployment in North India* (Palo Alto, CA: Stanford University Press, 2008).

Kasbekar, A., 'Hidden Pleasures: Negotiating the Myth of the Female Ideal in Popular Hindi Cinema', in R. Dwyer and C. Pinney (eds), *Pleasure and the Nation: The History, Politics and Consumption of Public Culture in India* (New Delhi: Oxford University Press, 2001), pp. 286–308.

Lee, D.-H., 'A Local Mode of Programme Adaptation: South Korea in the Global Television Format Business', in A. Moran and M. Keane (eds), *Television Across Asia: Television Industries, Programme Formats and Globalization* (London and New York: Routledge Curzon, 2004), pp. 36–53.

McMillin, D.C., 'Television, Gender, and Labor in the Global City', *Journal of Communication*, vol. 53, no. 3 (2003), pp. 496–511.

——, 'Outsourcing Identities: Call Centers and Cultural Transformation in India', *Economic and Political Weekly*, vol. 41, no. 3 (2006), pp. 235–41.

——, 'The Global Face of Indian Television', in M. Curtin and H. Shah (eds), *Re-Orienting Global Communication: Indian and Chinese Media Beyond Borders* (Chicago: University of Illinois Press, 2009), pp. 118–38.

——, *Mediated Identities: Youth, Agency, and Globalization* (New York: Peter Lang, 2009).

Mukherjee, A., and Roy, R., 'A System Dynamic Model of Management of a Television Game Show', *Journal of Modeling in Management*, vol. 1, no. 2 (2006), pp. 95–115.

Papa, M.J., Singhal, A., Law, S., et al., 'Entertainment-Education and Social Change: An Analysis of Parasocial Interaction, Social Learning, Collective Efficacy, and Paradoxical Communication', *Journal of Communication* (Autumn 2000), pp. 31–55.

Serequeberhan, T., *Contested Memory: The Icons of the Occidental Tradition* (Trenton, NJ: Africa World, 2007).

Thomas, A.O., and Kumar, K.J., 'Copied from Without and Cloned from Within: India in the Global Television Format Business', in A. Moran and M. Keane (eds), *Television Across Asia: Television Industries, Programme Formats and Globalization* (London and New York: Routledge Curzon, 2004), pp. 122–37.

Webster, J.G., Phalen, P.F., and Lichty, L.W., *Ratings Analysis: The Theory and Practice of Audience Research*, 3rd edn (Mahwah, NJ: Erlbaum, 2006).

Endnotes

1   Sony Television is based in Mumbai and owned by Multi Screen Media Pvt. Ltd. It was promoted as a joint venture with Sony Pictures International in 1995.

2   Phase 1 of the 2003–4 *TV Characters and the Formation of Cultural Identity* project attempted to understand, through qualitative fieldwork, the meanings favourite television characters had for teenagers in very diverse parts of the world. The study was sponsored by the Internationales Zentralinstitut für das Jugend- und Bildungsfernsehen, IZI (International Central Institute for Youth and Educational Television) at Bayerischer Rundfunk (Bavarian Broadcasting Corporation), Munich, Germany.

3   Follow-up fieldwork, sponsored by the IZI, formed Phase 2 of the *TV Characters* study.

4   Interviews with Sameer Targe, a Zee TV network executive based in New Jersey for a project on Indian television's transitional presence (see McMillin 2009), revealed that the network's focus on Gujarati urban life happened quite by chance. Plot development in the early 1990s catered to the Mumbai market, its primary viewers. Such programming was very successful in Mumbai and demonstrated continued popularity in other regional markets even in South India. Such success could most likely be attributed to the fact that private, regional networks were yet to develop their own in-house dramas. Currently, adaptations of Zee dramas abound in regional languages on their respective networks.

5   The other two paths industries may take are coercive morphism, where they are forced to comply, and mimetic morphism, where they imitate the market leader.

6   Some production details missing from this paragraph.

7   Almeida, A., Lulla, S., and Jaipuria, N., *Jassi Jaisi Koi Nahin?* (n.d.), online at: http://www.etstrategicmarketing.com/SmJul-Aug04/Strategic-Article10.html (accessed 12 August 2009).

8   Fieldwork for both phases was conducted in three stages. During the first, researchers and respondents conversed at length on the purpose of the project. The researcher became acquainted with the respondent's family and neighbours and was shown around the home, school and neighbourhood. Discussions focused on the general interests, rituals and television habits of the teens and their families. The goal was to get a feel for how the teens interpreted their lives (see Eder and Corsaro 1999). The second stage was conducted after the respondents had had at least two months to collect material about their favourite television shows and characters. Researchers or their assistants checked in periodically with the teens, answering questions they had along the way. At the end of this period, researchers interviewed the respondents. Semi-structured interviews took between two and three hours each where the respondent answered a variety of questions about what it felt like to be a teen, what pressures and victories she or he had faced, and what she or he felt about favourite television characters. In terms of television characters, questions focused on favourite and least favourite shows and characters, and

reasons for these choices. All interviews were informal, in-depth conversations during which the researcher took photographs of the respondent and her or his environment and browsed through the respondent's collected materials. The third phase included the opportunity for the researcher to seek clarification after a review of all fieldwork materials. The author thanks Professor Susheela Punitha for her assistance with the fieldwork.

9   Online forums such as bollywoodgate.com, apnicommunity.com and studentdoctor. net which boasted around 200,000 users each, brought together the diasporic fan base throughout the show's run. Some fans provided their own transcripts of the show, embellished with comments about their own lives. For example, user Shreya posted a detailed description of the 22 June 2006 episode on Indiaforums.com, where more is revealed about Mallika's machinations. Transcriptions and descriptions are conventionally written in a hybrid style, with English phrases intermingling with the vernacular. Personal anecdotes are often thrown in, to illustrate resonance between the fan's own life and the show.

Ugly Betty on Turkish
Television: Updating Popular Cinema

Laurence Raw

Jade L. Miller (2010: 213) remarked recently that the global success of *Yo soy Betty, la fea* (*I Am Betty, the Ugly One* [RCN, 1999–2001) has much to do with its culturally translatable content, including the big-city setting and the social and behavioural conflicts between the city *fashionistas* and those originating from more modest backgrounds. What she has overlooked, however, is the fact that the *telenovela* form might be equally translatable specifically because of its modest production values and repetitive shooting style comprised of establishing shots, close-ups and shot/reverse shot sequences. This is certainly the case with the Turkish adaptation *Sensiz Olmuyor* (*Won't Work Without You*), which played for two seasons on two different private television channels – the first debuting on Show TV in January 2005 and the second on Kanal D in May 2005. This short piece will suggest that director Taner Akvardar deliberately recreated the *telenovela* in the style of *Yeşilçam* melodrama, a low-budget, popular cinema that flourished in the Republic of Turkey between the 1950s and the late 1970s. This choice was designed not only to appeal to the viewing public's sense of collective nostalgia, but fulfilled a patriotic desire to prove that the Turkish *telenovela* could match anything produced in Colombia. At the same time, I suggest that in thematic terms *Sensiz Olmuyor* is very different from *Yeşilçam* (the product of a period in Turkish history where morality and class-difference assumed particular significance). *Sensiz Olmuyor* is the product of a society placing more importance on individualism rather than sustaining social distinctions. Image is seen as a means to achieve success, as well as maintaining personal integrity.

The attraction of *Sensiz Olmuyor* for local programme-makers and viewers alike must be understood in the light of social and institutional changes taking place in the Republic of Turkey since 1980. Inspired by Margaret Thatcher's example, the late Prime Minister – later President – Turgut Özal introduced a series of measures designed to promote private enterprise and reduce state control. Such policies led to the creation of a new, upwardly mobile middle class, whose habits were dictated by 'conspicuous consumption patterns shaped by material values, as well as an urge to stay away from the "real" social diversity within … [Turkish] society' (İlkücan 2004: 167). The better their lifestyle, the more rapidly they can ascend the social scale. Özal's reforms extended into the media sector: in 1990, the first private television station (Interstar, later renamed Star TV) emerged as a competitor to the state-run Turkish Radio and Television Corporation (TRT), and within a decade viewers were faced with a multiplicity of channels, many of them financed by major media conglomerates. Show TV is owned by Çukurova Holding, while Kanal D is part of the Doğan Group, whose other interests include newspapers, magazines and bookstores. Relying on advertising for their survival, these private channels are involved in cut-throat competition for what they identify as ideal viewers – the *nouveau riche* middle class with sufficient disposable income to purchase the products on offer. Hence the domination of the nightly schedules by lifestyle programmes, quizzes and *telenovelas* that represent viewers' interests, hopes and aspirations should come as no surprise.

Sessiz Olmuyor offers a prime example of this type of programming. The opening credits of each episode introduce the principal members of the cast, and subsequently cut to a mass of fashion-magazines spread across the floor. The camera pans the magazines, showing a succession of elegantly dressed models of both sexes as the opening titles appear. The action cuts to a shot of a dimly lit catwalk, and dissolves to a shot of Arda Gazioğlu's (played by Turkish pop star Emre Altuğ) apartment with the star crossing the frame. Further dissolves show three people enjoying an evening meal by the Bosphorus, Gönül Üstünsoy (Özlem Conker/ Yeliz Şar) surrounded by her adoring parents Orhan and Zehra Gazioğlu (Aslan Altın and Gülsüm Kamu) and Arda kissing Gönül's hand. The sequence concludes with a shot of Gönül looking out to sea on a ferry-boat crossing the Bosphorus.

The sequence expresses the characters' (and the viewers') preoccupation with public display: fashionable attire and a tastefully decorated apartment celebrate the achievement of those who have taken advantage of the free-market economy and moved up the social scale. Now they can enjoy the fruits of their lifestyle, such as eating a leisurely evening meal by the Bosphorus. At the same time, the credits suggest that individual success can only be achieved with familial support – a nod, perhaps, to the communal traditions that shaped (and continue to shape) the lives of most Turkish citizens, including those not fortunate enough to enjoy material prosperity. The credits end with another patriotic allusion: the ensuing action will take place in İstanbul, the only city in the world to span two continents.

In this kind of an environment clothes assume paramount importance in fulfilling one's social aspirations. Hence Gönül – unlike the central character in the American adaptation *Ugly Betty* – would never dream of dressing in the kind of eclectic manner that might encourage her fellow-workers to write a blog about her. Instead she dresses fashionably in knee-length skirts or pants – all supplied by the Turkish fashion-houses sponsoring the programme – with occasional sartorial embellishments such as a long, woollen scarf. Interior decor fulfils a similar function of advancing one's aspirations: Arda's living room is tastefully lit with sidelights on each of the four corners, while large pot plants are deliberately designed to make the room look smaller, focusing viewers' attention on the rosewood dining table and chairs, and the leather three-piece suite. This design underlines the significance of the living room in upper-middle-class social life as a performance space for dinner parties and other gatherings. In a review of the lifestyle programme *Yemekteyiz* (the Turkish version of the Channel Four hit *Come Dine With Me* [2005–present]), I emphasized the significance of the dinner party as an opportunity for the host to invite judgements from the guests both on the food and the decor. At the end of each week, the winner emerges as the person who has 'created the best lifestyle suitable for public display' (Raw 2010). Arda's apartment in *Sessiz Olmuyor* invites a similar reaction, prompting viewers to decide whether his choice of furniture, fixtures and fittings is appropriate to his social position as head of a large İstanbul fashion-house.

And yet as modern and forward-looking *Sessiz Olmuyor* is, it also looks back nostalgically to the immensely popular *Yeşilçam* style of film-making, which represented a high point in Turkish cinema in the pre-television era with over 200 films being produced in 1970 alone. The majority of them were produced by small companies (similar to the 'Poverty Row' studios during the studio period in Hollywood) on minimal budgets with a maximum of three weeks for shooting. The action remained resolutely studio-bound; if location shots were required, they were inevitably restricted to the Bosphorus and its environs in İstanbul (then, as now, the film-producing capital of the Republic of Turkey). Most directors adopted a no-nonsense shooting style predominantly comprised of close-ups, two-shots and shot/reverse shot sequences; despite the constraints placed on them, they believed that they were creating 'a new national cinema that proved highly popular with filmgoers ... rather than simply imitating Hollywood models' (Raw 2011: 8).

Sensiz Olmuyor directly references this tradition. In the first of a cluster of sequences from Season Two, episode 2 – broadcast on Kanal B (rather than Show TV), and with Yeliz Şar replacing Özlem Conker in the lead role, Gönül and her boss Arda are seen in a shot/reverse shot in Arda's apartment. Obviously surprised by Gönül's entrance, Arda walks round her and exits: the action shifts to a close-up of Arda and his current girlfriend Şebnem Tezel (Ebru Gürsoy). As Arda tries to explain Gönül's entrance, the dialogue unfolds in a further series of shot/reverse shots. The second sequence opens with an establishing shot of Arda's office as he confronts his hapless assistant Can (Okan Yalabık), and unfolds in a series of close-ups culminating in a long reaction-shot of Arda's expression. The final sequence in this cluster recalls the opening sequence, only this time it is Arda rather than Gönül who makes an unexpected entrance.

While this form of narrative structure might seem repetitive to non-Turkish viewers, it is this very repetitiveness that accounts for its popularity. Savaş Arslan remarks that film-going during the *Yeşilçam* era was invariably a family affair, especially during summer, when spectators purchased wooden chairs and watched films in the open air while consuming food and drink (Arslan 2011: 109). They liked their films to be structurally repetitive, as it gave them the chance to eat, drink and talk amongst themselves without losing the thread of what was going on. As a family show intended for primetime viewing (8–10 pm on Turkish private channels), *Sensiz Olmuyor* offers similar possibilities for television viewers.

The series thus communicates a nationalist message on two levels. First, it invites viewers to celebrate screenwriter Hayal Tacirleri's achievement in domesticating the Colombian source-text: less emphasis was placed on class conflict, and more on the clash between centre and periphery involving those who had grown up in metropolitan İstanbul, and those – for example Gönül – who came from families with their origins in more rural parts of the Republic of Turkey. Secondly, *Sensiz Olmuyor* emphasizes the importance of continuity – the fact that *Yeşilçam* has been successfully kept alive in television, while the film industry has changed beyond recognition. The same applies to most *telenovelas* (or *diziler*) broadcast on Turkish television, whether original or based on foreign formats, which tend to be constructed in much the same way. The bulk of the action unfolds in anonymous-looking interiors (apartments, office blocks), interspersed with occasional location-shots of districts in and around the Bosphorus.

If *Sessiz Olmuyor* seems so perfectly to express the concerns of its intended audience, we might wonder why it lasted only two seasons. There are two possible explanations: first, that there was simply no desire on the producers' part to continue. Turkish *telenovelas* depend for their success on repetition, hence it is not a difficult task to recycle the plots, characters and situations of *Sessiz Olmuyor* in an alternative format that might not require the payment of copyright fees to RCN, the Colombian television company that originated the series. Secondly, *Ugly Betty* began to be broadcast – in both subtitled and dubbed versions – on TNT and ComedyMax, two channels owned by Kanal D and Show TV respectively. Clearly both organizations felt it unnecessary to duplicate the format on their various televisual platforms.

To date, *Sessiz Olmuyor* has not been released commercially, either on DVD or download. During its short run it topped the ratings, due in no small part to the presence in the cast of singing star Emre Altuğ who, during the first season, released a commercially successful recording of the theme song. Nevertheless, the series represents a good example of how a global franchise has been domesticated, in an attempt to show how capitalism has contributed to a radical transformation of Turkish society, in which the statist mentality – that prevailed prior to 1980 – has been superseded by a spirit of free enterprise and personal (rather than social) ambitions, enabling individuals to fulfil their aspirations, if they are prepared to work for it.

Works Cited

Arslan, Savaş, *Cinema in Turkey: A New Critical History* (Oxford: Oxford University Press, 2011).

İlkücan, Altan, 'Gentrification, Community and Consumption: Constructing, Conquering and Contesting 'The Republic of Cihangir' (Unpublished PhD thesis, Bilkent University, Ankara, 2004).

Miller, Jade L., '*Ugly Betty* Goes Global: Global Networks of Localized Content in the Telenovela Industry', *Global Media and Communication*, vol. 6, no. 3 (2010), pp. 198–217.

Raw, Laurence, 'Yemekteyiz,' *Scope: An Online Journal of Film and TV Studies* (16 February 2010), online at: www.scope.nottingham.ac.uk (accessed 15 July 2011).

——, *Exploring Turkish Cultures: Essays, Interviews and Reviews* (Newcastle-upon-Tyne: Cambridge Scholars Publishing, 2011).

Esti Ha'mechoeret: Ugly Esti as a Local and Successful Israeli Telenovela

Amit Lavie-Dinur and Yuval Karniel

Esti Ha'mechoeret (*Ugly Esti* [2003–4]) was first broadcast in 2003 on channel 2 (Keshet TV), the most central and popular commercial channel in Israel, some years after *Yo soy Betty, la fea* (*I Am Betty, the Ugly One* [RCN, 1999–2001]) first appeared on the Israeli cable channel Viva. *Esti Ha'mechoeret* (hereafter referred to as *Ugly Esti*) proved one of the most successful TV series ever to air not only on the channel, but also on Israeli television. It was broadcast over three short seasons and consisted of 25 episodes, with Esti's makeover receiving a 32.6-per-cent share, a record for channel 2. The next phase of *Ugly Esti* was the spin-off *Elvis, Rosenthal, VeHaIsha Hamistorit* (*Elvis, Rosenthal, and the Mystery Woman* [Keshet Broadcasting, 2005]), which changed its title to *Elvis* for its second season in 2006.

Ugly Esti as a Local Israeli Telenovela

According to Jade L. Miller popular *telenovelas* succeed as both canned programming and formats because they combine universally appealing stories (rags-to-riches) and style (melodrama) with localizable specifics with which viewers can easily identify (2010: 198). *Telenovelas* are dramatic narratives full of romantic liaisons, improbable storylines and melodrama, and they differ from US and US-style soap operas in a number of important ways. They are limited-run enterprises: only 75–150 episodes are usually produced, and these episodes are shown over the course of 3–6 months by airing 5–6 nights a week in a single timeslot. The story arc is known prior to production and *telenovelas* tend to conclude with a happy ending and all loose ends wrapped up – in stark contrast to soap operas that can last for decades with meandering storylines. Additionally, unlike soap operas in the USA, *telenovelas* are frequently a success in primetime on major networks and are popular across age and gender lines (200).

Yair Dori is the man responsible for the *telenovela* finding success in Israel. An Argentinian national, Dori set up Dori Media Group (formerly Yair Dori Communications Ltd) to import movies, series and, most importantly, *telenovelas* from South America. Initially selling them to Israel Cable Programming (ICP), Dori quickly realized the potential of cable broadcasting as a way of distributing his beloved *telenovelas* and in April 1999, launched Viva, a channel devoted solely to the genre. Both the importation of *telenovelas* from South America and the screening of local remakes consolidated Viva's success in the cable television market and the channel fast established itself as among the top three niche channels in Israel and one of the top five nationwide[1] – and it was on Viva that *Yo soy Betty, la fea* first aired in the country.

Ugly Esti became the focus of controversy in 2005 when RCN Television (the Colombian company that holds the rights for *Yo soy Betty, la fea*) submitted a claim against Darset (a subsidiary of Dori Media) for copyright infringement. *Ugly Esti* was already in its third season and a brief look at the background to its inception proves illuminating. Although it is widely believed that *Ugly Esti* was a local adaptation of the original Colombian *telenovela*, *Yo soy Betty, la fea*, the Israeli *telenovela* was actually based on the 2000 Mexican remake *El amor no es como lo pintan* (*Love is not as they depict it* [TV Azteca, 2000–1]). Despite the Israelis having bought the rights to remake the Mexican version, RCN Television deemed *Ugly Esti* to have unofficially borrowed too many elements from the Colombian original (particularly the title), justifying court action. However, the case proved difficult to prosecute, as there was enough to distinguish the Israeli *telenovela* from the original Colombian version. For example, *Ugly Esti* was not structured like a daily *telenovela,* but more like the US weekly series, *Ugly Betty* (ABC, 2006–10). The narrative may focus on Esti Ben-David (Riki Blich), who, like Bea, is an intelligent but unattractive and unfashionable woman who wears braces on her teeth, oversized glasses and has curly, unruly hair; but, unlike her Colombian counterpart, she works not in fashion but, like her Mexican counterpart Alicia Ramírez Campos (Vanessa Acosta) in *El amor no es como lo pintan*, in advertising. Esti may fall in love and get her 'happy-ever-after' like Bea (and all the other Betties) but, like Alicia, she is already conducting an online flirtation with the vice-president of the company, Omer Rosenthal (Leon Rosenberg), the son of the playboy owner Tzvi Rosenthal (Oded Kotler). This narrative addition in fact gave *El amor* its reputation as a cross between the *telenovela Yo soy Betty, la fea* and 1998 Hollywood romantic comedy *You Got Mail* (Nora Ephron). The point, however, is how influential the *Yo soy Betty, la fea telenovela* has been on shaping contemporary storytelling, and rethinking fairytale romance mythology in particular, and, more importantly, how difficult it is to disentangle the original from adaptations and remakes as a consequence.

One factor that remains constant in each of the Betties is the importance of the father figure to the heroine, particularly when the mother is absent. Esti's father, Elvis Ben-David (Shaike Levi) is no exception, and is decidedly unhappy with the direction his daughter's professional life has taken. The Ben-Davids come from a lower-middle-class socio-economic background; Elvis is a retired police officer who lives with his new partner Ika (Nitza Shaul), an ex-convict. Esti's love affair with Omer, who is a member of the rich Israeli elite, combines global components of a Cinderella/Ugly Duckling story with a local one set in the midst of the Israeli social-ethnic split. It translates the Cinderella story, dare one say, into a redemptive Romeo and Juliet-type love affair: a girl of North African origin, Esti Ben-David, who falls in love with a man of European descent, Omer Rosenthal.

Popular Texts as Representatives of Culture and Society: The Israeli Case

Popular culture, as an institution, is an important site of education about ourselves and others (Esposito and Love 2008; Kellner 1995; Lipsitz

1998). Cultural critics regularly assert that it creates, as well as represents, cultural meaning and ideological understandings about race, gender, class and sexuality (Kellner 1995). In many ways representation not only reflects but also dictates significance. Some cultural commentators have suggested that since Barack Obama was elected President of the United States the media has increasingly used the term 'post-racial' to suggest that we have somehow entered a new age in which race is no longer an issue (we have moved beyond questions of race and race no longer structures our thinking or actions) (Esposito 2009: 521). While Obama's election may symbolize a new post-racial era in the USA, scholars such as Cornell West have argued that race matters and is 'America's most explosive issue and most difficult dilemma' (2004: 1). A more moderate claim is that the political and financial situation for people of colour is much better than it was 50 years ago (Jaynes and Williams 1989).

Ugly Esti was broadcast between 2004 and 2006 and moderately reflected ethnic and status conflicts within Israeli society. Such conflicts have in the past been represented in a sharp and stereotypical manner particularly in the *burekas* movie genre, popular during the 1960s and 1970s. The *burekas* movies are similar to the *telenovela* and based on stereotypical characters (poor/rich, male/female, North African/ European origin) chasing each other, but resolved in a happy ending with all financial, sexual and ethnic conflicts solved (Shohat 1989). Tension was introduced as a cultural-racial problem, often solved by inter-ethnic marriage among the younger generation. The optimistic endings created the illusion that inter-ethnic tensions can be neutralized, similar to the narrative resolution of the *telenovela* where the gap between classes is bridged through marriage. The *burekas* movies are mostly based on the ethnic conflict existing in Israel between the people of North African origin (e.g. Sephardim, those who immigrated from Arab countries and seemingly represent a faltering, primitive, inferior culture) and those of European ancestry (e.g. Ashkenazim, immigrants from Western nations who symbolize the Israeli cultural and financial elite) – and is a division dating back to when the new state of Israel was established in 1948 (Almog 1997). These ethnic differences were traditionally shown in movies in a ridiculous and highly stereotypical manner: the oriental figure was usually represented as poor, conniving and streetwise, in contrast to the rich, arrogant, impermeable and alienated European one. These ethnic conflicts are replicated in *Ugly Esti*, but are less extreme than those in *burekas* movies.

The two central families – the Rosenthals and Ben-Davids – represent the differences in class, ethnicity and status in Israel. The advertising office in which Esti works belongs to Zvi Rosenthal and his sons. Not only is the name Rosenthal of European extraction, but the family reside in a big villa in a rich and luxurious neighbourhood. Rosenthal's wife, Dina (Liora Rivlin), is a depressed and suicidal alcoholic. Needless to say, she does not work but lies around in bed drinking most of the time, giving the viewer ample opportunity to contemplate the size and grandeur of the family house. On the few occasions that she does leave home, she wears expensive, fashionable clothes, drives a large vehicle and radiates prestigious snobbery.

In complete contrast to the Rosenthals, the Ben-Davids are clearly representative of a lower class, their name leaving the Israeli viewer in no doubt about Esti's oriental roots. Her father Elvis and his new partner live in a small apartment house and their simplicity is emphasized by the casting of Shaike Levi in the role of Elvis and Nitza Shaul as Ika, his partner and Esti's eventual stepmother. Levi is a prominent Israeli comedian and was a member of the 'Ha'Gashash Ha'hiver' trio[2] whose work was seen to reflect folklore, often commenting on the gaps and differences between the Israel Ashkenazim and Sephardim. Levi and Shaul appeared in a 1976 comedy entitled, *Givat Halfon Eina Ona* (*Hill 'Halfon' Doesn't Answer*, Assi Dayan), which eventually became a cult movie.[3] Levi thus brings his status as a comedian to the father's character, granting a parodical-humorous interpretation understood only by Israelis. The Israeli oriental simplicity connected to the lower-middle class is always about the warm, smouldering family, mother's food, a conservative attitude towards women, and a deviousness that focuses on cutting corners and disregard for the law, especially rules and instructions that come from above.

The inter-family relationships are also based on stereotypical and ideological contrasts. *Ugly Esti* plays on Israeli notions that European familial ties are based on alienation that leads to unfaithfulness, lies and hypocrisy, while the families of Arabic origin enjoy loving, warm and supportive relations. Father Rosenthal is unfaithful to his wife and Dina busies herself only with intrigue in the home and beyond. The relationship between the brothers, Omer and Noam (Omer Barnea), involves jealousy, treachery and lies. The Ben-Davids, on the other hand, are a small family unit comprised of the father, Elvis, his partner Ika and Esti. The heroine may not live with her biological mother who is missing presumed dead,[4] but the Ben-Davids share love, closeness and care deeply for one another. Elvis is a devoted if not overprotective father. But his overprotection is justified in the narrative as it stems from deep love and genuine affection. The overwhelming message is that lower-class people may not have wealth or social standing, but enjoy warm and loving familial relations, whereas the elite may have money and status, but not close and heartfelt family ones. The connection between the two young people across the class divide is a trade-off, in which Omer grants Esti money and status while she offers personal happiness and a solid domestic life. The ideological message is that the lower class can climb the social ladder through marriage and bring value to society and culture. The series does not end in a wedding as is traditional in the *telenovela*, but it is clear that Esti has won Omer's heart.

Another value, no less important than the happy-ever-after marriage, is the myth of female beauty. Despite their long online flirtation Omer notices Esti only after she goes through a dramatic external change into a beautiful woman. She no longer wears braces or glasses, her hair is long and straight, and in the makeover episode she wears a tight, red dress that highlights her trim and well-toned form. The traditional notion of beauty is intertextually sustained through a combination of signs in media and society. Definitions of beauty can, of course, vary over time and between regions, but they are collectively represented by conventional codes and standards of feminine beauty, which in this case is denoted by a slim body and stylish dress, or what Jennifer Esposito defines as 'white, thin, upper-class, straight femininity' (2009: 527).

As in the Cinderella fairytale, the heroine wins love and success against the odds. Miller (2010: 205) explains that such universal stories are especially attractive when viewers can identify with the heroine. In this sense the story about an urban immigrant who achieves financial success and gains social status and romance in her new environment is especially popular where immigrants reside (Singhal and Rogers 1999: 36-9). This explanation is particularly pertinent to Israel, a relatively young nation-state only 63 years old. Until its establishment, the Ashkenazi people (those of European origin) made up 85 per cent of the Israeli population. Once the waves of immigration from Arabic countries began, the Ashkenazi population decreased to about 60 per cent (Almog 1997). Yet their demographic superiority increased the Ashkenazis' political and cultural hegemony, fostering an attitude of arrogance and patronage towards the 'faltering' oriental ethnic group. The inter-ethnic issue common to all the Betties, from Colombia to the USA, not only represents how the possibility of the American/Israeli dream can ultimately be fulfilled through marriage, but has more importantly transformed into a central and specific message in the Israeli text: the dream that through marriage women from all ethnic groups, even the Sephardim, can climb the social ladder and belong to the desired elite class – the Ashkenazi.

Works Cited

Esposito, Jennifer P., 'What Does Race Have to Do with *Ugly Betty*: An Analysis of Privilege and Postracial (?) Representation on a Television Sitcom', *Television & New Media*, vol. 10, no. 6 (August 2009), pp. 521–35.

——, and Love, Bettina, 'More Than a Video Hoe: Hip Hop as a Site of Sex Education About Girls' Sexual Desires', in Deron Boyles (ed.), *The Corporate Assault on Youth: Commercialism, Exploitation, and the End of Innocence* (New York: Peter Lang, 2008), pp. 43–82.

Jaynes, Gerald D., and Williams, Robin M. (eds), *A Common Destiny: Blacks and America Society* (Washington, DC: National Academy Press, 1989).

Kellner, Douglas, *Media Culture: Cultural Studies, Identity and Politics between the Modern and the Post-Modern*. New York: Routledge, 1995).

Lipsitz, George, *Dangerous Crossroad: Popular Music, Postmodernism and the Poetics of Place* (London: Verso, 1998).

Miller, Jade. L., 'Global Networks of Localized Content in the *telenovela* Industry', *Global Media and Communication*, vol. 6, no. 2 (2010), pp. 198–217.

Singhal, Arvind, and Rogers, Everett M., *Entertainment-Education: A Communication Strategy for Social Changes* (Mahwah, NJ: Lawrence Erlbaum, 1999).

Shohat, Ella, *Israeli Cinema: East/West and the Politics of Representation* (Austin: University of Texas Press, 1989).

West, C., *Democracy Matters: Winning the Fight against Imperialism* (London: Penguin, 2004).

Endnotes

1 Dori Media website: http://www.dorimedia.com/content.asp?page=history

2 The Ha'Gashash Ha'hiver was an entertainment band that was active for over 30 years, from the 1960s to the 1990s, and created a cultural pattern that influenced the Hebrew language and the Israeli lifestyle affecting almost every individual in Israeli society.

3 *Givat Halfon Eina Ona* is a satirical movie about the IDF after the 1973 war, which humorously criticizes the institution's high levels of bureaucracy and lack of organization.

4 Although her mother does return in the spin-off *Elvis, Rosenthal, VeHaIsha Hamistorit* [*Elvis, Rosenthal, and the Mystery Woman*] in 2005.

The Greek *Maria i Asximi*:
The Never-Ending Journey of a Myth

Betty Kaklamanidou

Maria i Asximi (*Maria the Ugly One* [Mega Channel, 2007–8]), the eighth adaptation of the Colombian *telenovela*, premiered in Greece on 1 January 2007, six years after *Yo soy Betty, la fea* (*I Am Betty, the Ugly One* [RCN, 1999–2001]) ended. The smart promotional campaign that ran in the weeks preceding the screening of the Greek pilot captivated audiences – expectations for the new show were high. The teaser proved ingenious. Airing every day for a few weeks before the start, it focused on Maria's point of view as she walked hesitantly around her new workplace meeting new colleagues. Seeing the shocked and horrified reactions of various characters, the audience could only speculate: how *ugly* was Maria? No one knew what she looked like. Even though the series' success was much anticipated as it followed the Mexican version, *La fea más bella* (*The Most Beautiful Ugly Girl* [Televisa, 2006–7]), the Greek audience had little idea of what to expect from the domestic adaptation. Viewers were not disappointed; and *Maria i Asximi* became the most popular show during its two-year run.

The original plan was that *Maria i Asximi* would be screened in the slot traditionally reserved for Greek soap operas – an early evening time period targeted primarily at children and women over 45 years old. The first season, however, broadcast much later, in primetime at 9 pm; while the second season moved to the earlier time of 7.15 pm as a lead-in to the 8 pm evening news. In a 2008 interview I conducted with Jo Frangou, one of the *Maria i Asximi* writers based at Mega Channel, she explained the reasoning behind the change: as the show debuted during the holiday season and with no other new programmes – neither from Mega nor the competition – the opportunity arose to put *Maria i Asximi* in a primetime slot with a view to eventually moving it to an earlier time of 7 pm after the summer. However, the steady and unexpected 40-per-cent rating rise allowed *Maria i Asximi* to keep its timeslot until the second season. According to Frangou, 'The transfer to 7.15 pm for the second season was at once a strategic move, since Mega could hold the first position without *Maria* in primetime; and secondly, a broadcast necessity as there were other series that were ready to air.'[1]

Whatever its time slot, *Maria i Asximi* proved immensely popular with audiences, and a worthy successor to the Colombian original. The experiences of Frangou and director Thanassis Tsaousopoulos are instructive of what went on behind the scenes and shed light on the processes involved in adapting and translating the Colombian *telenovela* for Greek audiences. Knowledge gleaned from the two interviews informs the first part of this chapter, while the second part explores the mythic subtexts running through *Maria i Asximi*. Utilizing the theories of Roland Barthes and Claude Lévi-Strauss, the chapter investigates the immense popularity of the show with particular focus on the myths that resonate in Greek culture.

Translating Colombian *Telenovela* into Greek Series

On Productions, one of the top three television production companies in Greece, originally purchased the rights to the Colombian *telenovela* from FremantleMedia. Frangou reported that once the deal was done, Mega became involved because the 'catchy' theme of the foreign format seemed to promise domestic success. Tsaousopoulos adds that Mega went ahead with the concept because market research and ratings data suggested that *Maria i Asximi* would be a solid and safe investment for them. Supported by Dermot Horan's remarks about the incontestable domination of 'the local soap opera … in most European territories' (2007: 113), it is possible to deduce that, as far as the television industry is concerned, Bea's transformation into Maria had less to do with the universality of the story than with contemporary TV business practice in a globalized capitalist market which looks to minimize risk. Low capital investment in a tried and tested (albeit foreign) concept allowed Mega to maximize returns rather than spend huge amounts of money on producing an original Greek series. Since the budget for any Greek production is tight, Alexandros Rigas, one of Greece's most successful television writers, playwright and actor, recommended neophytes Frangou and Rozi Riga as head writers because their salaries would be substantially lower than that of an A-list writer. Rigas initially took responsibility for the overall narrative structure of the Greek adaptation, but after the first months he left, leaving Frangou and Riga in charge of the dramaturgy.

According to Frangou, the Greek adaptation process proved 'adventurous'.[2] Not only were the two writers obliged to deliver 5 lots of 30 to 35 pages per episode per week for two different crews, but they knew little of the original *telenovela* as they rarely saw the Colombian scripts. In addition, the writers were consistently asked to keep location shoots to a minimum and to keep costs down, and there was never an opportunity for a second or third rewrite. Nevertheless, Frangou acknowledged that despite the restrictive working conditions and budgetary constraints, she and Riga enjoyed the experience, because they had absolute freedom with story, plot and character development. While the writers kept the basic premise intact, they altered and/or created new narrative features (characters, subplots) as the original contained elements that would not make sense for a Greek audience. After watching only a few episodes of the original *telenovela*, Frangou and Riga chose to omit several secondary characters they thought unnecessary and left out other elements they did not think would work in the Greek context. For example, neither Frangou nor Riga could understand the hostility faced by Betty because of her looks, and they were further shocked by the homophobic attitude towards the fashion designer Hugo Lombardi (Julián Arango – in the Greek version, Christo, played by Prodromos Tosounidis), which Frangou considers a result of Latin American machismo culture. These elements were modified in the Greek version to better speak of a domestic reality, while new subplots and characters were introduced depending on narrative requirements.

Another factor that partly explains the success of the original and its various adaptations, in contrast to most *telenovelas*, is that *Yo soy Betty, la fea* mixed comic elements with drama. This differed from the usual approach taken in the genre (Bignell 2004: 81) and constituted its modern evolution. Indeed, the Greek writers treated the original more as a romantic comedy than a conventional 'continuing drama' (ibid.) in the tradition of Brazilian *telenovelas*, and so incorporated comic elements into a traditionally dramatic format. More importantly, the metamorphosis of *Maria i Asximi* into a rom-com or dramatic romance (depending on the episode), along with its plot and the many issues it handled, had a significant effect on viewers and appealed to a much broader demographic as a consequence. Tsaousopoulos observed that turning *Maria i Asximi* into a comedy is rooted in his culture as Greeks prefer humour to drama and tend to turn even the most tragic event into something funny. The director concluded that it is through comedy that Greeks understand and critique themselves, as well as using the generic form to forget personal and social problems.

Another key factor in the successful Greek adaptation of the *telenovela* was casting. The production team initially wanted familiar faces in the lead roles, but settled instead for unknown actors. According to Tsaousopoulos, the team wanted someone with a completely fresh face to play the role of Maria. Several auditions were held, but it was not until a week before shooting that they cast Angeliki Daliani, along with Anthimos Ananadiadis in the role of Alexis Mantas. Of the casting, Tsaousopoulos adds that the production team avoided typecasting and chose instead those who looked ordinary, like someone living next door, rather than glamorous soap opera types (blonde, gorgeous women, or tall men with chiselled features). It is also worth noting that another reason the cast looked the way they did was to make visible the narrative realism of the show and facilitate a strong identification process.

The translation process from Colombia to Greece was enormously successful. Both Frangou and Tsaousopoulous credit the character of Maria for that success and while Frangou believes that it was Maria's identity as an 'outsider' that helped the audience identification process, Tsaousopoulos thinks it was her 'innocence, goodness, kindness and a little bit of naïveté [that] made us all search for our positive traits, those we had when we were kids and had to bury to survive' (2008). A closer examination of *Maria*'s structure, however, reveals a mythic subtext, a combination of the 'Ugly Duckling' and 'Cinderella' tales, which could account for the series' irresistible charm.

Anatomy of *Maria i Asximi*: A Transcendental Western Myth

As already stated, the story of *Maria i Asximi* remained close to the original *Yo soy Betty, la fea*. Like Beatriz Aurora Pinzón Solano, otherwise known as Betty (Ana María Orozco), Maria is intelligent, with two Masters degrees in finance. She lives with her adoring, if old-fashioned, parents, but is unable to secure a good job because of her appearance. Disheartened by prejudice and the often rude and insulting attitude of prospective employers, but encouraged by best friend Nicolas (Fotis Spyrou), a clearly overqualified Maria applies for a secretarial job at EcoModa. A major fashion house, EcoModa was established by Stefanos Manidas (Christos Nomikos and Yannis Evagelidis) and his wife Margarita (Ilias Labridou and Teti Shinaki)[3] but is now run by their son Alexis, one of Athens' most eligible bachelors and a notorious playboy, and recently engaged to Markella (Filitsa Kalogerakou), a dynamic, beautiful, but bossy and jealous woman. Alexis employs Maria as his personal assistant not only for her impressive résumé (which does not include a photo) but also because the only other candidate is his fiancée's best friend, Lillian Patrikarea (Ariel Konstantinidi) who he fears will spy on him. Maria soon finds herself having to conceal Alexis' various infidelities and lack of business acumen. In so doing, she quickly becomes indispensable to her boss but the sworn enemy of his fiancée, who is the first to suspect that Maria has romantic feelings for Alexis. Initially, Maria is 'rejected' by colleagues and treated with scorn by both her peers and superiors. She spends lonely moments crying in her little office but finds solace with her parents and Nicolas. Nevertheless, she never loses her kind heart or positive spirit and soon befriends her female colleagues. Moreover, it is through her ingenious plan to save EcoModa from bankruptcy and her close collaboration with Alexis that he finally sees the warm-hearted, sensitive woman behind the glasses and outdated clothes – and falls in love with her.

Maria i Asximi strictly adheres to the classic, three-act narrative structure, traced back to Aristotle and his seminal *Poetics*. Screen and television writer Christina Kallas-Kalogeropoulou notes that the Aristotelian structure denotes 'a complete, closed text with an unbroken unity and a calculated architectural design, as well as an entertaining ... and moral ... approach' (2006: 42). This narrative choice is widely used in mainstream Hollywood but is also employed in contemporary writing for television. Kallas-Kalogeropoulou claims that each episode of a TV series should convey 'the sense of a beginning, a middle and an ending, in other words, the sense of a complete story' (155) while simultaneously keeping the audience in a state of anticipation about what will happen next. *Maria i Asximi* conforms to this narrative structure. Each episode usually involves the dénouement of a simple plot while at the same time following Maria's narrative progress, her desire to be loved despite her appearance. Furthermore, it conforms to the basic narrative demands of the televisual, open-ended narrative by almost always leaving the audience with an unanswered question at the end of each episode.

The longer narrative trajectory of *Maria i Asximi,* however, held few surprises. Audience expectations were always that the glasses-wearing, moustache-bearing, thick eye-browed, insecure, awkward yet intelligent and good-hearted Maria would finally turn into a beautiful woman and realize her professional and personal dreams. After only watching a few scenes, it quickly became apparent that *Maria i Asximi* shared its central themes with other fairytales like 'The Ugly Duckling', 'Cinderella' and even 'Beauty and the Beast'.

So what explains this insatiable appetite for the same story? And why did Greek viewers keep tuning in day after day for two years if they knew how the story would end?

The answer is deeply rooted in the mythic qualities of the basic story premise. *Maria i Asximi* represents the 'eternal' myth of the persecuted and scorned outcast who blossoms, transforms and finally receives the respect, acceptance and love he/she deserves. The word eternal is put in inverted commas on purpose as, according to Roland Barthes (1979: 202), there may be ancient fables but no myth lasts forever as different cultures regulate and decide on the life and death of mythic language. Combining Barthes's view with Claude Lévi-Strauss's observation that 'the purpose of myth is to provide a logical model capable of overcoming a contradiction' (1963: 229) or 'the apparent resolution of a social conflict' (Stam, Burgoyne and Flitterman-Lewis 1992: 19), we can start to explain why Western society is not yet done with the 'Ugly Duckling' story; after all, cultures continue to 'categorize' people based on a specific set of rules (which vary over time) and tend to marginalize individuals who do not fit preset labels.

Furthermore, Barthes defines myth as 'a discourse ... a system of communication' (1979: 202–8). According to him, myth is a special system because it is a second-order, semiological one predicated upon an already existing semiological chain. For instance, in *Maria i Asximi*, this order is constructed as follows: the first sign (a concept/signifier and an image/ signified in the first system) is the ugly girl we see on our television and acknowledge as ugly Maria. The first sign is the 'literal' sign. We first see an ugly girl (signifier) and then we learn she is Maria (signified). In the mythic plane, however, ugly Maria becomes a signifier representing the signified ugliness and refers to those on the margins of society defined by unconventional appearance. In other words, on this second level, which is also known as the level of connotation, Maria acts a kind of 'index'.

This mythic subtext constitutes the basis of the *Maria i Asximi* narrative structure as well as its central appeal. Frangou admits that the series was rooted in the 'Ugly Duckling' and 'Cinderella' myths and stressed how, in a world filled with beautiful and assertive people, Maria's 'underdog quality', her kindness and childlike enthusiasm were the reasons viewers could not help but invest emotionally and desire to see her win. Tsaousopoulos adds that no matter how things change in our contemporary society, we continually return to these primitive myths that seem to run in our veins. Continuing, he observes that Maria possesses those positive traits of what Umberto Eco calls 'the mass superman',[4] with the difference being that she is an ordinary person. She may stumble over furniture, fall down and get hurt, and even suffer verbal insults, but Maria always finds the strength to go on. She finds solutions for everything and everyone, and in the end she teaches humanity to the 'bad' guys, transforming them into good ones. Anecdotally, during his many walks around Athens, Tsaousopoulos says that he encountered many young people who were once considered the school geeks or scared and shy Marias because they wore braces or glasses. For this reason he thinks that many people saw themselves in Maria, and this is why so many identified with her despite their own specific issues (awkward appearance, sexual orientation).

Maria i Asximi presents an intertextual play between fairytales and stories of the past and present, recycling a never-ending narrative that is still worth narrating in the twenty-first century. The 'Ugly Duckling' and 'Cinderella' subtexts, instantly recognizable and undeniably engaging, are the driving force behind the show, as they embrace a shared mythology of the Western world – one which still consists of cultures and societies that have difficulty in accepting diversity in appearance, behaviour or ways of thinking that are outside their own values and norms. According to Barthes, 'the role of the myth is to state and communicate, to explain and impose' (1979: 211). *Maria i Asximi* intended to spread the message that differences in outward appearance should be accepted and not laughed at. During the first season it succeeded in showing how Alexis fell in love with Maria despite her outward 'ugliness'. However, during the second season the rules of the myth dictated Maria's transformation and eventual integration into society with a good haircut, make-up and fashionable clothes. The higher ratings during and after her transformation prove that the audience wanted and anticipated this change. According to the AGB Nielsen Media Research database,[5] the series retained a weekly 30-per-cent share at the beginning of the second season, which increased to a striking 45 per cent after Maria's makeover.

Social Progress Meets Greek Neo-Conservatism: One Step Forward, Two Steps Back

Maria's narrative journey towards her final metamorphosis cannot be fully understood if not placed within its socio-political context insofar as, Jonathan Bignell points out, 'the meanings of television programmes are understood in relation to the cultural environment and expectations of viewers' (2004: 68). Betty travelled a long way from Latin America to re-emerge as Maria in Greece. The cultural background of Colombia, for example, is vastly different from that of Greece (despite both nations experiencing political scandal and corruption). Narrative adjustments were necessary if Maria was to be understood by the Greek audience – and may explain why neither the Mexican nor American versions found popularity in Greece.

Maria entered the homes of a small and troubled, neo-conservative country with a paradoxical attitude towards the United States. Greeks tend to blame the USA for everything that goes wrong domestically, because of a long, troubled political history involving American political and diplomatic intervention in the country. But, at the same time, Greeks do emulate the cultural trends coming from across the Atlantic – with music, movies and television, as well as fashion and ideals of beauty. Whereas US television is considered an example of what should be followed, intellectuals, critics and politicians more often than not attack Greek television as trash and not up to the task of entertaining and educating its audience. Despite comments that it deals only with social drama and has a negative outlook on life (Dambasis 2002: 231), reactions to *Maria i Asximi*, through its official Internet site, web forums (allowing teenagers to discuss the series and favourite characters),[6] video posts on YouTube, as well as articles in the print media, tell a different story. *Maria i Asximi* gave voice to underprivileged groups and addressed serious social issues, such as divorce and its effect on children, sexual harassment in the workplace, as well as the plight of single mothers. And this was despite the fact that it did so in a format that many in Greece deemed unworthy of scholarly attention, where the gap between 'high' and 'low' culture remains wide and the conservative cultural context privileges strict ethics and religious values, and is slow to accept change.

Maria i Asximi entertained and, at the same time, spread mainly positive messages about the sanctity of family, the importance of friendship, female solidarity, education and honesty, as well as the negative consequences of betrayal, cheating and duplicity. It was certainly not a subversive text. Nonetheless, it did acknowledge that Greek society has embraced positive influences, mainly concerning women and proving once again that 'it is often through television ... that women's issues have been most delicately and persuasively addressed' (Sayeau 2007: 59). Regrettably, however, the show also confirms that certain social norms will take much longer to change or adjust. For example, Greek men generally remain sexual or professional predators, homosexuality is tolerated, but only in certain social milieux, and uniformity and conforming to certain behaviours and appearance remains key to social integration. It should be noted that *Maria i Asximi* was produced in a broadcasting climate in which, in 2003, Mega had been fined €100,000 after it broadcast two men kissing in the primetime dramatic series, *Close Your Eyes* (2003–6). The Greek National Council for Radio and Television (NCRTV) considered the kiss a violation of broadcast ethics, and although the Council of State annulled the fine three years later, it is a good example of the continuing intolerance towards gay and lesbian rights in Greece. It explains, for example, why the representation of homosexuality in *Maria i Asximi* was stereotypical and focused on a single character, even though the narrative centred on the fashion world where homosexuality is accepted. Despite the fact that the gifted designer at EcoModa, Christo, is openly gay, and his sexual orientation is never treated as 'deviant' in the workplace at least, his histrionic and flamboyant behaviour (especially in the second season) did nothing but reinforce a televisual homosexual cliché – that of the two-dimensional cute, witty and cheerfully camp gay man – a non-threatening stereotype that the majority of the Greek audience is comfortable with. Frangou confirms this by saying that the writers 'preferred a stereotypical gay character, which would be played hysterically by Prodromos, and win the hearts and minds of the audience'. Finally and most importantly, while Maria's transformation closely followed the 'Ugly Duckling' script, it became a contradiction in itself by its implication that uniformity and conformity are the only ways to success and fulfilment. Not only did Maria become president of EcoModa (albeit under circumstances beyond her control) but her behaviour and demeanour also changed – gone was the clumsy young woman afraid to talk to her boss or even a waiter at the cafeteria – replaced instead with a fashionable, decisive and, more importantly, confident professional able to manage everything including confronting her old enemies and looking them straight in the eye.

Maria's Transformation: An Exclusively Female Affair

Since the series premiered in 2007, viewers anticipated the narrative culminating with the gauche, self-conscious heroine transforming into a beautiful and assertive woman. Rather than wait until the last episode, this moment arrived in the second season when ratings were high, which, in turn, allowed the network to postpone the narrative end. Maria's transformation took place during a business trip to Paris. Following revelations of the illegal plan she concocted to protect Alexis and the company from bankruptcy, Maria is forced to resign and accepts a job from Gina (Gina Alimonou), a public relations expert and the only person who has ever treated her with respect at work. Upon arrival in Paris, Maria once again finds herself immersed in the fashion world. Gina is preparing a show for a famous designer and Maria is taken on to help.

Unlike her colleagues in Greece, everyone in Paris treats her with respect and ignores her unglamorous appearance and awkward behaviour.

Maria's physical transformation took around three and a half weeks, beginning on Tuesday, 19 February (episode 212) and consisting of five different stages. First, her braces are removed; secondly, she buys new glasses after her old ones 'accidentally' break; thirdly, she buys a new wardrobe of fashionable clothes; fourthly, she goes to the hairdresser's; and, finally, she visits a beautician. Throughout her stay in Paris and during the gradual makeover, she remains clumsy, suspicious of everyone and prone to declarations of not belonging. Before her visit to the beautician (episode 228, which originally aired on Wednesday, 12 March 2008), she again sobbed to Gina that she did not want to go through the torture of becoming someone else. Her boss reassures her that the only difference will be the removal of unwanted facial hair which is naturally a torturous process played for laughs. Point of view shots punctuate the scene, echoing those from the series teasers, and used to create suspense for viewers. However, in the beautician scene, the point-of-view shots, a trademark of the series, intensify the claustrophobic and thriller-like ambience and slyly comment on what women must endure to uphold societal norms of feminine beauty.

The last step involves Maria's confrontation with Philippos (Manos Papagiannis), a Greek chef working in Paris who has been captivated by her inner beauty and good heart ever since they first met. The revelation of Maria as a beautiful swan is reminiscent of Julia Roberts in *Pretty Woman* (Gary Marshall, 1990). Just before Maria comes out of the bathroom, Gina leaves an expensive necklace on the bed for her, a gesture similar to that of Richard Gere's prior to Roberts' transformation from a street prostitute into a sophisticated woman. Furthermore, the moment Maria walks out of the elevator to meet Philippos, the soundtrack plays *She* by Eric Clapton, the title song of another Julia Roberts box office hit, *Notting Hill* (Roger Michell, 1999).

The scene of Maria's transformation ends with her walking in slow motion towards Philippos. The final reveal is the culmination of 228 episodes and more than 120 hours of viewing, and the protracted shot length allows both Philippos and the audience time to enjoy her metamorphosis into a beautiful woman. Despite the obvious allure of this, it is worth bearing in mind that the person behind Maria's makeover is not a man – but another woman. In keeping with the long tradition of fairytales, this benevolent woman has no ulterior motive when deciding to help Maria fulfil her potential. Gina is the archetypical fairy godmother, but with a modern twist. She may not give Maria the makeover with a magic wand, but she guides her in the right direction. Being a woman who has openly stated that she does not believe in marriage, Gina performs an act of sisterhood. First of all, she acknowledges Maria's professional abilities, hires her and takes her abroad; in a way, she is rescuing her from the 'ugliness' surrounding her at work and also taking her away from Alexis, the man who broke her heart. Although she is her boss, she treats Maria as an equal partner and a friend, takes her under her wing and shows her a new world, introducing her to people who embrace her as she is while boosting her young protégée's self-esteem through discussions, advice and a complete makeover. Gina's actions have significant connotations. On the one hand, they underline what can be achieved through solidarity among women and, on the other, they attack the norms of patriarchal hegemony, particularly in Greece, which dictate that a woman should only be transformed through the eyes or by the actions of a male suitor. The fact that *Maria i Asximi* treated Alexis (read: Prince Charming) as a secondary character and gave more television time to Maria, Gina and the other female characters must surely revise the meaning behind the 'Cinderella' myth – possibly calling for more female empowerment in Greece.

Are Foreign Formats the Future of Greek Television?

Yo soy Betty, la fea started a chain reaction and it is clear that its mythic structure resonated not only with a local Colombian but a global audience. It proved that in the era of globalization and proximity among nations, a television product could travel from one side of the globe to the other as long as it has a universal subject and promises substantial profit. More importantly, *Yo soy Betty, la fea* managed to question not only the omnipresence of American shows and formats in the global television market, but also the power of the Brazilian *telenovela* that traditionally dominated the countries of southern Europe (Bignell 2004: 81). More than half of the sitcoms and comedies Mega Channel has broadcast since the end of *Maria i Asximi* are based on foreign formats from different parts of the world: *I Polykatoikia* (*The Block of Flats* [2008–present]), recently green-lighted for a third season, is based on the Spanish, *Aqui no hay quien viva* (*No One Can Live Here* [Antena 2, 2003–6]), as is *Oikogenia Vlaptei* (*Family Hurts* [2009–10]), the Greek version of *La familia mata* (*The Family Kills* [Antena 3, 2006–9]). More than half of the series produced and broadcast by the three main private networks in Greece over the last three years have adapted foreign formats from Argentina, Canada, France and Denmark. Is this trend the future of Greek television?

For the foreseeable future, the answer is most definitely 'yes'. In the context of the recent financial (and political) crisis, one thing is for sure: as long as television executives are unwilling to invest in Greek productions because of higher costs and the continuous lack of prior marketing research and audience testing, and providing that the foreign formats keep advertisers and audiences happy, it will be a while before Greek television wins back its past autonomy. Tsaousopoulos was right when he predicted in 2008 that, for better or worse, *Maria i Asximi* started a trend that established new conditions in the television market with foreign concepts obtaining a significant part of the Greek television 'pie'. Despite originating in Colombia, the Greek *Yo soy Betty, la fea* will remain a point of reference, not only because of the influx of foreign formats in Greek television since 2007, but also because it showed that certain myths still have the power to capture the audience.

Works Cited

Aristotle, *Poetics,* trans. I. Sykoutris (Athens: Academy of Athens, 2004). (In Greek.)

Barthes, Roland, *Mythologies & Lesson*, trans. Kaiti Xatzidimou and Ioulietta Ralli (Athens: Rappa, 1979). (In Greek.)

Bignell, Jonathan, *An Introduction to Television Studies* (London: Routledge, 2004).

Dabasis, Giorgos, *Tin Epoxi tis Tileorasis* (Athens: Kastaniotis, 2002). (In Greek.)

Frangou, Jo, interviewed by Betty Kaklamanidou (Athens, 2008).

Genette, Gérard, *Palimpsestes, La littérature au second degré* (Paris: Seuil, 1982).

Horan, Dermot, 'Quality US TV, A Buyer's Perspective', in Janet McCabe and Kim Akass (eds), *Quality TV: Contemporary American Television and Beyond* (London: I.B.Tauris, 2007), pp. 111–17.

Kallas-Kalogeropoulou, Christina, *Screenplay. The Art of Narrative Invention in Film. 66 Exercises and 1 Method* (Athens: Patakis, 2006).

——, *Bio/Pic or the Life of Others, Script Development on the Basis of Biographical Material* (Athens: Patakis, 2009).

Lévi-Strauss, Claude, *Structural Anthropology* (New York: Basic Books, 1963).

Sayeau, Ashley, 'As Seen on TV: Women's Rights and Quality Television', in Janet McCabe and Kim Akass (éds), *Quality TV: Contemporary American Television and Beyond* (London: I.B.Tauris, 2007), pp. 52–61.

Radiotileorasi, no. 1830 (Athens: ERT editions.A.E, 10–26 January 2009). (In Greek.)

Stam, Robert, Burgoyne, Robert, and Flitterman-Lewis, Sandy, *New Vocabularies in Film Semiotics* (London: Routledge, 1992).

Tsaousopoulos, Thanassis, interviewed by Betty Kaklamanidou (Athens 2008).

Endnotes

1 All references to and quotes from Jo Frangou and Thanassis Tsaousopoulos are taken from interviews I conducted in 2008.
2 For reasons of confidentiality I cannot reveal some of the actual 'adventures' referred to here.
3 Both actors were replaced after the first two episodes.
4 The reference is to Umberto Eco's 1976 book of the same title.
5 http://www.agb.gr/gr/data/default.htm.
6 http://asximimaria.18.forumer.com/, http://clubs.pathfinder.gr/maria_asximi.

Czech *Ugly Katka*: Global Homogenization and Local Invention

Irena Carpentier Reifová and Zdeněk Sloboda

Since the 1990s, the Czech Republic has gone through a process of transformation. The country has advanced from an authoritarian regime to a liberal economy, where the post-socialist condition remains an influential discourse affecting how meanings are generated and fixed (Jakubowicz and Sukosd 2008). Implementation of the Columbian format of *Yo soy Betty, la fea* (*I Am Betty, the Ugly One* [RCN, 1999–2001]), which was adapted into a 73-episode serialization entitled *Ošklivka Katka* (*Ugly Katka* [TV Prima, 2008]), is a good example of how the combination of a social-realistic leitmotif with elements of fairytale and dramedy offers an opportunity to negotiate sensitive meanings concerning capitalism in a post-socialist world. In addition, it allows us to explore the dark side of the system, such as polarization and social difference, which Eastern European, neoliberal hegemonies present as the only viable and desirable social project. The basic assumption is that while Katka Bertoldová's (played by Kateřina Janečková) may come from a domestic world that appears ugly, the people living within it actually act beautifully, whereas her work environment is externally beautiful but is populated with people acting in ugly ways. The challenging intersections of some of the most effective 'engines' of this format,[1] as well as the issues related to a post-socialist agenda, motivate us to focus on oppositions like work/unemployment, social inequality/mobility, small private business/large corporations, and to study how Katka moves and mediates between these different worlds and what this movement could possibly mean.

Drawing on the fact that 'ugliness' is conspicuously and frequently articulated in relation to the socialist past, our main question relates to how meanings of 'ugly' and 'beautiful' are made visible within the narrative and how these meanings are linked to the broader post-socialist context of its reception. This framing is reinforced in an interview with the script editor of *Ošklivka Katka*, Valeria Schulczová:

> In the original story the rich people act differently and fit into a different social structure. The Czech Republic is more egalitarian, it has a strong middle class and a gap between the two ends of a social continuum is not so vast. The scissors of a social inequality had to be closed a little bit for the Czech version.[2]

To this end, our study explores the main narrative elements at work when indigenizing the story and domesticating cultural meaning. In drawing on the concept of 'cultural proximity', as emphasized by Joseph Straubhaar (2007: 197), the chapter specifies particular adjustments to the format with regard to the cultural and socio-historical context of contemporary Czech society.

Ošklivka Katka: The Production

The licence to produce and distribute an adaptation of *Yo soy Betty, la fea* was acquired by the Czech private broadcaster, Prima TV, from RCN Television S.A.[3] Prima TV adapted it and *Ošklivka Katka* was broadcast between March 2008 and April 2009, in 73 episodes. It was aired two episodes at a time, each lasting 50 minutes, per week, in primetime at 8 pm. In June 2008, transmission was interrupted by a football championship and, in July and August, Prima TV re-ran some old episodes. The scheduling pattern of two new episodes per week resumed at the end of August and, in October, TV Prima rescheduled *Ošklivka Katka* in primetime on Mondays. Ratings for the opening episodes reached 900,000 viewers, but they dropped to approximately 550,000 viewers. As a result, Prima TV abandoned further production and cut the number of episodes from 200 to 73.

The story is set predominantly in two environments: the poor Bertold family, living in a lower-class neighbourhood in Prague; and the wealthy Medunas, whose work is fashion. The Czech heroine, Katka's father František Bertold (Václav Vydra) is unemployed when the story starts and her mother, Zuzana Bertoldová (Jana Boušková), runs a shabby little grocery shop situated below their old-fashioned flat. Despite an excellent degree in economics, the desperately unattractive Katka loses her job in a bank because her superiors cannot compete with her intelligence. But a happy coincidence leads her to take up a secretarial job in the fashion company KM styl, as an assistant to the newly promoted, handsome, young director, Tomáš Meduna (Lukáš Hejlík). Katka must overcome many obstacles in the cruel world of glamour, particularly the constant criticisms of second secretary Patricia (Olga Lounová) and leading fashion designer Hugo (Lumír Olšovský). Despite numerous misfortunes, Katka slowly becomes acknowledged as indispensable, an economics expert and 'guardian angel' to Tomáš, whom she secretly loves. After a long and circuitous narrative, Katka, among other things, sets up a fictitious company as a cover for Tomáš's disastrous management of KM styl, and must deal with her boss pretending to fall in love with her to prevent her taking over his position. Katka's eventual makeover from ugly duckling to beautiful swan allows Tomáš to realize finally that he truly loves her and that she should be the company's new president. Like the other Betties, it is a familiar tale. But *Ošklivka Katka* also reveals further narratives of contemporary history and political transition, making it a prime example of how the global may absorb the local and how the popular may converge with the political.

Ošklivka Katka as an Element of the 'Glocalization Debate'

Our inquiry into specific post-socialist 'vernacularization' of the format is an extrapolation of a more general dilemma about a relationship between local invention and global homogenization of media products travelling in globalized flow(s).[4] It is widely recognized that globalization can endorse contradictory tendencies and produce diversity as often as homogeneity. Roland Robertson, with his treatise on 'glocalization', was among the first to popularize this point (Robertson 1995: 25–44). David

Morley and Kevin Robins see the ambiguity of globalization directly in television programming: 'As an antidote to the internationalization of programming, and as compensation for standardization and loss of identity that is associated with global networks, we have seen a resurgent interest in regionalization in Europe.' (1995: 17) Silvio Waisbrod refers to the 'Janus-faced' television industry (2004: 367), while others think that formats have the potential to support national programming in a local culture where canned shows (original series, either dubbed or unaltered) would have little appeal (Beeden and de Bruin 2009: 3).

International communication exchange has not always been understood as a process that includes adjustment to local cultures, however. Early perspectives of so-called cultural imperialism as debated by Herbert Schiller (1971) or Armand Mattelart (1984), for example, assume that the more powerful North and West regions imposed their values and cultural patterns on weaker, nation-based cultures in the South and East. This is supposed to happen through a one-way flow of mass communication with a language-independent television as its leading force (Tomlinson 2002). However, this thesis of early cultural imperialism underwent revision in the 1980s and 1990s. Strong Latin American and Indian television and film productions motivated scholars to propose the concept of 'contra-flow' (or reversed flow), which describes how mainly Brazilian and Mexican *telenovelas* were disseminated in the USA and some European countries (Biltereyest and Meers 2000: 394).

A further challenge to cultural imperialism emerged when Eastern European television markets opened up to the global circulation of international television shows. The new post-socialist markets offered scholars the opportunity to look for examples of a new wave of systematic bias towards foreign tastes and imperialist values. Despite the intellectual élite assuming the Americanization of television programming, studies in the Czech Republic have not discovered a massive surrender of local cultural preferences, which led to the cessation of this kind of research (Štětka 2007: 168). The way Eastern European television markets operate also helps to make oversimplifications in discourses on cultural imperialism visible; for example, if Columbian television sells a programme format to Czech television, is this a flow or a contra-flow? Which element is dominant and which is on the periphery of this transaction? What matters more in the television formats business – the fact that formats promote certain global sameness and homogeneity, or the fact that they allow for considerable regional distinctiveness? In further analyses of highly glocalized, post-socialist motifs in *Ošklivka Katka* we want to show that formats really do provide space for indigenous modifications.

Global and Local Chains of Equivalence in *Ošklivka Katka*

Serials and series have been a mainstay of Czech (formerly Czechoslovak) television production since the end of the 1950s (Reifová 2009). However, socialist and post-socialist programmes differ significantly in the ways that, for example, work and wealth are articulated or disarticulated. Unlike the old propagandist serials produced by communist television, 'in the new "capitalist" serials physical manual work is remarkably absent. ... Otherwise invisible work is made present only through its effects: wealth and social status' (Reifová 2008: 303). Negotiation of the meanings associated with gaining property, new class differences and social inequality – in a sense a kind of economic determinism – is an important paradigm in *Ošklivka Katka*.

The main organizing principle of the *Ošklivka Katka* narrative is the movement between conflicting oppositions. One of the basic engines of this particular global format is the conflict between two different worlds. It contrasts the world of interior goodness and outward ugliness (Bertolds) with the external beauty but inner lack of morality (Medunas). In the Czech adaptation this fundamental division is further emphasized by specific post-socialist elements that stand for economic transformation and the nation's contemporary history.

Effective tools that help us to see the construction of the counter-position of the two worlds can be found within discourse theory. For example, Ernesto Laclau and Chantalle Mouffe's notion of a 'chain of equivalence' (1985: 127–9) is of particular relevance: particularly, the idea of a discursive practice 'through which some possibilities of identifications are put forward as relevant while others are ignored' (Jorgensen and Phillips 2002: 44). In other words, the chain of equivalence articulates social elements that do not naturally belong to each other and could also be interconnected differently. In the case of the narrative of *Ošklivka*

Katka, it reveals the principal mechanism by which the global pattern is supplied with local meanings and particularly what happens when linking new (local, post-socialist) elements to already existing global chains and making them into new coherent wholes.

In the original global version, there is a core chain of equivalence in operation – the unprivileged world of inner beauty and outer ugliness is linked with poverty and the privileged world with wealth. This can be defined as the universal, global chain of equivalence in which identifications of ugliness/good character/poverty and beauty/ bad character/wealth are put forward. Our main point is that, in the Czech version, there is also a second level of equivalence that is added in the process of local adaptation. This level adds another systematically articulated element to the global chain – it is the presence/absence of a socialist past in visual and/or narrative dimension. The Czech adaptation takes up the global chain of equivalence and extends it with one added local element in both its branches. In the local version of the story, the unprivileged world is not only poor, but its poverty is amplified by many different links to socialism, its heritage and the iconicity of its life-style. Moreover, the global articulation of ugliness, good character and poverty is expanded upon with a tight linkage to socialist history. On the other hand the privileged and coherent world of beauty, bad character and wealth is totally immersed in the new era of capitalism, which is strictly disconnected from the nation's socialist past.

	diagetic world		global equivalence	local equivalence
	outside	inside		
Bertold family	ugly	pretty	poor	**associated** with socialist past
Meduna family	pretty	ugly	wealthy	**dissociated** from socialist past

Double history: 'We had special tools in the 1970s factory ...'

The capitalist world and the lower-class environment have different temporal characteristics created by specific history. The rich people connected to the Medunas do not have a past beyond 1989, no tradition back to the 'old times' of the socialist regime. In episode 7 old Meduna refers to the foundation of the company 18 years earlier (early 1990s) as the furthest point in time – no reference is made to how the rich characters in the serial lived or what they did before that time. In the case of the poor Bertold family, however, there are several connections with socialism and its everyday life. The concept of Katka's 'ugliness' is, for example, based on numerous references to ladies' fashions in the badly supplied socialist market. A good marker of how Katka's styling draws upon 'socialist' appearance is her similarity to Anna from a 1988 realist television serial *Boys and Men Chlapci a Chlapi* (*Boys and Men* [Ceskoslovenská Televize, 1988]).

Katka's hair and eyebrows are shaggy, a slight moustache can be detected on her upper lip; she wears big, old-fashioned glasses, braces on her teeth and no makeup. Her clothes are also rich with meaning. Katka is generally more warmly and sensibly dressed than the other female characters, she wears low heels, thick tights and heavy, below-the-knee-length skirts or ill-fitting dresses. From episode 38 on Katka acquires new glasses that are even bigger and uglier than the old pair, but she wears them because they are a gift from her father – the naive, unemployed do-gooder, František – who is the strongest link to the past for the Bertold family. Even though František lost his factory job after decades of loyal service, he still feels nostalgic for his work. He drives a rusting old Skoda 120, which is nowadays seen as an artefact that epitomizes Czechoslovak socialism, and he continues to find it difficult to establish his place in the new, harsh, capitalist world.

The Bertolds' flat and lifestyle are permeated with reminders of a socialist past, such as the food and clothes. Material signifiers of the past are not simply ahistorical props with purely aesthetic functions, but signs of lifestyle and objects of consumption turned into important points of historical reference within a process of resurrecting socialist memories in a post-socialist era. This material form of post-socialist nostalgia is frequently referred to as reification, or fetishization of the past (Reifová 2009: 64), although it can be interpreted as a cultural compensation for dislocated memory. For example, in the first episode the Bertolds eat bread and marmalade for breakfast, and in episode 2 the family enjoys a simple soup with Nataša (Liliana Malkina), an old, unkempt Ukraine woman.[5]

The equipment in the flat dates back to the 1970s and 1980s, as does the music that the family listens to. They live in Vystrkov, a fictional place located in the Prague neighbourhood of Žižkov.[6] Vystrkov is an isolated and unsightly suburb, with paint flaking off the houses, and populated by lower-class people, small-business (wo)men, retirees, unemployed street accordionists and young people represented by nerds such as Katka's friend Miky (Vojtěch Štulc), or skateboarders and graffiti artists. The Bertolds' life thus has clear connections to objects or patterns of behaviour inherited from the modest, underdeveloped, socialist past. The principal of profit and economic growth has not affected the Bertolds, nor has it impacted on their living standards or immediate environment. According to Jeremy G. Butler (2009: 139), set design has a narrative function of its own and serves as objective correlatives or symbols. Katka's mother may run several small businesses (a shabby grocery store, and later an Internet café), but the Bertolds are not motivated by the accumulation of capital. The family places more emphasis on sustainability than on progress, on community benefits rather than on individual merits. All these qualities are presented in a package with the retro elements of their living and clothing style linking the Bertolds more to a socialist past than a competitive capitalist present.

In contrast, the world of the wealthy Medunas has no bond with the 'primitive' socialist past. The family enjoys a flamboyant lifestyle, as if the socialist past had never existed: old objects and memories of bygone times are absent in their world. Visual ugliness in the serial is articulated through poverty – we rarely encounter it in the rich, capitalist world. The fashion designer, Hugo, remarks that the seedy, ugly outfits worn by Katka (episode 1) and later Nataša (episode 28) make him feel physically sick. The ugliness of the poor people who surround the Bertolds and populate their world is often emphasized by physical malformation. Nataša from the Ukraine (a direct reference to the former USSR) is missing some of her front teeth, and a homeless character who socializes in the family shop is blind. Tomáš´s girlfriend, Marcela (Michaela Horká), shows unerring social intuition when she recognizes Katka as an alien, somebody, who 'belongs to another category and you cannot drag her in among us' (episode 17). The worlds of richness/beauty and poverty/ugliness have two distinct histories belonging to different durations. 'Beautiful' people live in a world defined by a new and clear-cut beginning initiated in the early 1990s; 'ugliness' often draws its meaning from its continuity with the socialist past. Katka's transgression between the worlds of poor/ ugliness and affluent/beauty is underlined by the shift in her manners and tastes. In episode 6 she struggles (unsuccessfully) to eat sushi in an up-market restaurant; in episode 61 she has become a gourmet, and invites her parents to eat sushi at the same restaurant (where her father wants to complain about having been served raw fish).

Double Capitalism: Drudgery and the Shiny World

The beautiful/wealthy world is essentially rooted in the new capitalist business environment of the fashion clothing company and its glamorous lifestyle. Although the way that the entrepreneurialism of KM styl is presented differentiates between two generations of capitalism: the company's founding fathers (Meduna and Konečný) (Ladislav Frej) and the 'greenhorns' Tomáš Meduna and Daniel Konečný (Petr Štěpán). The story suggests that fair and useful capitalism is possible, but that it vanished with the 'founding fathers'. (Old Konečný dies in a car crash and old Meduna is about to retire.) The older generation is depicted as honourable entrepreneurs who pursued genuine values and were interested in the substance of business, while the next generation of capitalists (Tomáš and Daniel) care only about superficial glitz, glamorous lifestyles and luxurious façades. In episode 1 Tomáš enthusiastically shows his father the new designer desk he bought to replace the old one his father used, confirming that the son cares more about image than the core values of the business his father started. In contrast with the older generation, representing a capitalist sensibility based on protestant work ethics and an aesthetic life, the younger one does not share the same values, instead requiring visible signs and signifiers of status. Tomáš and his rival Daniel never stop fighting over the position of the company's president, for example. In episode 7 old Meduna scolds them for attacking each other and contrasts their priorities with the values held by the old generation of company managers – he reminds them that he and his best friend Konečný (Daniel's father) used to fight over who would *not* be president.

The two layers of capitalism reference the shift from a utopian to a dystopian socio-economic imagination in post-socialist Czech developmental discourse. Economic transformation started as a dream about performance-based justice in a capitalist economy that brings welfare and rewards to those who work hard. Overcoming artificial equality, in the aftermath of the socialist project, was important immediately after 1989 – all primetime television serials produced by public television in the 1990s dealt with privatization and the acquisition of wealth and additional properties (a castle, farm, hotel, hospital, florist's studio) (Reifová 2008: 303). Capitalist renewal was first grasped as a renaissance of real, authentic work that brings people closer to the economic principle. Only later did post-socialist society start to realize how important image, symbolic capital, the logo principle and the simulacra of the capitalist spectacle are. The shift from the old generation of hard-working manufacturers (old Meduna and old Konečný) to that of their hedonist sons (Tomáš and Daniel) refers to this shift from authenticity to superficiality, from fantasies dominated by production to the prevalence of consumption. What is even more important is that this capitalist schism is not framed as an irreversible dislocation. The gap between a generation of authenticity and that of image-making closes at the end and the unifying, reconciling agent is – as is usual in the series – Katka. Throughout the narrative, she epitomizes hard work, diligence and austerity. Such characteristics make her a kindred spirit to the old father Meduna and together they open Tomáš's eyes to where real value lies. Both forms of capitalism are shown to have strong managerial and business features and bridge a return to the healthy grassroots of the system which, in turn, refers to a post-socialist fantasy that sees the new economic order as a final and effective solution that cannot be altered.

The polarized environments of the rich Medunas and the poor Bertolds differ radically in terms of how work and the fruits of 'labour' are represented. The poor are always shown as doing 'hard' jobs requiring great physical effort that is not well rewarded. Jobs of the rich working in KM styl are, in contrast, often not visible; characters refer to a huge workload in the dialogue before (or after) a job has been completed, but the actual 'work' is rarely depicted. In the capitalist world, it is sometimes difficult to distinguish work from leisure with the borders between them being somewhat porous. The work of KM styl managers blurs with socializing and flirtation, as in episode 8 when Tomáš's friend Marek (Michal Zelenka) and Patricia meet after work in her modern, kinky apartment with the consultation soon turning into a sexual encounter. That same night, Katka and Miky (Vojtěch Hádek) develop a business plan, working through the night in Katka's bedroom with her mother supplying bread and glasses of milk to keep them going. In episode 13 Tomáš confuses work with a bowling competition, and in episode 24 he uses his workplace for an erotic encounter with a model. The rich Medunas talk about work and enjoy its rewards more than they are seen doing it. Upper-class work is mostly apparent through its indirect manifestations: profit (the Meduna's London residence or weekend house, in episode 61), duration (Tomáš and Marek work long hours on their papers, aided only by the light of a lamp in episode 8), related stress (Katka almost collapses after the alleged loss of data in episode 17) or responsibility (Tomáš and Marek use a dishonest supplier and almost drive the company into bankruptcy in episode 45). Lower-class labour is repeatedly constructed as involving hard work and physical drudgery. Mrs Bertold runs a small grocery and she is often heaving crates and boxes around the shop. Sometimes she complains about being exhausted or too tired as a result of her daily exertions, for example in the first episode she refuses dinner as she is too tired and later in the series she cries about the drudgery of shop work.

Specific demonstrations and definition of work are also connected to Katka. Although she is appointed as a secretary, she is a highly skilled businesswoman with a first class degree in economics as well as a PhD Christine Gledhill argues that the world of soap opera is characterized by structural oppositions and differences (2003: 362), in accordance with structuralist principles in which signs bear meaning only in relation to others (Danesi 2002: 39). Meanings contained within the character of Katka are created through the tension between her striking intelligence and an unattractive body. But Katka's intelligence and cleverness have an exact specification – equated with her ability to analyse finance and understand how the market operates. To underpin Katka's expertise, the scriptwriters often let her use specialist language and jargon. In episode 1 she introduces herself at the job interview as a person who masters 'financial database systems' and studies 'principles of the stock exchange business'. Katka's economic skills are also highly valued by her parents. Her father is proud of her abilities and believes strongly that 'she will go far' (episode 8). When Katka undergoes her 'transformation' in the last episode, not only does she become the beautiful swan, she also obtains a job as a financial executive officer in KM styl. Her parents receive the news with tears of joy as they chant: 'we have a daughter-director; we have a daughter-director ...' Quite simply, in the Czech version the main character's professional highlights are a talent for commercial transactions and an ability to enhance material estates or increase profits. It can be read as post-socialist enchantment with the market and uncritical worship of the skills that enable a neo-liberal economy to operate.

Social inequality is expressed strongly through scenes of material equipment in the worlds of the rich and poor. Surfaces speak, and meanings of difference are embedded in easily observable signifiers of misery and luxury. As well as ugliness, poverty is constructed through references to objects dating back to the times before the establishment of the free market at the beginning of the 1990s. As already discussed, the Bertolds' apartment is homely rather than elegant, furnished with items clearly from another era. The epicentre of the home is the kitchen, the room where the family gathers, where handmade tablecloths and other tasteless decorations predominate. The kitchen is not only cosy, but is also where various kinds of work take place (cooking, preparing things for the grocery store, doing the accounts, etc.). The heart of Tomáš and Marcela's apartment is the smart living room/bedroom. This space houses a double bed – sometimes covered with red satin bedclothes. Here, the emphasis is on pleasure and bourgeois vanity. The poor are set in a working kitchen, the rich in a voluptuous bedroom.

Throughout the series, images of class difference support an assumption that the worlds of the rich and poor are incompatible. Tomáš's parents look different from Katka's. They are always well groomed; his father is elegant and always sports a pocket-handkerchief and silk scarf, his mother wears mostly smart suits. The Medunas live in elegant houses, classic and expensive. (The London bedroom has a wooden-framed bed and white linen sheets. The weekend house is in a quiet street, with white picket fencing; their Prague flat has heavy curtains, gilt-framed pictures, French windows.) KM styl headquarters resides in a skyscraper in the business district and there are frequent shots of this tall building taken from below. Katka's first line in the series underlines her feelings of inferiority towards the company installed in this authoritative building – 'I knew the house was big – but I didn't know it was that big!' – confirming Hodge and Kress' argument that equilibrium (or its disruption) between subordinates and super-ordinates can be visually realized by (disruption of) symmetrical composition (Kress and Leeuwen 2006: 81).

An important way in which social class difference is represented is in an awareness of inequalities, presented only in the consciousness of the poor. They reflect on their problematic social position and are aware that their career paths differ from those of the rich; the rich take for granted their high standard of living and pay little attention to the alternative. In episode 1 a local in Vystrkov rides his skateboard and Katka tells him to be careful not to fall: 'Here, in Vystrkov, we all fall down and then get on our feet again.' In episode 13 Katka's parents acknowledge their lowly position and express anxiety that Katka will find a wealthy boyfriend in KM styl. In episode 28 Katka's mother watches a television broadcast of KM styl's fashion show and, overcome with emotion, almost weeps watching the glamour of the evening.

In some scenes where the characters play with images of their poor/rich identities and challenge them (are challenged by them), class difference is made to produce meaning in these moments of transgression. In episode 28 Péťa (Vojtěch Hádek) (the messenger and driver, occupying the lowest level in the company hierarchy) takes up chief fashion designer Hugo's directorial position during rehearsals for a fashion show. Péťa later crawls up the stage and marches self-confidently, parodying the patronizing, authoritative behaviour of the company powerbrokers. Péťa, being powerless, performs the transgression in playful style, creatively mocking power, in keeping with Mikhail Bakhtin's (2007) conception of the carnivalesque or John Fiske's (1988) theories of excorporation and popular resistance. Tomáš also finds himself in a situation where the image of his identity is challenged (episodes 42 and 43). Gay Hugo makes Tomáš wear a mask and go to a homosexual party dressed as Marilyn Monroe. On escaping, Tomáš ends up at Katka's house, where he borrows some of her father's outdated and worn-out clothes. However, Tomáš finds no pleasure in this 'travesty': on the contrary, he is irritated and worried about his reputation and loss of authority.

Summary: Katka as a Heroine of a Utopian Capitalism

Among the peculiarities of the two different worlds sketched above there is one component that continuously travels between the two poles and connects both – Katka herself. She is part of the ugly/good/poor world, but is the only character from this environment who has access to the beautiful/bad/rich world. She is a 'medium' communicating between two worlds, enabling comparisons and holding up a mirror to both. Katka is a typical popular heroine on a quest – a journey that takes her from one place to another (van Zoonen 2005: 109). The concept of a change or makeover from ugly duckling to beautiful swan is ever present. The Bertolds' shabby grocery store is renovated into an Internet café. The unemployed father becomes a freelance accountant. Tomáš changes from a cynical womanizer into a reformed sinner. Mervart (Josef Carda), the former accountant, changes from a fraud into a 'nice guy' who knows that money cannot buy love. Clearly it is not only Katka who is affected by the principle of change. It is omnipresent and works in both directions, as both worlds must change. The rich/beautiful world cannot stay as it is on the inside and the ugly/poor world cannot remain as it is on the surface. Katka operates as a 'medium', a moderator enabling circulation. She helps each world take the best from the other. The ugly world becomes nicer as she relinquishes her ugly duckling exterior and the beautiful world becomes morally reformed as Tomáš learns his lesson and starts to see real virtues instead of the superficiality of mere image-making. Post-socialist Czech adaptation eventually stages capitalism as a utopian land, which, if something goes wrong, allows for a return to its healthy and strong grassroots.

And the utopian equilibrium itself is established by the means of capitalist mentality – the exchange of beauty and goodness between the poor and wealthy worlds follows the pattern of profitable transaction. The exchange is personified in and arranged for by Katka and therefore we define Czech *Ugly Katka* as a heroine of a utopian capitalism.

Works Cited

Bakhtin, Mikhal, *Francois Rabelais a lidová kultura středověku a renesance* [*Francois Rabelais and the Popular Culture of the Middle Ages and the Renaissance*] (Praha: Argo, 2007).

Beeden, Alexandra, and de Bruin, Joost, 'The *Office*: Articulations of National Identity in Television Format Adaptation', *Television & New Media*, vol. 11, no. 3 (2010), pp. 3–19.

Biltereyest, Daniel, and Meers, Phillip, 'The International *telenovela* Debate and the Contra-flow Argument: A Reappraisal', *Media, Culture & Society*, vol. 22, no. 4 (2000), pp. 393–413.

Butler, Jeremy, G., *Television: Critical Methods and Applications* (Mahwah, NJ: Lawrence Erlbaum Associates, 2009).

Castelló, Enric, Dobson, Nichola, and O'Donnell, Hugh, 'Telling It Like It Is? Social and Linguistic Realism in Scottish and Catalan Soaps', *Media, Culture & Society*, vol. 31, no. 3 (2009), pp. 467–84.

Danesi, Marcel, *Understanding Media Semiotics* (London: Arnold, 2002).

Dorfman, Ariel, and Mattelart, Armand, *How to Read Donald Duck: Imperialist Ideology in the Disney Comic* (New York: International General, 1984).

Fiske, John, *Television Culture* (London: Routledge, 1988).

Gledhill, Christine, 'Genre and Fender: The Case of Soap Opera', in Stuart Hall (ed.), *Representations: Cultural Representations and Signifying Practices* (London: Open University Press, 2003), pp. 337–83.

Hall, Stuart, 'The Work of Representation', in Stuart Hall (ed.), *Representations: Cultural Representations and Signifying Practices* (London: Open University Press, 2003), pp. 13–63.

Jakubowicz, Karol, and Sukosd, Miklos, *Finding the Right Place on the Map: Central and Eastern European Media Change in a Global Perspective* (Exeter: Intellect, 2008).

Jorgensen, Marianne, and Phillips, Louis J., *Discourse Analysis as Theory and Method* (London: Sage, 2002).

Kress, Gunther, and Leeuwen, Theo, *Reading Images: the Grammar of Visual Design*, (London and New York: Routledge, 2006).

Laclau, Ernesto, and Mouffe, Chantalle, *Hegemony and Socialist Strategy* (London: Verso, 1985).

Moran, Albert, 'Configurations of the New Television Landscape', in Janet Wasko (ed.), *A Companion to Television* (London: Blackwell, 2005), pp. 291–307.

——, and Kean, Michael, 'Television's New Engines', *Television & New Media*, vol. 9, no. 2 (2008), pp. 155–69.

Morley, David, and Robins, Kevin, *Spaces of Identity: Global Media, Electronic Landscapes and Cultural Boundaries* (London: Routledge, 1995).

Reifová, Irena, 'Cult and Ideology: Serial Narratives in Communist Television. The Case of the Czechoslovak Television Serial Production of 1959–1989', in Nico Carpentier, Pille Pruulmann-Vengerfeldt, Kaarle Nordenstreng, et al. (eds), *Democracy, Journalism and Technology. New Developments in an Enlarged Europe* (Tartu: Tartu University Press, 2008), pp. 295–306.

——, 'Rerunning and "Rewatching" Socialist Television Drama Serials: Post-Socialist Czech Television Audiences between Commodification and Reclaiming the Past', *Critical Studies in Television*, vol. 4, no. 2 (2009), pp. 53–71.

Robertson, Roland, 'Glocalization. Time-Space and Homogenity-Heterogenity', in Scott M. Lasch, Mike Featherstone and Roland Robertson (eds), *Global Modernities* (London: Sage, 1995) pp. 25–44.

Schiller, Herbert, *Mass Communication and American Empire* (Boston: Beacon Press, 1971).

Štětka, Václav, *Mediální integrace národa v době globalizac* (Brno: International Institute of Political Science of Masaryk University, 2007).

Straubhaar, Joseph D., *World Television: From Global to Local* (Los Angeles: Sage, 2007).

Tomlinson, John, *Cultural Imperialism: A Critical Introduction* (London: Continuum, 2002).

van Zoonen, Lisbeth, *Entertaining the Citizen. When Politics and Popular Culture Converge* (New York, Toronto and Oxford: Rowman & Littlefield, 2005).

Waisbrod, Silvio, 'McTV: Understanding the Global Popularity of Television Formats', *Television & New Media,* vol. 5, no. 4 (2004), pp. 359–83.

Endnotes

1   Moran and Keane (2008: 156) use the term 'engine' to refer to innovations that have 'added value to television's bottom line at a time when conventional "finished production" genres are losing audience support because of strong competition from personalized media technologies'. In our opinion the term can be applied to any licensed content production technology. In the case of *Yo soy, Betty la fea*'s format (as traded by RCN Television S.A.), the 'engines' may, for example, be the social positions of the main characters (lower class versus high society) or the predominant environment (the fashion industry).

2   Interview with the script editor Valeria Schulczova on 25 June 2009. Transcription of the interview – archive ir.

3   Prima TV is a generalist channel which was launched in the Czech Republic in 1993. The licence is held by the broadcasting company, FTV Prima Ltd, owned by the Swedish media group, Modern Times Group MTG AB, onnline at: http://mavise.obs.coe.int/channel?id=44#section-2 (accessed 9 July 2009). Prima TV average rating in prime time in 2008 was 17.4 per cent (online at: http://www.ato.cz/ [accessed 9 July 2009]).

4 Format, according to Moran, is the 'set of invariable elements in a programme out of which the variable elements of an individual episode are produced' (2005: 296).

5 Realistic reproduction of culinary habits is also confirmed, for example by Castelló, Dobson, O'Donnell (2009: 467).

6 The literal meaning of 'Vystrkov' in Czech is something like 'in the middle of nowhere'.

Glamorously (Post) Soviet: Reading *Yo soy Betty, la fea* in Russia

Elena Prokhorova

Don't look, don't you look around
Stay just the way you are,
Remain yourself.
The whole universe will shine through your eyes
If love lives in your heart.

Be Not Born Beautiful/ Ne Rodis' Krasivoy, the song by Iulia Savicheva

The theme song addressing the awkward, bespectacled Russian Betty – Katya Pushkareva (Nelly Uvarova) – urges her not to look and to ignore the derision and judgemental stares of the new Russian elites. But not to look – for her and for us – is impossible: the sleek title sequence of the show displays the seductive pleasures of Moscow, the face-lifted, capitalist metropolis and the most expensive city in the world· (Sahadi 2007). Can this girl feel at home amidst the neon streaks of car lights, the rotating glass doors of modern skyscrapers, IKEA-styled offices and condos? And what if love, instead of illuminating the world, is just one more privilege of that glossy world, reminding you that you *are* an outsider? The globally circulating *Yo soy Betty, la fea* (*I am Betty, the Ugly One* [RCN, 1999-2001]) provided the Russian viewers with a format that gave positive answers to both questions, 'overcoming' class, economic and social conflicts of post-Soviet society via a healthy portion of comedy and a heavy dose of melodrama along the way.

The Russian version of *Yo soy Betty, la fea*, *Ne rodis' krasivoy* (*Be not Born Beautiful* [2005–6]) – the first part of the proverb 'be not born beautiful, but be born lucky' – premiered on 5 September 2005 on the STS channel. The Russian *telenovela*, possibly the closest and most faithful adaptation of *Yo soy Betty, la fea*, was a product of the co-operation between the A-Media studio and Sony Pictures Television International, the team that a year before had produced the highly successful Russian version of *The Nanny* (*Niania*, Sony, 1993–9). Whereas *My Fair Nanny* (STS 2004–9) was one of the most successful sitcoms on Russian television and pioneered a whole series of licensed American remakes,[1] *Ne rodis' krasivoy* became a cultural phenomenon in its own right. The commercial STS channel broadcast the show daily in Russia and the former USSR. The producers tentatively advertised 150 episodes, but the success of the show brought the total numberof this 'comedic melodrama' to 200 episodes.[2] The industrial pace of shooting – one episode per day – matched perfectly the shooting location: the vacant lots of the Moscow ball-bearing plant. One of the largest city industries since the 1930s, the plant, like many other Soviet-era enterprises, shut down in the 1990s, to be reborn in 2004 as shooting pavilions of the Media City corporation, a subsidiary of the A-Media company – one of the biggest producers of serialized dreams for post-Soviet consumers.

The US *Ugly Betty* may have been the first successful project out of Latin America to become a major hit on an American network, but in Russia audiences fell in love with Latin American *telenovelas* years before, during Perestroika – and they have long been standard fair on major television channels. The first of these was the 1988–9 Central Television broadcast of a shortened version of the historical Brazilian *telenovela Escrava Isaura* (*Slave Isaura* [UTC-3. 1976]), which was not only the first to be screened in Russia and Poland, but the most popular *telenovela* ever to be seen on Polish television. Two years later, Russians were crying together with the beautiful heroine of *Los ricos también lloran* (*The Rich Also Cry* [Televisa, 1979]), a Mexican production which attained cult status. The face of Marianna Villareal (Veronica Castro) appeared on posters and teacups, and on her visit to Russia in 1992 the actress received a royal reception, with crowds of adoring fans and a meeting with the then-president, Boris Yeltsin, at the Kremlin.[3] With the fall of the Soviet Union and the ensuing economic and social chaos, Latin American *telenovelas* continued to provide a welcome escape from the disorienting reality.

What is unique about *Ne rodis' krasivoy* is its appeal to multiple domestic audiences as, despite their popularity, *telenovelas* are targeted mostly at women.[4] According to Anna Borodina, the TV reviewer for the *Kommersant* newspaper, by late autumn 2005, the show was already rated number one among fiction programmes on Russian TV, stealing audiences from the major federal channels. Approximately one-third of viewers nationwide tuned in at 8 pm in Russia; in Ukraine the rating of the show was even higher: up to 58 per cent of viewers watched it more or less regularly.[5] With its focus on love and a woman's life in contemporary Russia, the show predictably drew female audiences. At the same time, recognizable character types and its setting in the Moscow fashion district and other hot spots of the still young consumer culture, allowed the show to reach groups that did not typically watch *telenovelas*: young, professional men and women whose lifestyle and work environment approximated those portrayed in the show. This so-called 'office Russia' is a peculiar euphemism for the 'middle class', which remains an elusive category in contemporary Russian society.

Old Stories, New Myths

The Ugly Duckling and Cinderella narratives are certainly not new to Russian culture. In fact Stalin-era musical comedies regularly featured female protagonists who started as humble and uneducated peasants and grew into respected and decorated collective farmers and workers, with a side benefit of love blessed by the Soviet state. The heroines of Ivan Pyr'ev's *Svinarka i pastukh* (*The Swineherd and the Shepherd* [1941]) and Grigorii Aleksandrov's *Svetlyi put'* (*The Shining Path* [1940], widely known as the Soviet *Cinderella*) were not just tokens of communist consciousness and the bright future; their transformation also testified to the possibility of combining women's happiness and careers. Late Soviet culture produced its own variations on the 'woman's lot' story. El'dar Riazanov's still very popular comedy *Sluzhebnyi roman* (*Office Romance* [1977]) combined the transformation-through-love motif with the 'taming of the shrew' plot. *Moskva slezam ne verit* (*Moscow Does not Believe in Tears* [Vladimir Men'shov, 1980]), a melodrama about three provincial girls who come to Moscow in search of personal and professional success, won the hearts of domestic audiences and earned the film an Oscar for Best Foreign Film. The film achieved a perfect fit between ideology and the fairytale: the heroine goes to bed an abandoned single mother in a factory dorm room and wakes up a factory manager, living in a modern apartment with a beautiful daughter. Twenty years of poverty and struggle disappear in this time warp. Her only problem now is to meet a man willing to tolerate her success.

It is not an accident that, 70 years later and in a country again building its ideology from scratch, a central popular cultural heroine is again a woman who fights for her happiness and wins. The difference is that heroines of the 1930s and 1970s fairytales lived in the 'best country in the world' and largely had to overcome their own weaknesses. Our Katya Pushkareva of 2005 is up against a formidable new reality: consumer capitalism and individualist ideology.

What Russians Want

Ne rodis' krasivoy addresses the central cultural conflict of post-Soviet culture: the negotiation between the traditional Russian (Soviet) values and the new corporate bourgeois ones. The vertiginous economic and political changes ruptured the fabric of everyday life, leaving people to cope with the trauma of the onslaught of new Russian capitalism, which left the majority of the population behind. The availability of consumer goods was tempered by sky-rocketing prices, financial instability and rising crime. But while lacking in 'bread' the emerging consumer capitalism provided plenty of 'spectacle'. The years of the Putin administration capitalized on the ideas of stability and prosperity, predicated on steady revenues from oil and gas sales. While the 2000s indeed showed a vast improvement in people's job security, salaries and public safety, the decade also widened the already enormous gap between the 'haves' and 'have-nots'. Yet 2004–6 became the apex of Russia's consumerism and glamour culture, fuelled both by the high oil prices and Putin-era mediatization of politics and everyday life.

Sony Pictures' move into the lucrative Russian market with ideas and format for locally produced series fulfilled a long-existing need. Up to the 2000s, the vast majority of domestic Russian TV productions were police and detective series as well as adaptations of literary classics. With no native sitcom tradition, Russian TV channels had to buy foreign (mostly North American) shows that enjoyed only a limited success because of the cultural gap and problems with translation. With the emergence of licensed productions, Russia acquired its own tradition of sitcom and dramedy. So seamlessly this transposition has worked that many viewers, in praising or criticizing the shows, persist in the conviction that they are uniquely Russian ideas.

The Russian Betty, Katya Pushkareva, is a mousy girl with glasses and braces who wears 'grandma' clothes. Despite being vastly overqualified for the job (she holds an economics degree), desperate for employment she applies for a position at a fashion company, Zimaletto, created by two new Russian families: the Zhdanovs and Voropaevs. The Voropaev parents are already deceased, but their three children, Aleksandr 'Sasha' (Ilya Lyubimov), a power-hungry egomaniac, Kira (Olga Lomonosova), who is engaged to Andrei Zhdanov (Grigori Antipenko), Pavel Zhdanov's (played by Georgiy Taratorkin) only son, and Kristina Voropayeva (Yuliya Rutberg), a 'new age' socialite who travels the world in search of new thrills, have been raised by the Zhdanovs. Zhdanov Senior feels his son is not ready to head the company, but the Board of Directors votes for him. Since Andrei is known for his womanizing, the father hires the unattractive Katya over Kira's friend Vika (Viktoria 'Vika' Klochkova, played by Yulia Takshina), a pretty, self-centred glamour girl. As is true of the other Betties, Katya quickly proves indispensable to the company. Not only is she a financial wizard and an excellent manager, but she also speaks fluent English and French and has a good reputation with bank managers who know her from her previous work with a German bank.

Originally, the scriptwriters wanted Katya to work in a publishing company, a job more fitting for a country that has traditionally read more than anyone else globally; however, things have changed and the scriptwriters decided that the glamorous world of fashion fitted the current cultural landscape and its resultant desires much better. Like any capitalist viewer, Russians prefer to see characters who are affluent and whose lives are above an ordinary, drudgery-like existence (Bogoslavskaia and Solntseva 2008). As if to confirm this point, in 2008, a special issue of the journal *Kultura*, which traces developments in Russian politics and culture, was dedicated to Russian glamour culture. According to the editors, during Vladimir Putin's presidency:

> Russian fascination with glamour was so immense that many commentators began to refer to it as the new ideology that the country had been searching for after the collapse of the USSR in 1991. One of the most popular panels at the international Ninth Russian Economic Forum in London in 2006 was 'Luxury as the National Idea'; one participant, Nikolai Uskov, editor of the Russian edition of *GQ*, went so far as to claim that glamour had superseded politics. He argued that 'politics was no longer about the "right" or the "left"; it was about appearances and the display of material culture that accrues to money and power'. Under Putin, the initial image of 'New Russians' underwent a transformation from vulgar and vicious criminals in brightly coloured jackets and gold necklaces to a hardworking, educated and stylish *haute bourgeoisie* (Rudova and Menzel 2008: 2).

This is exactly how the rich appear in the show: impeccably dressed, self-assured, well spoken and, on the surface at least, hard-working.

The blueprint of the globally circulating narrative proved to be an ideal forum for the new Russian 'national idea'. Unlike other television genres featuring Moscow elites (celebrity news, talk shows, reality shows), the world of *Ne rodis' krasivoy* gives the consumer paradise packaged in a narrative form which both legitimizes the desire to look and provides controlled outlets for populist anger. 'Elite' restaurants and clubs, fashion shows with invited celebrity guests, sports cars and oversized SUVs, and lots of money appear on the show as the normal and value-neutral lifestyle. What really made Katya Pushkareva the heroine of the decade was the mapping of the post-Soviet cultural conflict and desire onto the globally circulating narrative: the folkloric plot is interpreted through the codes of new Russian glamour culture, mixing curiosity about and resentment of the rich; celebration of merit and love rewarded, and satisfaction over the 'moral and social revenge of the recent outsider in the new Russian petit-bourgeois life' (Bogomolov).[6]

Describing the show, the producers claim that they went beyond the 'fairytale world of kindness and truth' depicted in *Yo soy Betty, la fea* in order to 'distract the viewer from the problems of corruption and drugs'. The Russians also claim to have not followed the Germans' introduction of a 'socio-political aspect into the show'.

> The Russian title of the serial is softer and more optimistic … [The Russian version] is about our contemporary life. Everything happens here and now. In our time and in our country. Every situation and every character are typical …. . Regardless of differences in their temperaments, their political and national features, people feel the same in any country. This is the key to the show's success. When a person wants to achieve anything he [sic] always sacrifices something, loses something. And often these are not financial losses – at times one risks losing one's self-respect. … What will the heroine do, what will she have to lose? – this is what the show is about. And also about what it means to put yourself on the line and what real Love is.[7]

Elaborating on the difference, one of the producers, Dar'ia Poltoratskaia, claims that previous versions (Columbian, Spanish, Israeli and German) were executed in the melodramatic mode. Everything happens 'almost seriously. Our serial is a comedic one, but it does not collapse into a sitcom but remains a lyrical comedy' (2007).[8]

The focus on contemporary Russian reality which becomes the playground for the archetypal tale tells as much as it conceals. Despite the disclaimers, *Ne rodis' krasivoy* shares its agenda with the German *Verliebt in Berlin* (*In Love in/with Berlin* [SAT.1, 2005–7]) and its melodramatic narration, tempered but not cancelled by the sitcom format, with the Columbian original. At the heart of the plot is the idea that consumer society is the norm; hence, either *you* need to change to fit in or, if you cannot, you must accept modernization as positive. Sitcom explores the norm, and registers or tries to guess people's ideas about themselves.[9] The delayed and slow introduction of sitcom on Russian television testifies to the unfinished business of modernization. Melodrama comes to the rescue, 'bearing witness to the underlying desires and impulses which fuel social process. In this respect melodrama feeds off the ideological conflicts that accompany social change' (Gledhill 1992: 118).

In Jesús Martín-Barbero's words, the driving force behind a *telenovela* plot is

> the ignorance of an identity ... [M]elodrama speaks of a *primordial sociality.* ... In spite of its devaluation by the economy and politics, this sociality lives on culturally, and from its locus, the people, by 'melodramatizing' everything, take their own form of revenge on the abstraction imposed by cultural dispossession and the commercialization of life. (277)

On the one hand, the heroine rebels against her invisibility, her lack of agency. It is not an accident that the show's most melodramatic scenes following Katya's discovery of Andrei's seduction plan take place not just in public places, but in the expensive and fashionable restaurant Richelieu, frequented by the rich and famous. Knowing that Andrei is ashamed to be seen with her, Katya refuses to be invisible and insists on 'going public' and, to aggravate him even more, she abandons her favourite orange juice for vodka. These scenes expose the 'guilty' new Russian man to the judgement not of Katya, but of the angry, cheated and dispossessed audiences.

If there is any doubt about the relative weight of comedy and melodrama both in the series' popularity and in its delivery of ideology, a look at the numbers tells it all. Slava Taroshina, TV critic for *Gazeta*, noted the correlation between plot developments and the show's ratings. According to her, the audience tuned out during the episodes that did not focus on Katya and Andrei's relationship. No amount of other attractions, including celebrity guests (Dima Bilan, Alina Kabaeva[10]) could compete with the dramatic twists and turns of the love plot (Rykovstseva 2006).[11] In fact, many viewers complained about the abundance of comic scenes that interfered with the melodrama. As the president of Telemundo Patricio Wills claims, the *telenovela* is driven by 'a couple that wants to have a kiss and a writer who doesn't allow them to for 200 episodes' (Martinez 2008). Katya and Andrei have to be together, and the expectation of the inevitable happy resolution of the love plot ensures the normalization of

Zimaletto as a place where miracles happen. The extended 'crisis' portion of the show is set around the New Year – the time when, since the Soviet times, feel-good fairytales were broadcast on TV.

Negotiating the Transition

Melodrama, however, is just one mechanism mediating the integration of the Soviet and the new Russian. For an audience that consistently prefers Soviet films over both post-Soviet and foreign, the show deploys a panoply of devices big and small that use Soviet representational codes to negotiate the transition. Russian film critic Iurii Bogomolov points out that if *Ne rodis' krasivoy* indeed provided identification material for an emerging middle class or 'office audience', then that audience remains Soviet at heart.

> Brought up on the ideas of collectivism and of the Big Brother's patriarchal care over its subjects, this audience massively rises up to defend their boss; acts as a women's collective which takes a sincere interest in the life of the protagonist; and enjoys Katya's social and moral revenge over the new Russian man.[12]

Perhaps most important to the show is collectivist ideology, the trope of re-education, and patriarchal social structure. Many licensed and homegrown Russian serials still rely on collectivist ideology. Often the individualist ideology of personal success is mediated through an archetypal story and framed by positive communal influence. Katya might have all the credentials for success but her career is 'super-motivated' – and is kept in constant check – by her family and her female work collective which shares communal values even though its members work in a new corporate environment.

Katya's family is also central to her definition as a character and the system of values around which the narrative is built. The family is ostensibly traditional, which within the parameters of the series means Soviet. Both parents are typical, salt-of-the-earth types: the father is a retired army colonel, the mother, also retired, is a housewife who spends her days baking delicious pies. Irina Murav'eva who plays Katya's mother, appeared in *Moscow Does not Believe in Tears* as one of the three friends who came to conquer Moscow. Unlike the protagonist (whose name is coincidentally Katya), who chooses education and a career, Liudmila (Irina Muravyova) aggressively searches for a well-to-do Muscovite husband. The plan initially succeeds: she marries a rising hockey star. Ultimately, however, the easy road she chooses proves the wrong one: her husband takes to drinking and drains money out of her. The actress's recent appearance in *Ne rodis' krasivoy* both signals cultural continuity and admits cultural change. As Katya's mother, she is quite matronly, has settled down and, while she wants her daughter to succeed at work and in love, she stands by the right values: education, hard work, honesty. The reformed man-eater of the Soviet brand pales in comparison with new capitalist sharks, but the stakes are higher too.

But the parents' role in the serial is much more than merely symbolic. Both fathers are instrumental in resolving the love plot and bridging the gap between Soviet and post-Soviet cultural landscapes. When the Board of Directors at Zimaletto hears false rumours that Katya is refusing to give back the company, Andrei's father invites Katya's father, Valery (Mikhail Zhigalov), to the office. Initial hostility notwithstanding, the older men instantly establish a mutual trust that rehabilitates Katya in Zhadanov Senior's eyes and triggers his later decision to make her the acting director of Zimaletto. The future of the fashion company is thus ensured by the unspoken but implied honourable army past of the Pushkarev family *and* the shared Soviet past in which both fathers take pride. Moreover, when Katya heads Zimaletto, she brings both her childhood friend Nikolai 'Kolya' Zorkin (Artem Semakin) and her father to the company. Pushkarev Senior is out of place in the corridors of corporate business and glamour, resulting in many comical encounters arising out of the clash of cultures. He is particularly outraged by Milko's 'non-traditional sexual orientation' as he calls it and Vika's narcissism and rudeness. As both are Katya's antagonists, the father's unfailing protectiveness also points to everything that he thinks is wrong in the new culture. But while Valery is incapable of fully integrating into the new world, his cameo presence in the Zimaletto office and his personal connection to Andrei's father suggests that the human decency and the shared values can reconcile the old with the new. Thus class conflict, having barely emerged, is diffused through comedy and the reassertion of patriarchy.

Katya's parents also play a major role in voicing and safely re-channelling populist anger against the new rich and their lifestyle. Katya's father is angry at her late working hours and puzzled at the purchase of an expensive SUV for NikaModa. Valery, however, is kept out of the loop regarding his daughter's whereabouts (doing business in fashionable clubs) and about the true nature of her relationship with Andrei. The father therefore interprets the situations within a military logic: Katya is Andrei's subordinate and should follow his orders. It is her mother, Yelena, who reads Katya's diary and gives Andrei a piece of her mind when he shows up on her doorstep. Unlike Andrei's earlier crises, which are designed to trigger satisfaction in the viewer, Katya's mother's anger at the lifestyle, superficiality and the less-than-honourable behaviour of the privileged Zhdanov is redefined through the melodramatic coda. Andrei's hurt and humiliation of Katya *as a woman* diffuses the implied class conflict. Moreover, this confrontation occurs during the last stretch of the show, after the audience has witnessed Andrei's own reading of the diary and how he is crushed both by the power of Katya's love and the extent of the pain he had inflicted. We know Andrei's love for Katya is genuine, and within the melodramatic logic of the *telenovela*, such complications will provide the sweet torture of delayed but inevitable resolution.

The successful resolution of the love plot means the integration of two incompatible worlds. On the personal level, both Katya and Andrei have to change. Katya learns to dress well and, as her fairy godmother – PR woman Yuliana Vinogradova (Natalya Richkova) – tells her, to 'get closer to reality', that is, to consumer capitalism. To help Katya forget Zimaletto, Yuliana employs her as an assistant and takes her to Egypt, one of the most popular and inexpensive post-Soviet tourist destinations/vacation spots, where they help organize a beauty contest. This is where Katya's transformation begins. In between trips to clothing stores, hair salons and meditation, Katya meets Mikhail 'Misha' Borshchov (Andrei Kuzichev) a promising young chef. A decent and caring guy, Misha signals Katya's impending transition in more than one way. Not only does he fall in love with Katya even before her transformation is complete, but he himself is an outsider in the glamorous world of fashion. Misha is a provincial from Novosibirsk, and his ultimately successful integration into the new culture (he opens fashionable restaurants in Moscow and St Petersburg) gives hope for ambitious and talented young people.

In the end, Katya, the glamorous proletarian and her reformed vice-president husband, Andrei Zhdanov, preside over Zimaletto. The wise and benevolent patriarch Zhdanov Senior intends to supervise business from London. This ending legitimates new corporate culture, preserves the Zhdanov family heritage (of which Katya is now part) and simultaneously restores social justice and meritocracy. Even the capricious diva Milko, who quits Zimaletto in protest against democratizing fashion, is rehabilitated: right before the wedding he returns to the company that is his family.

This corporate family also includes the members of the 'women's committee'. Their stories and resolutions mirror Katya's. While at the end of the show she is Zimaletto's boss, her professional success only matters if she is with Andrei. In representing gender issues, the show remains thoroughly traditional. At the beginning, all but one member of the 'collective' are unmarried. Two are single mothers, two others cannot find a date: one is too tall, the other one is a child of a Russian woman and a sprinter from Kenya who participated in the 1980 Olympic Games in Moscow. The only married woman in the group is overweight and is constantly dieting or having liposuction. The last episode celebrates consumer-friendly gender equality: Katya and Andrei will be a team in business just *like* they will be a married couple in life. The message perfectly echoes the resolution of the gender issue: in the last episode which features Katya and Andrei's wedding, all members of the 'women's committee' find their personal happiness: new boyfriends, fiancées, pregnancies.

Reinstating the Glamour

With Katya's return as the president of the company, the serial actualizes the famous line from 'The International': 'We have been nought, we shall be all!' (and vice versa). The resolution, however, is the reversal of what history had in mind: social justice, like 'The Marseillaise' (playing in the background), is no more than a *mise-en-scène* for the triumph of a more democratic version of consumer capitalism. Katya's daily-changing fashionable outfits, together with the makeover of the entire women's collective, promise to the surrounding female workers in identical work clothes the pleasures of consumption.

The issues of class and economic status are also diffused through the focus on appearance as the only obstacle in the way to success, according to the series. Guest stars on the show are mostly women, and their cameo roles fulfil the double function of adding to the glamour of the show itself and providing nationally accepted (that is, media-created), examples of successful women. In a curious twist, these media celebrities, such as former Miss Universe Oksana Fedorova, show kindness to the less-than-glamorous Katya, even sharing with her their own stories of the thorny road to success and celebrity status. The viewer is expected to feel satisfaction from these instances of equality, as well as from the fact that the celebrities behave like normal people, complete with heartbreaks and, by gosh, financial troubles in their past. But equally clear is the implication of their little speeches: the 'normal person' identity (kind, decent, average) should be *overcome*. 'One should fight' (*Nado borot'sia*), is the refrain of the show. The star image is simultaneously glamorous and projected as authentic and inspiring: my past and character is why I am so successful today. Yet one cannot but help wondering: can Katya – smart, efficient and ironic – buy these self-congratulatory stories?

Like a Hollywood musical then, *Ne rodis' krasivoy* deconstructs the illusions of glamour only to immediately restore them. Jane Feuer writes that Hollywood musicals 'give pleasure to the audience by revealing what goes on behind the scenes ... to demystify the production of entertainment. But the films remythicize at another level that which they set out to expose. Only unsuccessful performances are demystified' (443). The scapegoats of the show and the targets of criticism are exactly those characters, who in Feuer's words, deliver 'unsuccessful performances': the power-hungry Alexander and the self-absorbed, money-grabbing Vika. Both are punished for wanting capitalist pleasures without working for them.

The optimistic message of social integration in *Ne rodis' krasivoy* only concerns the younger generation. The older generation of Katya's parents is addressed through validation of their values (through the legitimizing figure of the new capitalist Zhdanov Senior). But throughout the narrative we also observe the economic improvement of the Pushkarevs' life. At the beginning of the serial the father is laid off from his job. By the end, they buy a new car, the father is employed as an accountant at Zimaletto, and they even talk about a vacation abroad.

If the intention was to read the melodramatic plot as a familiar tale with a predictably satisfying outcome, the desires and the commercial potential inscribed in the fictional world of the serial are real enough. A fashion company, Sela, which launched a fashion house, Zimaletto, with branches in major Russian cities, bought the brand name from the producers. For those who cannot afford the high-end prices of the Moscow fashion business, there is a vicarious consolation prize: A-Media is developing a game portal, 'Play at Zimaletto', where visitors can 'join the company's work. As virtual employees they fulfil characters' assignments, take part in business talks, create new collections, and organize seasonal fashion shows'.[13] More importantly, by participating in the virtual project young Russians can feel as though they are middle-class in training. In Philip Schlesinger's words, 'the media not only reflect national and cultural identity but play an active role in the *constitution* of the collective cultural identity' (quoted in David Morley and Kevin Robins 2006: 294). In February 2008, Putin announced the goal of narrowing the income gap and bringing the proportion of the middle class to 60–70 per cent by 2020 (Radio Free Europe Newsline 2008). The Russian media will undoubtedly go along with the project, circulating feel-good, uplifting tales of social integration and personal success much like those contained in *Ne rodis' krasivoy*.

Works Cited

Baldwin, Kate, 'Montezuma's Revenge: Reading *Los Ricos También Lloran* in Russia', in Robert C. Allen (ed.), *To Be Continued ...: Soap Operas around the World* (London and New York: Routledge, 1995), pp. 285–300.

Bogomolov, Iurii, 'Proshloe kak priem', *Seans*, vols 35–6 (August 2008), online at: http://seance.ru/n/35–36/kinotv-3536/proshloe-kak-priem/ (accessed 9 September 2009).

Bogoslavskaia, Kira, and Solntseva, Svetlana, 'Konstruirovanie 'serial'nykh real'nostei', *Iskusstvo kino*, vol. 7 (2008), online at: www.kinoart.ru/magazine/07–2008/media/soc08032 (accessed 15 December 2009).

Doane, Mary Ann, 'The Moving Image: Pathos and the Maternal', in Marica Lunday (ed.), *Imitations of Life: A Reader on Film and Television Melodrama* (Detroit: Wayne State University Press, 1991), pp. 283–306.

Gledhill, Christine, 'Speculations of the Relationship between Soap Opera and Melodrama', *Quarterly Review of Film and Video*, vol. 14, nos. 1–2 (1992), pp. 103–24.

Feuer, Jane, 'The Self-Reflexive Musical and the Myth of Entertainment', in Barry Keith Grant (ed.), *Film Genre Reader II* (Austin: University of Texas Press, 1995), pp. 441–55.

Martín-Barbero, Jesús, 'Memory and Form in the Latin American Soap Opera', in Robert C. Allen (ed.), *To Be Continued ...: Soap Operas around the World* (London and New York: Routledge, 1995), pp. 276–84.

Martínez, Laura, 'The Faces of Hispanic TV', online at: http://www.multichannel.com/article/87278-The_Faces_of_Hispanic_TV.php (2008) (accessed 20 January 2008).

Morley, David, and Robins, Kevin, 'Spaces of Identity: Communication Technologies and the Reconfiguration of Europe', in Valentina Vitali and Paul Willemen (eds), *Theorizing National Cinema* (London: BFI Publishing, 2006), p. 293–303.

'Ne rodis' krasivoi: istoriia fil'ma', online at: www.amedia.ru/nrk/rubric/23.html (accessed 12 September 2009).

Radio Free Europe Newsline, online at: http://www.rferl.org/content/article/1144049.html (11 February 2008) (accessed 30 July 2011).

Rudova, Larissa, and Menzel, Birgit, 'Uniting Russia in Glamour', *Kultura*, Special Issue 'Glamorous Russia' (6 December 2008), pp. 2–3.

Rykovtseva, Elena, 'Provody seriala *Ne rodis' krasivoi*', Radio Svoboda Program (6 July 2006), online at: http://www.svobodanews.ru/articleprintview/163523.html (accessed 23 September 2009).

Sahadi, Jeanne, 'World's Most Expensive Cities', *CNN Money* (19 June 2007), online at: http://money.cnn.com/2007/06/15/pf/most_expensive_cities/index.htm?cnn=yes.

Zvereva, Vera, 'Televizionnye serialy: Made in Russia', *Kriticheskaia massa*, vol. 3 (2003), online at: http://magazines.russ.ru/km/2003/3/zvereva.html (accessed 25 April 2012).

Endnotes

1   For example: *Liuba, deti i zavod* (*Liuba, Children and the Factory* [STS, 2005]) based on *Grace under Fire* (ABC, 1993–8); *Shastlivy vmeste* (*Happy Together* [TNT, 2006–present]) based on *Married with Children* (Fox, 1987-97); *Dom kuvyrkom* (*House Upside Down* [STS, 2009–resent]) based on *Full House* (ABC, 1987–95); *Voroniny* (*The Voronins* [STS, 2009–present]) based on *Everybody Loves Raymond* (CBS, 1996–2005).

2   In Spring 2008, A-Media announced the beginning of work on the sequel to the show. The A-Media site has also created an interactive project '*Don't Be Born Beautiful. A Sequel*', which invites viewers to post their ideas for future episodes. (Online at: www.amedia.ru/nrk/new/.)

3   For a discussion of the show's meaning in the Russian context see Kate Baldwin, 'Montezuma's Revenge: Reading *Los Ricos También Lloran* in Russia', in Robert C. Allen (ed.), *To Be Continued ...: Soap Operas around the World* (London and New York: Routledge, 1995), pp. 285–300.

4   Surveys indicate that, despite the increased production and relative popularity of licensed and domestic sitcoms, TV audiences in Russia still prefer more traditional soap operas. *Karmelita* (RTR, 2005–present), a serial about a passionate and illicit love between a Gypsy girl and a Russian man, consistently beats sitcoms in ratings and viewer loyalty. One way to account for this is the high percentage among the audiences of middle-aged and older women, for whom TV viewing is the primary leisure activity. See, for instance,

http://wciom.ru/arkhiv/tematicheskii-arkhiv/item/single/11639.html?no_cache
=1&cHash=2a52183d14.

5   Elena Rykovstseva, 'Provody serial "Ne rodis' krasivoi"', Radio Svoboda Program (7
June 2006), online at http://www.svobodanews.ru/articleprintview/163523.html.

6   Iurii Bogomolov, 'Proshloe kak priem', *Seans*, vols 35–6, online at: http://seance.ru/
n/35-36/kinotv-3536/proshloe-kak-priem/.

7   '*Ne rodis' krasivoi*: istoriia fil'ma', online at: www.amedia.ru/nrk/rubric/23.html.

8   Interview in the documentary film *Be Born Beautiful. The Story of Success*, Aleksandr
Nazarov. Neomedia, 2007.

9   According to Vera Zvereva, because the post-Soviet Russian identity and the social
composition and tastes of the audience are still in flux, producers are guessing
instinctively which kind of imaginary world the viewers are ready and willing to
see. '"Novye russkie" serialy, online at: www.uni-konstanz.de/FuF/Philo/LitWiss/
Slavistik/.../tez.-Zvereva.doc.

10 Dima Bilan is a pop singer who in 2008 won the Eurovision Song competition. Alina
Kabaeva is a Russian gymnast who holds multiple world and Olympic titles. Her star
career in sports, however, was overshadowed by the rumours of her alleged affair with
and pregnancy from Vladimir Putin.

11 This programme aired the day before the much-anticipated finale of the show featuring
Katya and Andrei's wedding.

12 Iurii Bogomolov, 'Proshloe kak priem', *Seans*, vols 35–6, online at: http://seance.ru/
n/35-36/kinotv-3536/proshloe-kak-priem/.

13 http://www.amedia.ru/zimaletto/.

Travelling Narratives and Transitional Life Strategies: Yo soy Bea and Ugly Betty

Paul Julian Smith

From Threat to Resource

In the credit sequence of *Yo soy Bea* (*I Am Bea* [Telecinco, 2006–9]) the Spanish daytime serial based on the Colombian *Yo soy Betty, la fea* (*I Am Betty, the Ugly One* [RCN, 1999–2001]) (which premiered on 10 July 2006), Pinzón Bea (Ruth Núñez) the timid, mousy heroine (thick eyebrows and glasses, disfiguring braces on her teeth), walks nervously into the campus-like office complex of fictional fashion magazine *Bulevar 21*. Her working-class father and plain childhood friend are left behind at the gate, worriedly watching as she begins a new life, at once glamorous and perilous.

In the pilot episode of *Ugly Betty*, which premiered on ABC on 28 September 2006, the Latina heroine (plumper and feistier than Bea, but still boasting prominent eyebrows, glasses and braces) tries to gain access to the offices of 'Meade Publications' for the interview she had arranged sight unseen. The sequence is shot in the gloriously ornate lobby of the Woolworth Building in Manhattan, which features an extended marble staircase, down which Betty Suarez (America Ferrera) will be marched by an officious underling. We cut to her modest family home in Queens (also an authentic location in the pilot), where Betty's young nephew Justin (Mark Indelicato) is watching a flagrantly melodramatic *telenovela* on TV with visible scepticism.

Both scenes suggest in a similar way that the show to follow will be a travelling narrative: the protagonist will undertake a journey that is at once geographic, social and metaphorical. But they also hint that this unique example of a transnational *telenovela* (shown in some 70 countries around the world [Rogers 2007: 14]) will offer its faithful viewers local life strategies, teaching them how to negotiate the metamorphosis that is the key feature of the story. Outside the USA at least, where the series structure can have no definitive ending, the ugly duckling from the wrong side of town will finally be transformed into a sleek swan and marry her initially feckless and thoughtless, and now hopelessly devoted, boss.

Where once globalization was widely thought to herald the homogenization or Americanization of culture, it is now more likely to be seen in the way that is suggested by the twin Betties above: as inseparable from a renewed intensity of local, regional or national characteristics. In the case of audiovisual media in general, and of television drama in particular, research has repeatedly suggested that since the 1990s local audiences in Europe prefer domestic production in primetime, which is widely held to be 'closer' to their own experiences. Foreign programming, whether from the United States or (for Spaniards) Latin America, once widespread in the evening, is now often confined to minority timeslots during the day or late at night, lacking as it does the key attraction of cultural proximity (Buonanno 2008: 96).

The Eurofiction Working Group, led by Milly Buonanno and based at the European Audiovisual Observatory, has charted this rise in the fortunes of Spanish television drama, with Spain reaching a higher production level and seriality index in 2002 than the other big European territories (Eurofiction). This suggests that, in spite of the continuing presence of foreign shows in marginal timeslots and on minority channels, Spanish producers have successfully secured the fidelity of domestic audiences to long-lasting local dramas that have found a secure place in national affections and living rooms. The figures for 2006 from Lorenzo Vilches's more recent survey of Spain in the Iberoamerican Television Observatory report confirm the dominance of local fiction in 2006. Mario García de Castro has also documented the unique features of the successful 'evolution' of Spanish TV fiction since the 1990s, such as their increasing engagement with social issues, complexity of narrative, and address to a sought-after, commercial target audience.

This article treats an apparent anomaly in this scenario: *Yo soy Bea* is, as mentioned earlier, the hugely successful Spanish adaptation of the Colombian *telenovela Yo soy Betty, la fea*. As Vilches notes (181), this is the only show in its genre and timeslot to figure amongst the top ten Spanish productions of its opening year and the only one to be adapted from a foreign format. As a control to test the cultural specificity of the Spanish *Bea*, this chapter contrasts it with the equally successful US primetime dramedy *Ugly Betty*.

Perhaps the most extensive and influential typology of *telenovela* is that of Martín Barbero and Sonia Muñoz, which examines production, reception and textual composition in Colombia, *Betty*'s original home territory. And it would clearly be possible to examine *Bea* (and the US *Betty*) using his methodology. First comes the structure and dynamic of production (1992: 30). Transferred to a Spanish context this would include such questions as the marginalization of the *telenovela* in Spain since the early 1990s, when it has only rarely leapt the scheduling fence (as in the case of *Bea* specials) into primetime; and the belated decision to make the US version not a daytime soap or sitcom but a bigger-budget, long-form dramedy. The context of industrial and communicative competition amongst Spanish and US networks also comes under this heading, with Tele5 successfully confronting the most competitive market in Europe and ABC attempting to win back network viewers lost to cable and connect with a fast-growing Latino demographic.

Secondly, according to Jesús Martín-Barbero and Muñoz's methodology, the two shows could be said to reveal distinct social uses and ways of seeing. Habits of consumption and family routines are implied by format and timeslot, as are spaces of circulation, such as the home, neighbourhood and workplace (31–2). Vital here in Spain is the post-lunch or *sobremesa* timeslot, which has come to be seen as a 'second primetime' and can even (as in the case of *Bea*) attract larger audiences than in the evening. Qualitative evidence for audience reception is available here both from trade press coverage of the programmes and from Internet forums, unusually active in the case of *Bea* and *Betty* from the first episode ('Bea' posted an extended and extraordinarily popular blog written in the first person and directly addressed to 'ugly-surfers' or 'feonautas' [yotambiensoybea]).

Martín-Barbero and Muñoz's final area is cultural competency and collective imaginaries (33). It is clear that, in the case of the *Betty* format, these are implicitly embedded in the very different textual composition of the shows, in spite of their common ancestor in Colombia. Social actors, conflicts and places, spaces, times and symbolic oppositions, and forms of narration and media language reveal significant variants between Spain and the USA. For example, the dominant ethnic theme of *Betty* is wholly absent in *Bea*, whose overall look is, unsurprisingly, much less glossy than its bigger-budget American sister. TV syntax (35–6) thus also testifies to the persistence of national cultures, markets and business interests, with the two shows looking very different from each other. An initial hypothesis would be, then, that even within a rare, indeed uniquely, successful transnational format such as *Yo soy Betty, la fea*, European drama continues to be specifically tailored to domestic audiences and is distinct from both Latin American and North American forms.

Travelling Betties

In 2001, the Spanish trade press attributed the 'renewal' of interest in the *telenovela* by local audiences, hitherto absorbed by reality shows, to just one title: the Colombian *Yo soy Betty, la fea* broadcast on national network Antena 3 (Sánchez Tena 40). By early 2006 (just before the summer launch of *Bea*), however, *Television Business International*'s territory guide to Spain makes almost no reference to the genre. The broadcast scene is said to be 'in a state of flux' with the recent launch of two new terrestrial channels (Cuatro and la Sexta) into an already crowded national marketplace (2007a: 1).

This changing situation brings opportunities for travelling fictions, however, as the new channels have schedules to fill and are 'thus opening doors' to foreign product. Cuatro, said to be 'aimed at a younger audience', has acquired quality US series both old (*Friends* [NBC, 1994–2004]) and new (*House* [Fox, 2004–present]) (10). La Sexta, meanwhile, also said to be targeting a 'young urban audience', has Mexico's Televisa (the world's biggest Spanish-language TV group) as its major stockholder (27). *TBI* writes that 'it has not always been easy to sell shows into Spain' and that previous 'outside involvement … has traditionally come from Latin

America, which could deliver the passion, emotion, and unique sense of humour that resonates with Spanish audiences' (27). Televisa will, however, have now to 'branch out in programming terms': its traditional output of *telenovelas* is no longer 'relevant' to its target audience for the new channel. While the established generalist channels (Tele5, Antena 3 and the public TVE1) would still take the lion's share of viewers, the fragmentation and diversification of the audience noted by Lorenzo Vilches (2007) took an international turn with the new minority broadcasters.

One year later, *TBI*'s territory guide to Latin America covered the 'new fashions' in *telenovela*, writing that: 'Helpings of violence and action have been added to staple themes of romance and heartbreak ... mov[ing] the novela away from being a genre mainly watched by housewives' (2007b: 15). Moreover 'better production values' are the result of increased competition amongst powerful local producers. The latter are 'hoping eventually that they will be able to compete with US series for worldwide dominance' (17). But the evidence for this outcome seems sketchy. The 'local tastes' of, say, Buddhists in Asia reject the violence newly fashionable at home, while US and European audiences continue to resist 'prime time shows stripped across the week' (17).

Once more, *Betty* is the unique case on which the optimistic view relies. As a format it has achieved higher ratings than the channel average from Germany to India; and the US version has achieved the same stellar performance at home on ABC as it has abroad on Britain's Channel 4 and throughout Scandinavia (16). The *Betty* franchise has thus (supposedly) 'opened a window to the world for Latin American programming'. However, one executive from Disney-ABC admits that while *Betty* has 'brought a Latin American format into a US network', 'the *telenovela* hasn't really travelled yet'. The 130 daily episodes of the Colombian original were 'compressed' into just 13 weekly programmes in the USA (16).

Variety's review of the US dramedy ('*Betty* discovers America') is also ambivalent. Calling attention to the show's hybrid origin ('this adaptation of a popular Spanish [*sic*] *telenovela* – liberally adorned with swatches of *The Devil Wears Prada*'), the reviewer struggles with the tone of the piece, claiming the 'sweet, storybook quality to Betty's underdog status clashes, sometimes awkwardly, with an overly broad comedic tone (Lowry 2006: 68); or again that 'the series ... oscillates from screwball comedy ... to florid soap elements' (82). It concludes that 'creatively the episodic trick will be to prevent the show from becoming too silly or repetitive'.

An extended account of *Ugly Betty*'s scripting process in the official publication of the Writers' Guild of America also focuses on generic hybridism (which can lead to incongruity) and the shift from serial to series form (which can lead to repetition). The 'Americanization of the *telenovela*' was carried out by a writing team as diverse as the adaptation's target audience. Creator Silvio Horta defines himself as a first-generation Cuban American who always preferred 'traditional network fare' to the *telenovelas* on the TV in his Spanish-speaking household (Martínez 2007: 18). Other writers had experience working for *telenovelas* at Televisa, for US Anglo or Latino-based sitcoms, and even for medical drama *Grey's Anatomy* (ABC, 2005–present). The team admit that *Ugly Betty* 'has traveled an improbable path' (20). The 'dilemma' was that 'by its very nature [*Betty*] did not lend itself to open ended plotlines'. But the 'most popular series in worldwide television history' had special characteristics, given here as the combination of 'drama with humour' and a 'depth' that came from Betty's place as 'the moral centre in an immoral world', an element vital to the Colombian original with its particular stress on the theme of corruption.

The aim of the US writing team was to 'fuse the deep emotional draw of the *telenovela* with the fast-paced glitz of a hit network sitcom'. The 'problem' was to 'take a nightly episode concept with a definitive ending and turn it into a once-weekly hourly episodic with open-ended plotting, while attracting the same loyal following that has made *telenovelas* so popular' (21). To this end five episodes of the original were compressed into one of the US adaptation; and the show was structured 'to satisfy the true *telenovela* aficionado with a thematic ending while tantalizing the soap addict's need to follow an ever-developing plotline' (ibid.).

To this hybrid end, the team thus combines Latina and Anglo writers (one of the former says 'I *am* Betty'), with gay writers scripting gay characters and comedy and drama specialists even working in separate rooms. 'Silliness' is undercut by 'dark elements' and the 'harsh reality' of Betty's father's arrest by the immigration authorities (22). 'Stand-alone plots' are resolved in a single episode. 'Continuing plots' lend 'added depth' to family life in Queens, as important as work life in Manhattan. For example, in 'Lose the Boss' (1: 9) Betty struggles with a photo shoot, editor-in-chief Daniel is depressed over his courtship of Sofía (Salma Hayek), Daniel's nemesis Wilhelmina (Vanessa Williams) plots to take over the magazine, and Sofía plots to take Betty away from Daniel. All of these subplots are resolved, while the immigration drama of Betty's father is left open.

Beyond screenwriting, the ambitions of the series are shown in its stylized cinematography and production design, which attempt nonetheless to remain 'grounded in some sense of reality' (Oppenheimer 2007: 56). *American Cinematographer* wrote that 'broad comedy' required 'wide-angle lenses' and 'low angles' to 'show off the architecture' in the main office set (57). The cool palette of *Mode* magazine in Manhattan ('offset by wild splashes of orange') is contrasted with the 'vibrant, warm colours and well-worn furniture' of the family home in Queens. And the generous spaces of the first set (produced by glass doors and partitions, circular architectural flourishes, and reflective surfaces) are contrasted with Betty's 'small and narrow' home into which only one camera will fit. Although after the pilot the show was shot in a Los Angeles studio, an uncannily convincing sense of varied urban exteriors is produced using digital plates shot on Betty's modest Queens street, while a 43-metre (140-foot) TransLite backdrop of Manhattan wraps around the high-rise office set.

This close attention to localist realism even within stylized exaggeration is significant. Ben Silverman (later to be president of rival network NBC) further claims that *Ugly Betty* has revived the political dimension of comedy, pioneered in the USA by Norman Lear in the 1970s: 'Through emotion, through character, through comedy, conversations about race, about class, about differences and distinctions within our everyday life, *Ugly Betty* tangibly connects with real life.' (Martínez 2007: 23) It is perhaps no accident, then, that a show with such ambitions to present encounters with the other (Latina or gay) should be a travelling fiction that engages both a new and fleeting sense of place and a new *Mode* of temporality, half way between the evolution or metamorphosis of the serial and the repetition or iteration of the series. We can now move on to see how Spanish producers offered their own, newly indigenized, life strategies to devoted fans of *Yo soy Bea*.

Yo soy Bea: Production, Reception, Text

Specialist website formulatv.com gives a detailed account of *Bea*'s production process over two years (formulatv). As the series came to an end with the climactic wedding episode, script co-ordinator Covadonga Espeso spoke on 21 June 2008 of the collective process that required seven writers each for plot and dialogue. Espeso claims that it was only through 'team spirit' that they could 'stretch' 180 Colombian episodes into more than 460 in Spain. Espeso insists that, unlike the original, their version was taken from 'reality', from the everyday life of Spanish women, and their Bea (unlike Colombia's Betty) was a 'normal' girl you might meet in the street. Nonetheless, she admits that it was a 'crazy' job to extend the story as they did (on Tele5's orders) and to sustain the show's top ratings in its timeslot. The challenge was to keep inventing situations without falling into 'absurdity' (Eurofiction: 2007).

At the press conference held as shooting began on the series two years earlier (19 May 2006), Tele5's head of broadcasting Alberto Carullo had stressed the process of indigenization. While the story is, he says, 'universal' and 'timeless', the aim of the adaptation was to make Spanish audiences feel the plot, language, dialogue and situations were 'their own'. Creative director Mariana Cortés stated, along the same lines, that, while remaining 'faithful' to the original, the new version would 'distance' itself from Colombian 'caricature'. More specifically the protagonist's 'family structure' had to change to make it 'believable' to Spanish audiences: the innovation here is that Bea has no mother or siblings and has cared for her widowed father alone for two years. While Bea will be physically 'transformed' she will become 'attractive but not spectacular'; and the theme of 'personal evolution' and 'increasing self-confidence' is equally important (all from Eurofiction: 2007 website cited above).

In spite of this 'modernization' of characters and plotlines (said to include 'suspense' and 'high comedy'), Tele5 claims that *Bea* remains a genre piece, fulfilling no fewer than nine characteristics typical of the *telenovela*: sentimentalism, a happy ending for the central couple, easy-to-follow stories, simple dialogue, female-centred narrative, family complications, high drama and suspense, everydayness and local colour, and easily recognized, archetypical characters. These general points are combined with the specific attractions of the *Betty* format, which are said to be originality, suspense, due to the belated 'transformation' of the star, whose real appearance is kept under wraps, the memorability of the characters, and the moralizing 'message' that brings together two timeless fairytales: the Ugly Duckling and Cinderella.

It was not immediately clear that Tele5 and independent producer Grundy (later attacked by unions for the 'abusive practices' of overwork and unfair dismissals [2 March 2008]) could achieve this balancing act of memory and modernity. By 10 August 2006, Tele5 was already trumpeting *Bea*'s success, however, and seeking to associate it with *Ugly Betty*'s imminent bow in the USA. This attempt at international triangulation was supported by local stunt casting. On 9 November 2006, it was announced that, in a special primetime outing to mark the 100th episode, Jesús Vázquez, popular gay host of Tele5's game and reality shows, would guest star in the undemanding role of the ex-boyfriend of *Bulevar 21*'s art director, the queeny Ricardo 'Richard' López de Castro (David Arnaiz).

Future specials tied the show in to viewers' calendars and extended the franchise: one plot timed for Valentine's Day coincided with a look-alike contest on a talk show (13 February 2007). When a local singing star visited the set the next month (13 March 2007), *Bea*'s Internet chat room registered a record 5,480 unique visitors and 57,330 hits. For the 200th episode, in which the unreliable Álvaro Aguilar Velasco (Alejandro Garcia Tous) somewhat prematurely proposed marriage to Bea, Tele5 announced (6 May 2007) that every episode of the show had been number one in its timeslot, with over 3 million viewers and a 32.4 per cent share. While the 300th episode was less happy (Bea is briefly dispatched to prison), it gave Tele5 a chance to parade more statistics to the press: the production had so far required 10,872 pages of script, 6,000 scenes, 142 actors, 3,500 costume changes, and 123 locations (28 September 2007).

In the last year of production, writers continued to add major new characters and foreshadowed the final marriage with a gay wedding episode, also timed for Valentine's Day (14 February 2008). The climactic transformation or makeover episode was scheduled for a primetime Sunday, when it attracted a huge 8 million viewers (6 June 2008). It was followed by a unique personal appearance by the cast when *Bea*'s hen night took place by the iconic Puerta de Alcalá in the centre of Madrid (9 June 2008). After the primetime wedding episode (19 June 2008), *Bea*'s Internet alter ego took the time to thank faithful fans in a final blog posting which mentioned many of them individually by name (Bea forum, 'Hasta siempre').

Not all viewers were so enamoured of the ending. Some complained on the show's forum that the wedding was wrapped up too quickly and implausibly: Bea quite literally stepped into the shoes of a new character, the pretty blonde Be Berlanga Echegaray (Patricia Montero), who walked out of her own dream wedding and thus allowed the central couple to take her place. Others even claimed that a humorous dance performed by the newlyweds was stolen from US sitcom *Friends* (NBC, 1994–2004) (Bea forum, 'Enigmas'). Hence Tele5's demand to 'stretch out' *Bea* to twice the length than was originally intended clearly tried the patience of some viewers as much as it did the creativity of the writers and the endurance of the crew. Tele5 hoped, nonetheless, that *Bulevar 21* could continue with a new and less original protagonist, the conventionally good-looking Be. It was a conservative moral shared by cosmetic brand Nivea, whose sponsorship of the final episode on the channel's own website featured a tagline that could not have been further from the series' original premise: 'Beauty is freedom.'

In spite of its producers' claims to be distinct from the Colombian original, then, *Yo soy Bea* seems at first to attest to a certain standardization of offer across the huge region that is Iberoamerica. While *Bea* is ostensibly based in the modern capital Madrid, it often returns to 'eternal' themes more typical of a pre-industrial Spain (typically, *Bea* goes back to her unseen *pueblo* for the Christmas vacation). Although the rather primitive central premise (Ugly Duckling or Cinderella) is thus set within a supposedly sophisticated setting (the fashion magazine workplace), it is no surprise, then, that in the final episode Bea's wedding will require her to give up the chance of a glamorous job in Miami. And in spite of the claims that *Bea* is less caricatured than the Colombian *Betty*, the Spanish version retains a good number of farcical and melodramatic elements (pratfalls and murder mysteries). Finally, while *Bea* is said to be especially adapted to Spanish social circumstances, it allies itself to some extent with the regressive 'neutral' tendency of Miami (once more) and Mexico. The accent is standard Castilian (only Richard, the unsympathetic gay art director, speaks with a Sevillian lisp); and, defying contemporary Spanish demography, there is not one immigrant or person of colour amongst the regular cast.

The office location, often shown in establishing exteriors, is a bland, concrete campus shaded by trees that could be anywhere. While *Ugly Betty* is so insistent on the distance between Manhattan and Queens (between glamorous, treacherous work and dull but cherished home), *Bea*'s physical and social geography is sketchy indeed. *Bulevar 21* does not benefit from the handsome urban backdrop glimpsed through the windows of *Mode*, and nor does *Bea* feature aerial shots of Madrid to rival those of the towers of Manhattan that welcome us back from commercial breaks to *Betty*. Where rare authentic locations are used in *Bea* they tend to be anonymous and suburban: a school in comfortable Pozuelo de Alarcón, the Xanadú shopping mall 32 kilometres from the city centre are cited in the credits. There are few local references in the script and no mention of current affairs or politics.

In similarly traditional fashion, dichotomies remain mainly Manichean (evil Diego de la Vega Rivillas [Miguel Hermoso Arnao] will ceaselessly scheme against Álvaro) and morals are still conservative (single motherhood is permitted only to a supporting character, the receptionist Maria Jesús 'Chusa' Suárez (Carmen Ruiz), whose child longs for a father's attention). Wilfully or perversely, *Bea* thus chooses to neglect the potential for metropolitan sophistication that its milieu would appear to offer so readily. Rare film or fashion references are readily accessible to the widest of audiences. When *Bulevar 21* holds a costume party, staff come dressed in Marilyn's floaty white gown from *The Seven Year Itch* (Billy Wilder, 1955) or Audrey's little black dress from *Breakfast at Tiffany's* (Blake Edwards, 1961); when Bárbara Ortiz Martín's (played by Norma Ruiz) shoe suffers an injury in a catfight with Bea she complains 'My Versace is broken!' Far indeed from the giddy heights of *haute couture* with which the show's milieu is supposedly obsessed, the credits list some 30 everyday local brands that have paid for placement on *Bea*'s crowded sets.

It is not clear, then, that *Bea* (a unique success) is in the tradition of 'popular Spanish realism' that García de Castro believes has been vital to both the history of Spanish TV fiction since broadcasting began and its recent renaissance since the late 1990s. If anything, *Bea* would seem to have most in common with the *teleatro* of the 1960s, with its stagey set, dramatic moments, stereotypical characters and focus on a very long-suffering female who is prone to moralizing. The sense of the everyday and of the present prized in subsequent Spanish television is much attenuated here by the almost complete lack of reference to social issues explored by the new professional series of the 1990s.

While the rapid rhythm of daily drama still permits occasional exteriors (the entrance to an apartment building in the first week of the first season; the playground of the school in the last), *Bea*'s spaces of home, work and leisure (the inevitable staff cafeteria) are indistinct and undistinguished. Where the US *Betty*'s lavish workplace set is shot to show up its depth and height through trademark circular features and frequent low angles, *Bea*'s office set is so small that, when the heroine first arrives, a fashion shoot, complete with bikinied 'babes', is taking place in what appears to be a corridor or entrance hall (embracing all the girls, Álvaro kisses Bea by mistake and grimaces broadly). It is true that performance style is (as in current Spanish primetime series) relatively naturalistic and Ruth Núñez's timid Bea is genuinely affecting; but this novelty is undercut by the cheesy musical prompts used to underscore comic or dramatic plot points that come straight from the most traditional of *telenovelas*.

Even compared to contemporary Latin American production, reviewed by *TBI* above, *Bea* seems somewhat conservative. An early hint that *Bea* might be dabbling in the new trend to incorporate violent action is quickly disabused. If Álvaro finds the bloody footprints of his missing sister Sandra de la Vega Rivillas (Ana Milán) in the shower (cue *Psycho* reference), she will soon turn up live and well and masquerading as a cleaner in the *Bulevar 21* office. But *TBI*'s survey of Spain is perhaps more fruitful than its coverage of Latin America in offering a hypothesis for *Bea*'s success. With the new free-to-air national channels opting, we remember, for smart US imports to snare young urban audiences, a space opened up for a traditional *telenovela* for a broader demographic. *Bea*'s local characteristics are thus evident but not excessively marked by an old school *costumbrismo* (local colour) that is perhaps now rendered embarrassing by the newly sophisticated production values of primetime series made both at home and abroad. In a difficult balancing act, *Bea* thus reconciled the modern with the old and familiar.

If the daytime *Bea* kept one eye on primetime (Tele5 scheduled frequent special episodes for evening viewers), then it also carefully situated itself in transit between Latin America and Spain. Spanish viewers were, of course, already fully aware of the Colombian original of the format that had revived the fortunes of *telenovela* in their country just five years before. Yet, was it an accident that the decor for the main *Bulevar 21* set (against which publicity shots of the cast were also taken) features prominent patches of red and yellow, the colours of the Spanish flag? The art design thus hinted at the need to familiarize the potentially troubling alterity of a fiction that had travelled so far even before it had begun.

Crossing Bridges

Pobre muchacha cuando llega a la oficina
¡Ay! Que se pone nerviosita 'perdía'
Que los tiburones se la zampan con papitas fritas
Y es que es ella tan inocente y tan enterita

¡Ay! Pobre niña que has caído del cielo
Y desde el limbo caes y bajas a este mundo de lagartas

Ya no se puede ir por el mundo derrochando el amor
En esta vida hay que saber capear
A ti te falta veneno y te sobra corazón
Así vas a llegar a Santa 'na' más

Poor girl, when she gets to the office/ Oh! she goes all nervous/ the sharks will eat her up with fried potatoes/ and she's so sweet and innocent too./ Oh! Poor little girl, you've fallen from heaven into this hell, this world of lizards./ Now you can't go around being lovey dovey/ In this life you need to know how to fight back./ You've got too little venom and too much heart./ All you're set for now is to become a Saint.

In a typically canny example of cross-promotion, Edurne, a graduate of Tele5's reality contest *Operación Triunfo*, sings the theme tune of *Yo soy Bea*. The rap-style lyrics stress the defining characteristic of Ruth Núñez's performance as the title character: her timidity. She is a little girl with too much heart and too little 'venom', all at sea in a dangerous workplace full of sharks and lizards. Bea's personality could hardly be further from America Ferrera's Betty, who, in spite of identical reversals and humiliations, remains as feisty as she was in the pilot episode.

Likewise, Núñez's physical type is less subversive of beauty norms than that of Ferrera, who was, before *Betty*, best known for the feature *Real Women Have Curves* (Patricia Cardoso, 2002). Unlike the rounded Latina, the fragile Núñez is model-thin, already ready for the transformation that will be effected by a strapless gown and perilous heels. Furthermore, while *Bea* deals mainly with class and taste (wealthy Cayetana's spaghetti-strapped little black dresses versus Bea's frumpy mid-length skirts and sensible shoes), it does not address the questions of ethnicity that are centre-stage in *Betty*, with its richly detailed Mexican-American family and ruthless African-American executive Wilhelmina, struggling to reconcile glamorous work with a neglectful father and alienated daughter. Moreover, the gay theme is much stronger in the US *Betty*, with episodes focusing on the coming out of assistant Marc St James (Michael Urie) to his mother and the education of Betty's effeminate young nephew Justin. In spite of his marriage in a late episode to a man who also has to come out to his family, *Bea*'s Richard is an unsympathetic caricature by comparison.

It follows that *Betty*'s humour is much more based on the coded references of camp than is *Bea*'s and its media references are condensed and allusive (for example, when Justin says he saw '*Prada*, like five times', the viewer must know that he is referring not to the fashion label but to a then recent feature film, *The Devil Wears Prada* [David Frenkel, 2006]). While *Betty*'s guest stars impersonate fashion figures (Gina Gershon's grotesque parody of Donatella Versace, James Van Der Beek's sleazy version of the boss of American Apparel, lightly disguised here as 'Atlantic Apparel'), *Bea*'s guest stars, pop singers and TV presenters, pretty much play themselves. Surprisingly perhaps, the US show also has a much stronger sense of family than the Spanish, with Betty supported by a loving, if meddlesome, father, sister and nephew, while Bea is reduced to the widowed father who is here less sympathetic than in the USA. In spite of the importance of family to the *telenovela*, then, *Bea* responds closely to changes in Spanish demographics, which have made such claustrophobic family structures newly typical.

Most evident is the difference in the role of travel between the two versions. Betty's family speak often of their origins in Mexico and visit that country when her father Ignacio (Tony Plana) is deported. On her first day at *Mode*, the new secretary sports an unlikely Guadalajara poncho. Salma Hayek, one of the show's producers, takes a featured role as a Latina editor and temporary love interest for Daniel Meade (the Spanish Álvaro played by Eric Mabius). A touching scene between Betty and Daniel takes place on an emblematic Brooklyn Bridge, reminiscent of that game of bridge-crossing which is a symbol of the life strategy of new beginnings and for Buonanno a privileged motif in the ever-renewed series television (2008: 128). In *Bea*, on the other hand, journeys are either unseen or unmade (the Christmas vacation in Fiji or the job offer in Miami); and, in a lost opportunity, the serial makes little explicit reference to its continent of origin, in spite of the fact that Latin American immigrants make up a large and growing community in Spain. While one plotline focuses on a proposed merger with a Mexican media company (frustrated by the evil Diego), no regular characters from the continent appear. *Bea*'s narrative universe would thus seem to be disturbingly homogeneous.

Bea's aesthetic also feels flat. The cramped red and yellow sets cannot compete with *Betty*'s sense of space and place, even though so much of the latter is shot on green screen. *Bea*'s occasional vertical wipes are also no match for the frequent and varied iris effects used in *Betty* to link sequences. Moreover, *Betty* skilfully crosscuts between multiple plot strands (Spanish 'multitrama'). This tendency that climaxes in the first season's finale 'East Side Story' (23:1) which crosscuts between Betty's foiled romance with an accountant, the car crash of Daniel's sister Alexis (Rebecca Romijn), the announcement of the forthcoming marriage of Wilhelmina and Daniel's father Bradford (Alan Dale), Daniel's mother Claire (Judith Light) escaping from prison, and the shooting of Santos (Kevin Alejandro), Betty's sister Hilda's (played by Ana Ortiz) fiancé, all to the poignant soundtrack of Justin's performance in his school production of West Side Story. A long delayed kiss between Bea and Álvaro offers a more traditional and less complex source of pleasure in the Spanish finale.

But this is, of course, not to compare like with like. A day-time serial stripped across the week could hardly be expected to have the production values of a once-a-week primetime series, which thinks nothing of recreating the Brooklyn Bridge on digital plates. And Spain does indeed have a history of evening drama on generalist channels that approaches the sophistication of the US series on which the newer minority stations rely for their ratings (the US *Betty* premiered on Cuatro on 10 June 2008).

Unlike *Betty*, which incorporates fragments of a spoof *telenovela* into its episodes and posts them on its website (ABC, 'Telenovela'), *Bea* does not explicitly acknowledge its debt to Latin America. But I would argue that this is because bi-locality or interculturality are already implicit in *Bea*'s production, reception and textual composition. Thus the punishing rhythm of shooting and scheduling five times a week associated *Bea* with the *telenovelas* screened in the same timeslot in Spain. The habit of consumption implied by the *sobremesa* timeslot also implied a connection with rival or neighbouring shows in the schedule that originated in Mexico or Miami. As we have seen in the producers' launch of the serial, the Spanish version was inseparable from the Colombian original in the minds of the programme makers. They thus attempted to distance their version from certain social actors (e.g. the Colombian family structure) and certain kinds of textual composition (e.g. the exaggerated performance style), even as they held on to others (the Ugly Duckling motif, the intrusive music cues).

Ugly Betty sought to confuse reality and fiction to some extent, with ABC publishing a book of the series that mimicked the fictional *Mode* (ABC, 'Book'). In what is perhaps its most important innovation, *Bea*, a daily visitor to its fans' homes, went much further with Tele5 launching a monthly magazine called (as in the show once more) *Bulevar 21*, with a print run of 300,000 (vayatele.com). Social uses and ways of seeing were also expanded and exploited through the integration of *Bea*'s blog into the show itself and the direct communication with individual spectators. While many may have been disappointed by the final wedding episode, others vowed never to forget Bea and Álvaro, with many uploading their own treasured compilations of clips (often set to new music tracks). Some six months after *Bea* ended (14 December 2008), YouTube still hosted 30,000 clips from the show.

The travelling narrative thus finally became a life strategy, founded on that definitive ending and final metamorphosis that can only be provided by the serial, however long its climax is postponed. The Spanish *Bea* may thus be the ugly sister of the US *Betty*, lacking the latter's glamorous production values, sophisticated dialogue and complex plotting, but, as its title suggests (with the two words 'Betty' and 'fea' fused into the single 'Bea'), it constitutes a skilled form of cultural condensation: a carefully indigenized revision of a foreign format reworked as a resource in a way that makes it distinct from both Latin American and North American norms.

Works Cited

ABC, 'Book', online at: http://abc.go.com/primetime/uglybetty/index?pn=book#t=0 (2008) (accessed 14 December 2008).

ABC, 'Telenovela', online at: http://abc.go.com/primetime/uglybetty/telenovela/sinsofthe heart/index (2008) (accessed 14 December 2008).

Bea Forum, 'Enigmas de la boda', 21 June 2008, online at: http://yosoybea.mforos. com/1162016/7106495-enigmas-de-la-boda/ (accessed 14 December 2008).

Bea Forum, 'Hasta siempre feonautas', 24 June 2008, online at: http://yosoybea.mforos. com/1161970/7114623-hasta-siempre-feonautas-martes–24-de-junio-de–2008/ (accessed 14 December 2008).

Buonanno, Milly, *The Age of Television: Experiences and Theories* (Exeter: Intellect, 2008).

Eurofiction (Milly Buonanno and the European Audiovisual Observatory), 'Television Fiction in Europe', 18 November 2007, online at: http://www.obs.coe.int/oea_publ/ eurofic/ (accessed 14 December 2008).

Formulatv, '*Yo soy Bea*: noticias', 1 September 2008, online at: www.formulatv.com/ series/108/yo-soy-bea/noticias/3.html (accessed 14 December 2008).

Formulatv, 'Series', 1 September 2008, online at: http://www.formulatv.com/series/108/yo-soy-bea/ (accessed 14 December 2008).

García de Castro, Mario, *La ficción televisiva popular* (Barcelona: Gedisa, 2002).

Lowry, Brian, 'Betty Discovers America', *Variety* (25 September 2006), pp. 68, 82.

Martín-Barbero, Jesús, and Muñoz, Sonia, *Televisión y melodrama: Géneros y lecturas de la telenovela en Colombia* (Bogotá: Tercer Mundo, 1992).

Martínez, Julio, 'You Are So Beautiful: *Ugly Betty* and the Americanization of the *Telenovela*', *Written By*, vol. 11, no. 3 (1 April 2007), pp. 18–23.

Oppenheimer, Jean, 'Prime-Time Pros,' *American Cinematographer*, vol. 88, no. 3 (1 March 2007), pp. 50–9.

Rogers, Jessica, 'The Plain Truth about Betty', *Broadcast* (12 January 2007), p. 14.

Sánchez Tena, Jesús, 'Trece años de telenovela en España', *Cineinforme*, vol. 755, no. 1 (March 2003), pp. 40–3.

'Territory Guide to Spain', *Television Business International* (February/March 2007a).

'Territory Guide to Latin America', *Television Business International* (May 2007b).

vayatele.com, 'Bulevar 21 en los kioskos', 30 June 2007, online at: http://www.vayatele.com/2007/06/30-bulevar-21-en-los-kioskos (accessed 1 September 2008).

Vilches, Lorenzo (ed.), *Mercados y culturas de la ficción televisiva en Iberoamérica*. (Barcelona: Gedisa, 2007).

yotambiensoybea [blog and forum]. Tele5, online at: http://www.yotambiensoybea.com/lowres.asp (accessed 1 September 2008).

Our Betties, Ourselves

Dana Heller

This is the story of a modest but ambitious Columbian soap opera. It is a story of life imitating fiction, for just as Beatriz Aurora Pinzón Solano took the Latin American fashion empire by storm and found romance with her wealthy, handsome boss, *Yo soy Betty, la fea* (*I Am Betty, the Ugly One* [RCN 1999–2001]) took the global television industry by storm, won the love of viewers across Latin America and around the world, and went on to become the most popular *telenovela* of all time. It has also become the most imitated, with adaptations in 19 countries (at last count), including China, Turkey, the Philippines and the Republic of Georgia. Indeed, when we speak of the Betty phenomenon – or 'Bettymania', as it is known among fans – we speak not of Betty but of Betties. We speak of multiples, pluralities, profusions. As the poet Walt Whitman sung of himself, Betty is 'large' ... she 'contains multitudes'.

And as the poet further wrote, she contradicts herself. Our Betties are at once local and global, particular and universal. By loving our Betties we learn to love and manage the contradictions and tensions of the international television trade's commercial traffic in format franchising, as well as the processes through which commodities produced for global licensing and distribution become adapted to local, regional, national storytelling practices and cultural traditions, so as to make them seem indigenous in terms of the feelings and fantasies they produce and the affective spaces they open up. By comparing and contrasting our Betties we position ourselves as *de facto* media comparatists and cultural translators. By examining our Betties, we hold a mirror to ourselves, or to our own nationally produced myths and aesthetics that are responsive to familiar strategies of day-to-day consumption, sense-making, and television-viewing practices. Our Betties speak our language pregnant with highly specific, vernacular forms of global awareness, which, in turn, manifestly reshape the conventions of national television programming in concert with the development of new media technologies, emergent political economies and transformations of traditional narratives of cultural identity and belonging.

This collection of essays is the clearest evidence yet that the Betty phenomenon stands, for good or ill, as the best available case study on the *techné* of global television, not only because of its market value but also because it voluminously illustrates the negotiations that are enacted between national tastes and transnational media flows. In these enactments, each locally produced Betty represents her own version of a global narrative, a set of complex relations that are unique to every location and replete with their own underdog mythology, their own fantasies of triumph and redemption. This, we could say, is the essence of Betties everywhere: they are ungainly women, abject and subordinate to the international beauty industry, an image-driven world in which they appear superficially inappropriate. But there is much more beneath the surface and this is where our Betties reveal their complex affiliations. For no matter what language they speak, no matter what geeky outfits they wear, our Betties universally serve as sites of intense local struggle with the style mandates of global consumerism. On the one hand, they all have the moxie and the heart to succeed in the wider world. On the other, their success suggests critical resistance to cultural cosmopolitanism – and the consumer traffic in international women's self-fashioning – that has stigmatized them as 'ugly' to begin with. This is the story of Everybetty. As incongruous labourers in the unyielding economies of gender and beauty, they are themselves – always themselves – and yet they are as adaptable as the television format they star in.

Indeed, the gendered visual rhetoric of 'ugliness' that underwrites the format presents us with mediated flashpoints of similarities and differences that are key to a rudimentary understanding of Bettymania on a global scale. Like Pierre Bourdieu's notion of 'taste' (1984), concepts of ugliness are socially and culturally produced and connected to processes of global mass culture and practices of consumption. As a global commodity, the basic storyline of *Yo soy Betty, la fea* yields to the commercial flow of television's international marketing objectives as well as to locally manufactured economies of desire, power and romance. However, at first glance what is most striking about the various adaptations of *Yo soy Betty, la fea* is not how different our Betties are, but rather how very much the same they appear. In each instance, Albert Moran's 'pie principle' of television format adaptation applies, as the 'crust', or generic structural container that is Betty's physical embodiment, is consistently made up of similar 'stock' elements such as the thick-rimmed glasses, orthodontic braces, bushy eyebrows, social awkwardness and a carefree lack of personal fashion sense (1998: 13). These comedic tropes, in combination with our Betties' cleverness, spunk and loyalty make them readable as ubiquitously forlorn, but otherwise earnest and admirable character 'types'.

However the affective labour that our Betties perform – the 'filling', if you will – must be understood as rooted content. In this process, global stories are disaggregated into indigenous stories designed to suit local aesthetic preferences. According to Gerhard Zeiler, chief executive of RTL Group (Europe's largest TV, radio and production company) this is the biggest opportunity in the age of global television formats: the 'content business', by which he means story-telling, or the challenge of tailoring global stories 'just enough to suit local tastes while staying true to the original idea'. And this is what all our Betties are ultimately about: 'a good story, emotionally told', and preferably told in one's own familiar affective idiom (Edgecliffe-Johnson 2007: 12).

Take *Ugly Betty* (ABC, 2006–10), the United States' adaptation of *Yo soy Betty, la fea* that premiered on Disney-owned ABC on 26 September 2006. Starring America Ferrera as Betty Suarez, a Mexican-American, first-generation college graduate from Queens, New York, the American Betty fused two familiar US genres, the sitcom and soap opera, into an hour-long, weekly comedy with a quirky, camp sensibility and a large, multiracial cast of actors. The plot would have been equally familiar to viewers of Telemundo: after landing a job as assistant to Daniel Meade (Eric Mabius), the womanizing editor-in-chief of *Mode* (a high-status fashion and lifestyle magazine modelled on *Vogue*), Betty Suarez gradually befriends her boss and earns his respect and admiration, if not his romantic interest, which the series hints at but never resolves. Rather, over four seasons *Ugly Betty* focused on its protagonist's stalwart ability to guide Daniel through the malevolent manoeuvrings of his power-hungry creative director, Wilhelmina Slater (Vanessa Williams) and her flamboyantly gay assistant Marc St. James (Michael Urie), and the personal crises of the highly dysfunctional Meade family, which includes the philandering mogul father, Bradford (Alan Dale), an alcoholic mother, Claire (Judith Light), and brother, Alex, who fakes his death to undergo sexual reassignment surgery, reappearing as Alexis (Rebecca Romijn). In contrast, Betty's caring and big-hearted, working-class family includes her widowed father, Ignacio (Tony Plana), her sister, Hilda (Ana Ortiz), and Hilda's son, Justin (Mark Indelicato), who over the course of the series comes to realize that he is gay.

As *Ugly Betty* progressed over the course of its four-season run in the United States, its aesthetic blend of comedic and melodramatic formats took shape alongside a distinctive fusion of themes. Discourses of national and sexual otherness – immigrant minorities and LGBTQ minorities – became increasingly central to the series' narrative arc and character development. Camp humour, evident in the series' deployment of over-the-top theatricality and excessive performativity, signalled its availability as a queer television text. Moreover, the series demonstrated an apologetic willingness to champion, discretely and indiscreetly, the debased status of women, illegal immigrants, non-whites and queers. From humiliating references to Betty's weight to her sister Hilda's struggle as an unwed, single mother; from Marc St. James's never-ending boyfriend woes to Alexis Mead's fight for dignity as a transgender M2F; from the discovery of Ignacio Suarez's illegal immigration status to his grandson Justin's coming-out narrative; *Ugly Betty* channelled the aspirations of outsider praxis into the wholesome mainstream of US popular prime-time television.

It achieved this by championing the 'outlaw body' as a figure of denaturalization, a tool for reappropriating cultural authority on behalf of ethnic, gender, class and sexual outsiders. These 'spoiled identities' (to use sociologist Erving Goffman's term for individuals who are faced with managing any stigma of deviance that might cause them to be discriminated against or judged negatively) are strategically linked throughout the series (1963). These characters were also discursively linked to the ongoing US 'culture wars', specifically to debates over same-sex marriage, President Barrack Obama's nomination of the first Hispanic justice, Sonia Sotomajor, for the US Supreme Court, the rash of anti-gay bullying in schools and the controversial construction of a series of concrete barriers along the 3,140-kilometre (1,951- mile) USA-Mexico border, purposely aimed at preventing the illegal crossing of Mexicans into the Southeastern United States. Against a steady, fulminating talk-radio backdrop of homophobic, anti-abortion and anti-immigrant (read: Mexican) politics, *Ugly Betty* highlighted time and again the extent to which ideologies of misogyny, racism and the demonization of sexual minorities become damagingly interwoven at key moments in US history. By connecting Betty's story arc to other 'ugly' characters, the series became, in many ways, a commentary on an oppressive system of bodily segregation whereby certain manifestations of otherness, in appearance and behaviour, are construed as dirty, inappropriate and possibly even outside the law.

Take, for example, Betty Suarez herself. In the series' pilot, pointed reference is made to the fact that she is not only style-challenged in the eyes of *Mode* employees, but fat. When she is rejected for an interview with Mead publishing because of her looks, she pleads with the supervisor to give her a chance based on her extensive knowledge of their publications. 'I know most of your magazines inside out,' she explains. 'I try to devour all that I can.' 'Clearly,' the supervisor responds sarcastically. Betty's roundness is a significant register of her incompatibility with the size 0, botox-crazed denizens of the corporate fashion world. It is also an indicator of her homeliness, or her status as an ordinary young woman from the working-class boroughs outside of Manhattan. Additionally, Betty Suarez's ostensible girth is a trait that sets her apart from other Betties around the world, most of whom (including the original Betty [Ana Maria Orozco]) have been played by slim actresses.

As observed by fans and critics during the show's first season, Betty's articulation as a plus size girl requires considerable suspension of disbelief, since America Ferrera's curvaceous figure can, in fact, hardly be called fat. But here we need to understand fatness not so much in its materiality, but in the perplexing context of changing bodily norms, medical industry reports of a national 'epidemic of obesity' that threatens the lives of children and adults, a multi-billion dollar diet and weight loss industry, as well as the comedic denigration of fat in mainstream popular culture as weak, non-conforming and lazy. In the contemporary United States, making sense of fat is no simple matter, as witnessed in reality shows such as

The Biggest Loser (NBC, 2004–present), where bodily norms, disciplinary enforcement, emotional injustice, as well as a desire for space in which to renegotiate the contract between bodies and the world, invariably reveal the dire consequences of violating aesthetic conventions. Given all this, however, we should not assume that Betty Suarez's coding as a chubby Chicana provides a source of cheap amusement. Quite to the contrary, it is perhaps *Ugly Betty*'s most potent political metaphor.

But how does Betty's body mass – fuelled by her father Ignacio's legendary Mexican cooking skills and domestic nurturing – come to be regarded in American society as a problem related not only to aesthetics (or the culture's preference for super-skinny female bodies) but to politics? To begin with, as feminist critics have long observed and sought to analyse, the female body – in its material and symbolic permutations throughout Western history – constitutes a field of volatile and contradictory political struggle. To the extent that the exterior of the body was throughout much of history believed to reveal its inner nature – its core predisposition – the measurement of fat on both the male and female body became part of an interpretive process. Increasingly, female corpulence was read to suggest a loss of male control over female sexuality, threats to public health and hygiene and an open defiance of patriarchal authority. The threat of unrestrained female disobedience, the polluting influences of which were often politically linked to urban, African-American and immigrant women, was medically codified through the appearance of excessive fat on particular parts of the body, for example the buttocks, stomach and thighs.

My point is that when we speak of the discursive history of fat in the United States we are speaking, wittingly or not, about the unavoidable confluences of racist, sexist, classist and nationalist ideologies as they become materially and even corporally manifest at particular historical junctures. In this regard, Susan Bordo's 1993 watershed work, *Unbearable Weight: Feminism, Western Culture, and the Body* continues to be of central importance for scholarship on the body precisely because of her recognition that the body – and in particular the female body – cannot be reduced to a mere system of trope and effect, but needs also to be understood as a concrete product of the culture that shapes it and guides its everyday material practices. Bodies like Betty's may be metaphoric, but they function as metaphors with real weight and force. The body makes flesh of history. It literalizes and naturalizes the longings and anxieties that arise out of social contests for power. And when we analyse representations of fat women in American popular culture we often find them functioning as 'the unknowing medium of the historical ebbs and flows of the fear of woman as "too much"'(Bordo 2003: 163). *Ugly Betty's* discursive deployment of female corpulence onto the scene of urban high fashion and global media power brokering establishes, in Angela Stukator's words, a 'revolutionary cultural politics ... that releases the body from the restrictions of socially sanctioned gendered, racial, and sexual roles?' (2001: 211).

But perhaps to speak of Betty's body in such figurative terms is a stretch. Let us consider a more concrete example of *Ugly Betty's* engagement with the affective substance of 'local' or national identity by turning to the season 1 story arc of Ignacio Suarez. In this subplot, Betty's concerns over her father's heart disease prompt her to shop for an affordable heath care plan for him. In the process, she encounters the frustrations that have animated the national debate over the costly, profit-driven, US health industry and inadvertently discovers a dark secret: Ignacio is an undocumented immigrant who has been working under a false social security number. Years earlier, his application for a US visa was denied for having murdered the first husband of his deceased wife back in Mexico, where she was the victim of domestic violence. The couple entered the United States illegally to escape prosecution in Mexico. In order to provide for his two US-born daughters and give them a better life, he continued living and working illegally in the USA.

Ignacio's immigration backstory, spreading over two seasons of the series, is a compendium of indignities and abuses. Cheated by an unscrupulous immigration lawyer and sexually harassed by a caseworker, who places him under forcible house-arrest, Ignacio's efforts to find legal recourse for obtaining US residency-status are processed through the series' signature aesthetic of camp melodrama, a nod to the Latin American *telenovela* from which it derives. But the story nevertheless resonates emotionally, if not viscerally, for anyone who has attempted to navigate the perilous landscape of US immigration law and the mystifying bureaucracy that oversees it. When his illegality is discovered, Ignacio is deported back to Mexico, where, unbeknownst to him, he is the target of a 30-year revenge plot that was set in motion by his wife's ex-husband before his murder. Betty follows him to a country that she knows from stories but has never seen, in the hope of helping him obtain a visa. Although she is unsuccessful, the journey nevertheless affords her an opportunity to connect with her cultural and familial roots, as she learns the truth about her parents' identity from relatives who would otherwise be strangers to her. In the second season, Ignacio's immigration subplot is resolved when Betty discovers Wilhelmina Slater, now engaged to Bradford Mead, in bed with a clandestine lover and accepts a 'buy-off' that pays for an immigration attorney who secures Ignacio's legal residency.

In its duration and complexity, Ignacio's story of secrecy, false identity, family loyalties, government corruption and – finally – justice obtained through a private payola agreement, would seem an unlikely narrative turn for a romantic comedy. But I would argue that the content of his story works to humanize the instabilities and paradoxes that are themselves the very stuff of what we recognize as 'national' identity in a 'nation of immigrants', where some are more welcome than others. The emotional and political crosscurrents that crystallize in Ignacio's dilemma underscore the usefulness of affective content in analysing national format adaptation. However, for many viewers of the series Ignacio's story arc was an unflinching acknowledgement of the country's broken immigration system and its Spanish-speaking victims. Its potential to move people – voters above all – was not lost on political fund-raisers. In 2010, Tony Plana recorded a Spanish-language advertisement for comprehensive US immigration reform that was produced and funded by the grassroots coalition 'Reform Immigration for America'. Aired during *Ugly Betty*'s final season, the ad was targeted at television markets in Nevada, a state with one of the higher proportions of Hispanics who are also registered voters.

At the time, Plana expressed surprise that *Ugly Betty* would take on such a hot button political issue, but he claims to have learned something from the experience. 'It was a lesson for me that people wanted more out of television than just entertainment,' he admits (DiBranco, 2010). In the advertisement, Plana grimly warns Spanish viewers about the rising tide of anti-immigrant sentiment, his voice set against a visual montage of homes being raided by police and angry white mobs waving patriotic placards with messages such as 'I want YOU out of my country.' Plana encourages viewers to call upon congress to enact reform lest they, and their families, face the mounting tide of prejudice. For viewers of *Ugly Betty*, Plana's appeal referenced the struggles of the character he played on the popular series and this lent an undeniable authenticity to his dire warnings. Clearly, this is the effect that producers hoped for, particularly as predictions of a Republican sweep in the upcoming November mid-term elections elevated the urgency of their campaign before a congress dominated in both houses by Democrats. In the end, comprehensive immigration reform failed to garner the support that it needed to pass. However, *Ugly Betty* – both the series and the cast members – became influential players in the campaign to generate sympathies and influence voters' hearts and minds.

Similarly, as the problem of youth suicide and anti-gay bullying permeated the US news media, we should consider the character of Justin Suarez, Betty's precocious nephew.

How does Justin's lack of conventional masculinity – his signalling of homosexuality – destabilize mainstream representations of Latino machismo in American culture along with the televisual representation of children and teens as queer beings? Against a background of blustery national debates over the status of illegal working immigrants and their children, in addition to court challenges to the federal government's 'Defence of Marriage Act', which effectively blocks immigration sponsorship for bi-national, same-sex couples, even those who may be legally married in their state of residence, anxiety around Justin's deconstructive performance of Chicano masculinity and his coding as a future gay male subject create discursive convergences that are contextually charged and atypical for a primetime network comedy. Moving beyond mere topicality, his story arc persistently collapses questions of civil rights into a performance where ethnic and sexual differences intertwine.

Indeed, from the show's inception in 2006, at which point Justin was a pre-teen, the character exhibited a distinctive effeminate manner, in addition to a pronounced love of cable fashion networks and Broadway musicals. Although the character's sexuality was never directly broached until the show's final season, such 'winks' to a presumably savvy audience seemed evidence enough to support speculation that Justin was destined to be gay. His storyline further supported such speculation by including a number of oblique yet judicious references to his struggle with the recognition that he is 'different' from other boys at school. In the late first-season episode, 'Derailed' (1.16), Justin obtains, through his Aunt Betty, two tickets to see the Broadway musical production of *Hairspray*. As an ardent lover of musical theatre, he is beside himself with excitement. His parents, who never married, are at odds over Justin's lack of proper masculine interests. His mother, Hilda Suarez, supports her son just the way he is. However, his hard-gambling, macho father, Santos Reynoso (Kevin Alejandro), believes that the boy could benefit from some toughening up and suggests that they spend more quality time together. For their first outing, Hilda arranges for the two of them to attend *Hairspray*, an activity that she knows Santos will disapprove of.

As Justin eagerly anticipates the show, an approaching snowstorm threatens to complicate the father-son commute into Manhattan. Another complicating factor is Santos, who is angered to discover that Hilda has secretly arranged for him to see a Broadway musical with Justin instead of something more manly. He refuses to go and, moreover, suggests that Hilda's indulgence of Justin's theatrical passions may be responsible for the 'way he is'. He proposes that the three of them spend time together on the E-train from Queens to Manhattan, where Hilda and Justin will see the show while he watches basketball in a sports bar. Hilda reluctantly agrees; however during the ride into Manhattan, the predicted blizzard descends upon the city. The train comes to a grinding halt when the electric system fails. Already late for the opening curtain, Justin becomes emotionally distraught. His only expressed regret is that his father will never appreciate the 'satisfaction' of *Hairspray*. Hilda tries to comfort her son with the reminder that he knows the book by heart and could act out the show himself if he wanted to. Inspired by these words, Justin delivers a solo performance of *Hairspray* on the E-train, for his father's enlightenment. He belts out the show's opening number, 'Good Morning, Baltimore', as subway passengers look on with amusement and irritation. Santos shrinks with embarrassment at his son's flamboyance. But when a male passenger suggests that the show has gone on long enough (and calls Justin a 'fairy' under his breath), Santos rises to his son's defence. In a calm, assertive tone, he tells the passenger to be patient while his son finishes performing, and to be certain to clap when it is over. With this, the entire subway car breaks into applause. Santos sits back down and approvingly tells his son to continue, since he is eager to find out what happens next – the story is indeed satisfying, he admits.

Of course, *Ugly Betty*'s reference to the Broadway musical production of *Hairspray* needs to be understood as part of the commercial process known as product placement or embedded marketing, when branded products are conspicuously inserted within the storyline of a movie or television show for the purpose of promoting them. Throughout the course of *Ugly Betty*'s four seasons, the show regularly promoted a number of products, from office equipment to cell phones to Broadway theatre productions such as *Hairspray* and *Wicked*. However, there is more that we can say about 'Derailed' and its use of *Hairspray* to advance Justin's ongoing developmental storyline within the over-arching narrative of a series that traffics playfully in queer images of gender and sexuality while addressing dicey social issues such as illegal Mexican immigration. Specifically, we should note the episode's linking of the performative satisfactions of Broadway theatricality with the implicit coming-out process of a Chicano-American boy whose father cannot accept his son's difference until he is compelled to confront the ugliness of his own homophobia in the casual slur of a stranger.

In particular, *Hairspray* (a musical about a fat girl who becomes an unlikely television celebrity, with a best friend who is in love with a black boy and a mother who is a man in drag) would seem to lend itself to recent debates over social exclusion and commonplace practices of othering, visibly manifest in the struggle for recognition and visibility among LGBTQ youth, and in the effort to counter stereotypes of immigrants (Latinos and Chicanos in particular) as economically and linguistically unassimilable into the utopian sensibilities of mainstream cultural production. We see this in Santos who, despite his initial resistance to the overwrought extroversion of Broadway theatricality, is able to transcend traditional Chicano machismo long enough to appreciate with his son (and within his son) the satisfactions of a queer-friendly musical.

In other words (and notwithstanding that Justin's storyline is one of several storylines in the episode), much more is derailed in 'Derailed' than an evening at the theatre. Indeed, the classical Oedipal trajectory of father-son identification is diverted, along with the conventional popular culture template of Chicano hyper-masculinity. Santos is transformed by his son's assimilation of *Hairspray*. The musical provides him with a pedagogical context for learning to accept difference in his son, while for Justin it provides a hopeful context for imagining his emancipation from oppressive strictures of patriarchal hetero-normativity. In this way, *Hairspray* helps reinforce *Ugly Betty*'s signature destabilization of gender. And when Santos is accidentally killed in the second season – the random victim of a grocery store shooting – Justin's tragic loss is somewhat mitigated by his sudden liberation from the pressure of paternal expectations.

In the final season of *Ugly Betty*, Justin becomes romantically involved with Austin, a schoolfriend who is questioning his own sexuality. In a series of episodes that won accolades from LGBTQ media watchdog groups and youth organizations, Justin comes out, first to Betty's gay co-worker, Marc St. James, and finally to his accepting mother and new step-father, Bobby (Adam Rodríguez), by dancing with his boyfriend at his mother's wedding. As two teenage girls watch them wistfully from the sidelines, *Ugly Betty* demonstrates once again its penchant for transgressing mainstream American cultural values – in particular, the privileging of hetero-normative family values – while at the same time earnestly supporting the narrative conventions (such as the resolution of Hilda's story arc through marriage) that generate those values.

This, of course, is a core component of the series' distinctive deployment of popular camp, the pleasurable properties of which – irony, hyperbole and inverse valuations of good taste – constitute a comprehensive critique of the category of the 'natural'. From its inception, the series took bold critical advantage of camp's capacity to upend categorical distinctions between surface and depth, naturalness and artifice, normalcy and queerness, beauty and ugliness. However, *Ugly Betty* further mobilized its camp sensibility to address changes in the composition of the American social body along with the aesthetics that have conventionally underwritten our notions of American beauty, romance and privilege. The articulation of local content – the stuff that makes the American adaptation feel so American – is not its campiness but rather its knowingness with respect to the inevitable migrations of people, sexualities and cultures across the arbitrary boundaries of nation, class and gender, despite the material and ideological concrete walls that are built to separate us from others. At the same time, the series undeniably champions the power of US consumer capitalism to assimilate our individual differences and make Americans of us all.

The US adaptation of *Yo soy Betty, la fea* thus confronts and overleaps isolation and disenfranchizement in a neo-liberal nation, where injustices enacted against those deemed ugly are as varied as they are similar. In this way, *Ugly Betty* affirms the relevance of the American Dream – the nation's perennially beloved makeover mythology – wherein the working class triumphs over the privileged and powerful to emerge transformed, morally sanctified. And it enacts this affirmation while coyly acknowledging that we owe this particular triumph to the migrations of a Latin American *telenovela*, a property that we bought and sanctified as our own.

Ultimately, the success of Betties around the world rests on their migratory traces, their juxtapositions of global sentiments and native structures of feeling that are never separable yet always responsive to the dynamics of history and place. And from this standpoint, it would be wrong to assume, as some critics of global media have, that the transnational merchandising of television formats is tantamount to the homogenization of global media space. Nor can we say that global media produces internationalism or cultural cosmopolitanism as the pure antithesis to national identities. As Ien Ang demonstrates, to assume such would be to ignore 'the fact that what counts as part of a national identity is often a site of intense struggle between a plurality of cultural groupings and interests inside a nation, and that therefore national identity is … fundamentally a dynamic, conflictive, unstable and impure phenomenon' (2003: 369).

Such struggles do not occur monolithically, of course, but in contexts that communicate the continually changing configuration of social bodies and their cross-identifications. That is where *TV's Betty Goes Global* comes in. This volume enables us on a global scale 'to see the resemblances between our own stories and those of others, calling ever more attention to the structural unities that underlay seemingly diverse experiences' (Lipsitz 1990: xiv). Investigations of this expansive nature require that we hold in place multiple complex systems. From this perspective, the study of globally marketed television franchises such as *Yo soy Betty, la fea* may be viewed as a contribution to translation studies or to the effort to imagine a comparativism of media cultures overall, in the sense that Michal Riffaterre understands it as an attempt 'to explain what is lost and what is gained in translations between the distinct value systems of different cultures, media, disciplines, and institutions' (1995: 67).

The essays in this volume demonstrate that our Betties, like ourselves, are mobile and tractable flashpoints of surprising collaborations between home and the world. They may be managed yet unsettled; they are variously and continuously brokered. Over time, they may be softened, sexualized, radicalized, domesticated, cross-dressed, or coutured, all of which becomes evident when we pay attention to the trajectories of their ambitions, the private/public architecture of their relations to family and co-workers, the articulation of female fragility over female robustness, the dynamics of their native intelligence. Similarly, our Betties' abilities to manage contradictory discursive positions will become legible in format elements that contextualize human movement and manage the ways in which bodily meanings are fashioned: costume, set design, music selection, the staging, production and editing of flashback segments, advertisers, cast interviews and cross-media references and promotions, and the 'chatter' generated by viewers at home and across various media platforms.

And while global television is often thought to disrupt existing forms of national identity, the essays in this compilation collectively demonstrate that it also offers opportunities for strengthening them. In such a precarious environment, the triumph of *Yo soy Betty, la fea* may reside in the fact that it empowers national versions of culture, thickening loyalties to place through a mass media allegory of transformation and expanding opportunities for all the world's uglies. The possibility, contradictory though it may seem, recalls Bruce Robbins's premise that 'forms of global feeling are continuous with', rather than contrary to, 'forms of national feeling' (1999: 33). And if this is the case, any critical effort to decipher what it is that makes Germany's 'Lisa' feel German or China's 'Wudi' feel Chinese will need to be situated in these multiple exchanges and flows as we seek to make sense of a nationalized internationalism, communicated through television formats that beautify the world we know.

Works Cited

Ang, Ien, 'Culture and Communication: Toward an Ethnographic Critique of Media Consumption in the Transnational Media System', in Lisa Parks and Shanti Kumar (eds), *Planet TV: A Global Television Reader* (New York and London: New York University Press, 2003), pp. 363–75.

Bordo, Susan, *Unbearable Weight: Feminism, Western Culture, and the Body* (Berkeley and Los Angeles: University of California Press, 2003).

Bourdieu, Pierre, *Distinction: A Social Critique of the Judgment of Taste*, trans. Richard Nice (London: Routledge, 1984).

DiBranco, Alex, '*Ugly Betty's* Undocumented Dad Fights for Immigration Reform', 10 February 2010, online at: http://news.change.org/stories/ugly-bettys-undocumented-dad-fights-for-immigration-reform (accessed 25 April 2012).

Edgecliffe-Johnson, Andrew, 'Local TV Lights up Global Sets', *Financial Times* (13 September 2007), p. 12.

Goffman, Erving, *Stigma: Notes on the Management of Spoiled Identity* (New York: Simon and Schuster, 1963).

Lipsitz, George, *Time Passages: Collective Memory and American Popular Culture* (Minneapolis: University of Minnesota Press, 1990).

Moran, Albert, *Copycat Television: Globalization, Program Formats and Cultural Identity* (Luton: University of Luton Press, 1998).

Riffatere, Michel, 'On the Complimentarity of Comparative Literature and Cultural Studies', in Charles Bernheimer (ed.), *Comparative Literature in the Age of Multiculturalism* (Baltimore: Johns Hopkins University Press, 1995).

Robbins, Bruce, *Feeling Global: Internationalism in Distress* (New York and London: New York University Press, 1999).

Stukator, Angela, '"It's Not Over Until the Fat Lady Sings": Comedy, the Carnivalesque, and Body Politics', in Jane Evans Braziel and Kathleen LeBesco (eds), *Bodies Out of Bounds: Fatness and Transgression* (Berkeley: University of California Press, 2001), pp. 197–213.

Episode

Ugly Betty, 'Derailed', 1.16, dir. James Hayman. Writers: Silvio Horto and Cameron Litvack (ABC Broadcast, 15 February 2007).

Index